Working Together
to Get Things Done

Issues in Organization and Management Series

Arthur P. Brief and Benjamin Schneider, *Editors*

G P 8 7 0 0 7 7 8

Working Together to Get Things Done

Managing for Organizational Productivity

Dean Tjosvold
Simon Fraser University

Lexington Books
D.C. Heath and Company/Lexington, Massachusetts/Toronto

Library of Congress Cataloging-in-Publication Data

Tjosvold, Dean.
  Working together to get things done.

  (Issues in organization and management series)
  Bibliography: p.
  Includes index.
  1. Work groups.   2. Organizational effectiveness.
I. Title.   II. Series.
HD66.T56   1986   658.4'036   85-40108
ISBN 0-669-10834-0 (alk. paper)

Published simultaneously in Canada
Printed in the United States of America
Casebound International Standard Book Number: 0-669-10834-0
Library of Congress Catalog Card Number: 85-40108

The paper used in this publication meets the minimum requirements of American National Standard for Information Sciences—Permanence of Paper for Printed Library Materials, ANSI Z39.48-1984. ∞™

87 88 89 90   8 7 6 5 4 3 2

To My Family

Contents

Foreword

Arthur P. Brief
Benjamin Schneider

I t is axiomatic to say that people in work settings get things accomplished by working together; the extent to which people's activities are coordinated at work is *the* defining characteristic of organization. And yet, in the history of thought on organization and management the issue that attracts the least research attention and often the least emphasis from management concerns cooperation, coordination, and the effectiveness of groups.

In this book, Dean Tjosvold has written about working together to get things done. The book is about cooperation, coordination, and work group effectiveness. But, more importantly, it is about organizational effectiveness. Tjosvold helps both the researcher and the manager appreciate the centrality of cooperative behavior in the life of organizations and shows how cooperation can be facilitated and organizational effectiveness enhanced. He does this through development of a relatively simple framework for understanding cooperation and then applies the framework to grappling with managing and understanding such key organizational processes as power, conflict, decision making, and stimulating and implementing innovation, as well as the creation of top management teams.

A key feature of the book is that it preserves a focus on people, as individuals, while it emphasizes the way we work in real organizations. This is no easy task since cooperation, coordination, and work teams obviously are not the focus of the study of individuals—at work or elsewhere. But Tjosvold has a good way of showing how, by cooperation and coordination, we carry out our individual goals while moving organizations to effective functioning.

Finally, Tjosvold has written a book that not only summarizes what we know about the antecedents and consequences of cooperation but shows how to *achieve* cooperation, even under conditions that might be inhibitive. For example, how can cooperation be achieved when groups are in conflict? Or when groups are competing? By providing explicit guidelines in such cases, and by showing how the best-run companies in the United States handle such situations, Tjosvold provides a service to managers and to the future of cooperation and effectiveness in work organizations.

Acknowledgments

I gratefully acknowledge the many researchers, managers, and observers who have contributed to the ideas and research used to write this book. David W. Johnson, my mentor at the University of Minnesota, and his mentor, Morton Deutsch at Columbia University, helped me to understand cooperation and organizations. Colleagues at Pennsylvania State University—Bill Rabinowitz, Deno Theavos, and Paul Weener—supported my early work. My colleagues at Simon Fraser University—Bob Andrews, Rich Field, Tom Janz, Steve McShane, Larry Pinfield, Bob Rogow, Jerry Ross, Bill Wedley, and Mark Wexler—enriched my perspective. The insights and experiences of many managers and students have stimulated my thinking.

Ben Schneider and Art Brief, the series editors, and Bruce Katz at Lexington Books made useful suggestions. Mary and Margaret Tjosvold demonstrated many ways to use the book's ideas and procedures. Bill Swanson helped to develop an approach to presenting the material. Jenny Tjosvold commented on my work and, with our sons, provided a rich, warm environment for work. I am indebted to these and many other people.

Introduction

Organizations get things done. They solve problems and create valued goods and services. They make steel and television sets, they sell bonds and clothes, they heal the sick and educate the young, they unionize workers and unite professionals, and they run local and national governments.

Organizations are amazingly useful and flexible tools, but from the largest and most complex to the smallest and simplest, they demand skillful management to make them work. Management is the expertise, knowledge, and techniques needed to harness and coordinate the energy and skill of people. Managing people is the key to a productive, successful organization.

Managers are expanding our knowledge of what makes organizations effective. Entrepreneurs develop organizations to exploit opportunities, market new technologies and inventions, create a world economy, and support new lifestyles and values. Banks now have the organization and technology to offer extensive, instantaneous worldwide investment and foreign currency services. Home-health companies provide nursing and housekeeping that the frail elderly need to live independently in their homes. Drawing largely upon their own experiences, managers are experimenting with organizations and restructuring the way we work and live.[1]

Managers use various methods to transform organizations. They develop strong corporate cultures to create a common vision, invite employees to participate in solving problems, form project teams, and share profits.[2] These innovations—with different labels and histories—all function to improve productivity and the quality of life by getting people to work together more effectively.

The significance of teamwork is no accident. The basic rationale of an organization is to take advantage of the various abilities, backgrounds, and interests of its members. A company's success depends on the combined energy and skill of its employees and departments. An architect and engineer must work together to develop an attractive, practical plan; marketing and production personnel must collaborate to make a high-quality product that sells.

Widely read books such as William Ouchi's *Theory Z* and Tom Peters's and Robert Waterman's *In Search of Excellence* have inspired managers to innovate. They describe how managers have achieved excellence and show that even large companies can be productive and humane by creating a cohesive, committed work force. These and other books have convinced many managers of the need to work together and the value of teamwork. What managers now need are reliable, systematic means to get employees to work together effectively.

This book identifies ideas, strategies, and procedures that will improve teamwork and thus enhance organizational productivity and the quality of work life. Managers and management educators will find this book's summaries of ideas and findings from organizational behavior, social psychology, and related disciplines useful to deepen their understanding and sharpen their skills. They also will find here the procedures and skills needed for effective collaboration between individuals and groups within an organization. Skillful management is the key to the great potential of organizations; as this book points out, the key to skillful management is getting people to work together to devise strategy, solve problems, and get things done.

This book develops an approach to understanding teamwork that integrates considerable empirical research and shows how working together motivates, gets jobs done, and solves problems. The framework can be used to analyze the many ways employees work with each other. It helps managers to understand strong, open relationships as well as troubled ones. The approach encompasses leadership, power, conflict, and participative management.

In addition, this book helps to bridge the gap between research and practice. Studies, incorporated in the book's approach, have powerful implications that can be used to improve coordination on the job and to make organizations more productive and humane. The approach can help managers improve how they work with individuals and employees as a group, and it can facilitate collaboration among departments. The approach also suggests effective ways to work with customers, suppliers, marketing agents, experts, competitors, and others outside the organization.

This book briefly summarizes theories and their research support, discusses the practical applications of ideas, and suggests plans of action. But it is not a how-to book in the narrow sense of the term; there is no simple, concrete plan that will necessarily work wonders for you. If I had such a plan, I would tell you. The fact is that effective, appropriate action depends on the specific situation and people involved. The strategy that works for your competition does not necessarily work for you. You must understand the ideas and approaches, think about what they mean for the specific circumstances you face, and decide on the specific actions that will be most effective for your situation. This book can help you develop goals, analyze situations, make wise choices, and act on your choices.

An important advantage of this book is that it presents ideas that have been developed systematically through empirical research. They have withstood repeated, vigorous testing by many investigators over many years and have been found to work. Researchers, like managers, are interested in the practical; both want to distinguish ideas that work from those that merely happen to be fashionable or sound good. Researchers put ideas to repeated tests to determine their usefulness to understand and influence behavior. Yet I must add a caveat: This book is not the final word on management procedures. These procedures must be further refined. I hope that managers and researchers will continue to test them in their work.

Although it is based on research, this book is really about hopes and possibilities. It does not try to describe how organizations function as much as it attempts to portray how organizations can be successfully managed. It examines the choices managers have and the decisions they must make. We sometimes feel powerless in organizations, but we create and control them— they do not control us. Employees and departments do not inevitably bicker and force decisions on each other, nor do they automatically cooperate and coordinate their work. Organizations and their managers must create the values, attitudes, assignments, norms, and procedures in which employees work together productively and humanely.

For hundreds of years philosophers, heads of state, and business leaders have called for cooperation among people; this book simply continues the theme. The suggestions are similar to the practices of many effective managers and well-run departments and companies. Indeed, my studies show that managers, executives, and workers in many organizations in several countries have developed creative, effective ways to manage conflicts, solve problems, and collaborate productively.

Many managers know the theories and ideas discussed in this book, but on an implicit, unarticulated basis. Savvy managers can use this book to improve their explicit understanding of teamwork, as well as to discover biases and shortcomings in their thinking and help them develop their methods to facilitate cooperation. Human beings have been cooperating for tens of thousands of years, but only recently have we begun working together in complex organizations that must incorporate the ideas of many specialists and cope with intense international competition. Managers must understand teamwork thoroughly and refine their methods to help people cooperate in today's organizations.

I have written this book for professional managers in all types of organizations as well as for management researchers, educators, and consultants. In some sections I discuss previous literature to place my arguments in context. These sections will mean more to those readers already familiar with management-research literature, but a background in research is not required to understand and use this book.

I have tried to communicate without confusing jargon, although I have used a few specialized terms because their specific meanings are important and cannot be conveyed by more common expressions. Moreover, I have written directly without stopping to remind readers of all the exceptions and caveats. I have taken cases and examples from public accounts and from my own experience working with organizations. I have altered these latter cases to protect confidentiality, and a few of them combine material from more than one situation. To avoid sexist language, I have used plural pronouns and alternated between male and female pronouns when the plural was awkward.

Managers, philosophers, and social scientists have worried that organizations suppress the human spirit, force compliance, foster conformity, and create the organizational man. Managers and researchers have wondered whether individual aspirations can be reconciled with company objectives. Now, however, there is a growing recognition that life within organizations can be rich and rewarding, that being organized helps being human. There is no fundamental incompatibility between individual aspirations and organizational success. Organizations provide great opportunities for human learning and satisfaction. Organizations contribute valued goods and services to society and enhance the lives and abilities of the persons who work in them. But organizational excellence demands skillful management so that people work together to get things done.

Part I
Teamwork and Organizations

1
Working Together and Management

*B*ob Clinton broke into a half-smile for the first time that morning as he met Jenny McCollough, a new member of his commercial loans–health care group at Midwest National Bank. "It's not banking and health care that are sleepy," she said, laughing, "it's me!"

Riding the elevator to their offices, they chatted about their handling $150 million in loans for Abbey and City health-care companies, which both wanted to buy nursing homes near their hospitals. The deals had to be closed before the state's reimbursement policy took effect the following Monday. Winded by the exhilaration, Bob and Jenny joked about the "easy life" of a banker with one of their colleagues, Fred Johnson, who was already at his desk poring over applications.

Bob glanced at his calendar, asked Sandy Hamel, his secretary, about any additional appointments, and began planning his day. He would get caught up on the nursing home loans at the regularly scheduled team meeting. He wanted everyone to realize what had to be done before the deadline and that everyone needed to pitch in. These clients were important customers who had to be well served, but the loans had to make sense, the details had to be handled correctly, and the loan committee had to be fully satisfied. Team members should not hesitate to ask him or each other for help.

He also remembered that before the meeting, he had to tell Fred to call Dwayne Oxman in the bank's public finance division about a new vehicle Dwayne had discussed; it might just be right for the Simmons project. He also would try to arrange a time when the group could consider Dwayne's offer to discuss some of the more useful new finance instruments. Fortunately, Dwayne liked to keep abreast of these developments and could talk about them in ways loan officers could understand. After the meeting, he needed to talk with Jack Dobson in the real estate division—why was Jack so *slow?—to expedite the construction loan for Health West's congregate apartments for the elderly.*

Then he had to talk with the boss, Duncan Foster, about getting another person and more secretarial assistance. He went over his pitch: "Duncan, we have assistant vice presidents typing their own letters when they should be investigating new loans." Duncan probably would be cool; he wanted the company to slow down, be more conservative, and stop making so many loans. Luckily the chairman was progressive: Bob might just get what he wanted. Time did not really allow for the racquetball game with Wilbur from personal banking, but he decided to go ahead anyway; he needed a workout and could still make it back for lunch with Tom Kneller from Health West.

Relieved that his first afternoon meeting began at 1:30, Bob got his coffee cup and headed off to the group meeting by way of Fred's office.

Bob Clinton, like managers everywhere, works, laughs, and learns with colleagues and customers. To work in an organization and to strive for excellence in management demands knowledge and interpersonal skills. All employees must work with others; their relationships determine their effectiveness and the quality of their work lives. Managers and executives must be especially skillful, for their job is to help others do their jobs more efficiently and work together.

Large and small, profit and nonprofit organizations need teamwork. Midwest National does not rely on Bob, Jenny, Dwayne, and others just to do their own thing; it needs them to share information and ideas and to coordinate their efforts. Only if employees work together to solve problems and complete tasks can organizations be productive. Working together is not just something that would be nice for a company; it is essential for success.

People make or break a company. Executives and researchers tell us that employees are an organization's most important resource. People are more important than a company's products or technology. People, after all, decide the products and services to offer, the tools and technology to be used, the employees to be hired, and the strategies to market products. And people use the technology, sell the goods, and do all the other necessary tasks. Because they are aware of the value of people, companies have human resource departments, and universities teach human resource management. An organization is not made up only of people, however, but also of their interactions.[1] Only when employees exchange information and assistance are decisions made and work accomplished.

Understanding how people can work together has a great practical payoff. At Midwest National, Bob, Jenny, Fred, and their colleagues do the many tasks, answer the many questions, and know the strengths and weaknesses of the loans much better when they work together rather than alone. Working with each other and with Dwayne in finance helps them to learn useful job skills.

Poor work relationships court disaster. If Jenny makes assumptions rather than risk looking stupid to Bob, or if she does not dare ask a colleague to check her work, the resulting bad loans could cost the bank millions of dollars. Poor collaboration leaves decision makers uninformed and workers unassisted; it disrupts the exchange necessary for solving problems and completing tasks. For many employees, the people make their job. If working with others is a joyless struggle, their job becomes a burden, and they seek employment elsewhere. Companies depend on individuals to perform their tasks effectively, but success depends even more on the coordinated performance of individuals and groups.

The study of cooperation in organizations is intellectually exciting and challenging as well as practically useful. Observing a typical day at Midwest National Bank stimulates curiosity and exploration. How were Bob and Jenny able to laugh about being stressed? What is behind Duncan Foster's commitment to conservative practices? How does he see his contribution to the bank? What are his true feelings toward Bob? Working with others is a window through which we can better understand and appreciate our colleagues and ourselves.

Striving for Excellence

Managers are experimenting to find humane, productive ways to organize. Established as well as emerging firms challenge traditional principles and procedures and experiment with creative ways to manage. Impressed with the morale, élan, and profits of strong culture companies, executives and managers around the world want to strengthen their own corporate family to bind employees to the company and improve productivity. Keen interest in participative management, project teams, quality of work life programs, quality control circles, parallel structures, labor-management problem-solving groups, and other innovations all attest to the efforts to create humane, profitable organizations.

Popular management innovations are attempts to strengthen teamwork. Strong corporate cultures create a community of employees who care about each other, appreciate each other as human beings, and feel part of a team dedicated to common goals.[2] Project teams bring persons with a variety of backgrounds, views, expertise, and interests together to work closely to accomplish a common task. Sales representatives, marketing researchers, production specialists, and product researchers work as a group to develop a new product. Participative management asks employees to join with their managers to identify and solve problems and to improve productivity and the quality of work life. Workers and union officials join management and engineers to develop an alternative to the assembly line. Developing productive, rewarding teamwork is an essential part of the pursuit of excellence.

Improved teamwork is not only the aim of management innovations, but also is necessary to implement them. *In Search of Excellence* lists eight attributes that characterize excellent companies and should guide other companies' management.[3] For example, excellent companies are biased toward action and eschew repeated analyses; they stay close to customers to learn and fulfill their needs; they are lean by reducing administrative layers and the number of people at the top; they stick to the knitting.

These practices, while informative, are only rough guides to organizational excellence. Surely, not every organization should be biased toward fast action. Swift decisions have cost some companies dearly. Failure to analyze before action may threaten a company. Even if the principle of lean staff applies to a company, it still must decide which staff positions to retain and who should fill them. To stick to the knitting, companies must identify their strengths and the reasonable options they should pursue. Staying close to customers is generally useful, but the company must decide which customers will be its future base. Nor is listening to customers, even by the chief executive officer (CEO), sufficient. Persons who listen must communicate their findings to relevant managers, who together must develop an understanding of the market and respond constructively.

Characteristics of successful companies must be applied wisely, not simply imitated. Managers must be able to adjust, alter, and even ignore generally useful practices to fit particular situations. They must assess the issues, dig into the problems, and develop solutions that work for them. But how are they to do that? They need to share information, exchange views, and discuss opinions to create their plans. Even the best principles, procedures, and programs demand that employees work together to implement them. Working together is necessary to introduce innovations and achieve organizational excellence.

What Makes an Organization Productive?

An organization is a network of interpersonal and intergroup relationships designed to accomplish established goals.[1] It takes people and resources from the environment, uses them to provide products and services, and markets its products and services to the environment. It carries out these functions through the coordinated effort of employees.

An organization requires the following:

1. Employees who have the knowledge, technologies, and skills to transform resources into products and services and are committed to completing their tasks and achieving company goals.
2. The capacity to identify obstacles, opportunities, and other problems and to solve them.
3. Strategies to market outputs and adapt to the environment.
4. A management process that integrates people and resources into a system to achieve the organization's goals.

By working together, employees become more knowledgeable and committed, are better able to solve problems, and can help devise strategies to adapt to the environment. Managers are the architects of the teamwork that makes organizations productive.

Organizational Productivity and Teamwork

> *The highest and best form of efficiency is the spontaneous cooperation of a free people.*
> —Woodrow Wilson

Organizations touch every aspect of life; we increasingly work, worship, relax, exercise, and eat in them. They are powerful and flexible. They coordinate the efforts and knowledge of several persons to manage $100 million investment portfolios; they coordinate hundreds of people to explore space; they coordinate thousands of people to build automobiles.

Organizations owe their immense potential and usefulness to the simple yet profound principle of division of labor. All organizations divide work, but they use many different methods. Some manufacturers divide the tasks by product lines and assign a group the responsibility for one line; others assign major tasks to departments of production, marketing, research, and accounting.

With these separate responsibilities, departments and individuals concentrate on their work and develop their expertise. Specialists are needed to keep abreast of the expanding knowledge and complex developments necessary to run most companies. Specialization works for individuals as well as the company. Employees are not overwhelmed with too many different tasks and develop a sense of competence and expertise.

To capitalize on division of labor and specialization, departments and individuals must combine efforts and avoid duplication, but coordination can be elusive. Employees may be much more concerned about their department's objectives than company goals; doing their own individual task well may seem the ultimate objective, not contributing to the department. The development of specialized expertise and outlooks further impedes communication. The computer repair specialist, the marketing representative, and the customer speak different languages.

Many traditional ways to improve teamwork are ineffective. Slogans such as "Fight the Competition, Not Each Other," demands that everyone cooperate, and procedures such as transfer prices and liaison offers are by themselves insufficient to achieve coordination. Consequently, many managers are firefighters; they try to stop infighting and struggle to get departments and individuals to work together.

Teamwork is essential for a productive organization. Through employees working together, a company transforms resources into products and services. Collaboration is needed to develop the commitment and skills of employees, solve problems, and respond to suppliers and markets. Working together is not just nice but is the key to an effectively managed organization.

Employee Competence and Commitment

Loyal, skilled employees are the heart of a productive organization, for they make the company productive and identify and solve problems. Companies want employees who value their jobs and develop their abilities. Competent persons must be motivated to join the company, contribute to it, and remain in it even in times of trouble. Employees must be integrated into the company.

How employees work together greatly affects their learning and commitment. Employees become motivated to complete their assignments and become committed to company goals as they talk with supervisors and colleagues. Through such discussion they come to understand the importance of their assignments and the value of company goals.

Working together directly affects motivation and productivity. Employees can share their expertise and make it more likely that goals will be reached; otherwise, they undermine confidence and motivation. Employees learn on the job. Workers learn through observation and informal instruction how to operate machines, develop ideas and products, manage their time, and communicate. Managers learn how to supervise, discipline, motivate, and inspire from observing their own manager and deciding to imitate or reject that style.[4]

Current knowledge indicates that teamwork in organizations not only satisfies an important human need to feel connected and valued, but also facilitates learning, social competence, feelings of self-worth and self-control, and social and psychological well-being.[5] Well-structured, effective teamwork is richly rewarding to individuals; co-workers make work enhancing and invigorating. Respect for executives and managers also strengthens employee commitment to the organization.[6]

Problem Solving

Inevitably problems develop as goals are not achieved, tasks are not completed, norms and rules are not followed, and misunderstandings occur. The organization also must monitor its technology and productivity and take advantage of opportunities to become more effective. Coordination is critical for problem solving and decision making. Superintendents and workers must exchange information and ideas to improve their work methods and resolve conflicts. Managers should discuss their views thoroughly and challenge each other's positions to make wise decisions on technology, procedures, and investments.

Adaptation to Environment

Markets, suppliers, value and skills of recruits, available technologies, stockholder demands, and other aspects of the environment continually change, and organizations must cope with these changes to survive and prosper. New niches must be discovered and new products introduced to keep abreast of changes in consumer preferences, the competition's offerings, research and development's discoveries, and pressures to demonstrate an acceptable return on investment.

Executives who are able to discuss their opinions and information about a new product are apt to make a decision that keeps the company's products current and marketable. Coordination between the organization and the environment is essential. Listening and working with customers can help employees to develop new products, discover quality-control problems, and develop marketing approaches.[7] Employees also must work effectively with investors, government officials, competitors, suppliers, marketing agents, union officials, researchers, and consultants to identify and solve various problems.

The Manager's Role

> I will pay more for the ability to deal with people than any other ability under the sun.
>
> —John D. Rockefeller

Managers must be skilled in working with others. They oversee, encourage, plead, cajole, and threaten employees to complete and coordinate tasks. Throughout the day, managers assign jobs, give pep talks, enforce deadlines, knock down barriers, discuss problems, and provide assistance. They work with employees, colleagues, superiors, suppliers, customers, and other departments.

Although there are differences in how managers use time, studies show that all managers work with and through others and live in an interpersonal, verbal world. Superintendents might interact with twenty-five to fifty people a day; managers have fewer interactions but contact more people outside the organization.[8] Managers have been found to communicate orally, usually face to face, about 75 percent of their office time. Managers continually talk, listen, and exchange information, but they give few orders and make few decisions.[9] Some managers are alone about one-third of the day, but usually for less than half an hour at a time.[10]

The findings that managers live in a high-activity, intensely interpersonal world, are continually interrupted, and do little independent reading and thinking have been interpreted to mean that managers are not systematic planners.[11] Studies indicate, however, that managers spend much of their day in scheduled and informal meetings. Executives were found to have four scheduled meetings that averaged sixty-eight minutes apiece plus an additional four unscheduled meetings each day.[12] Managers plan, but they plan together.

Aren't managers trapped by this intensely interpersonal, meeting-oriented environment? Without these constraints, wouldn't they become independent analysts and decision makers? Managers' own estimates of their time suggest that they value their interpersonal world. Managers consistently have been found to overestimate their time alone and underestimate their time with others.[13] They report that their interactions are invigorating and fulfilling. Most of us have had bosses who want face-to-face, eye-to-eye discussions; the telephone is not good enough. For instance, the two senior executives of a large corporation agreed to participate in research conducted by an MBA student that I supervised, but they insisted that he read the questions to them.

Teamwork and the Bottom Line

The need for coordination is built into all organizations, is part of their basic workings, and defines the manager's job. Yet many managers and researchers have doubts that working together is vital. One reason for this skepticism is that the bottom line impact of coordination has not been documented. The fact that how employees work together affects their commitment and competence, problem solving, adaptation to the environment, and the manager's role may seem vague to those who think in numerical terms.

A new method estimates the bottom line impact of interaction.[14] On the basis of structured interviews, five important dimensions that distinguished effective versus ineffective interaction were identified. One dimension, for example, tested the effectiveness of combining ideas and information to solve problems versus avoiding discussing the problem. Managers were asked to indicate the frequency with which employees interacted ineffectively and the extent (in dollars) to which these interactions resulted in unprofitable time and the number of days projects were delayed.

Ineffective interactions were estimated to result in more than $10,000 in time spent per employee per year. When project delays of $750 per day (due to idle equipment and inflation) were considered, the total reached $35,000. Ineffective interaction among departments was particularly costly. Even if the managers' estimates were too high, these results underline the fact that teamwork is critical and that the inability to work together undermines productivity and costs a great deal.

As John F. Donnelly, president of Donnelly Mirrors, notes:

> People can get satisfaction from a group effort as well as from individual effort. This is a good thing for business, because in an industrial organization it's group effort that counts. There's really no room for stars in an industrial organization. You need talented people, but they can't do it alone. They have to have help.

Employees must work together to make their organization succeed. Yet the idea that the individual is the basic building block of organizations persists. Frederick Taylor and other forerunners of modern management assumed that the key to an effective business is to select and motivate individuals correctly. Traditional American values reinforce this emphasis on the individual.[15] The individual is celebrated in folklore and studied in the social sciences. Values extol the virtues of rugged individualists and decry the "organizational man."

These traditions have made it more difficult to appreciate the importance of coordination, and researchers have not fully developed the implications that employees are mutually dependent. Still, tasks get done, problems are solved, innovations are implemented, and goals are achieved through people exchanging information, discussing issues, and supporting each other. By working together, managers and employees strive for and attain organizational excellence.

The Study of Teamwork in Organizations

Research on how employees work together potentially has a great impact on knowledge of organizations and management practices. Human relations and group dynamics research enjoys a rich and comparatively long history. Classic management studies focused on employee interaction. The Hawthorne studies of the 1930s showed that supportive leadership dramatically improved organizational life and productivity, and that workers often created informal groups to restrict their productivity.[16] In the same decade, Kurt Lewin, the father of contemporary social psychology, demonstrated that leadership could be studied systematically and that democratic compared to autocratic and laissez faire leadership resulted in intrinsic motivation and less aggression against group members.[17] In the next decade, Coch and French[18] found that workers who were asked to plan how to implement new technology used it to promote their productivity. Throughout the 1970s, research on group dynamics surged.

Recently, though, interest in group dynamics has waned. Research has become diverse and fragmented, making its potential contribution unclear. Attempts to characterize effective work relationships appear overly simplified and intensify suspicion that the research has little to offer. Many contemporary management researchers doubt that findings are persuasive or germane to the actual work of an organization. They charge that the research is ideologically motivated, removed from the reality of organizations, and not very relevant to the basic objectives of organizations. Despite managers' interest in interpersonal relations, researchers have concentrated on turnover, commitment, absenteeism, staffing, and organizational structure.[19] Considerable research from organizational behavior, social psychology, and related disciplines is, however, available to help managers understand and improve how employees work together.

Fragmentation

Researchers use a variety of perspectives and methods to study collaboration. Leaders' structuring of work and expressing consideration, group processes that mediate task groups, openness of ideas and feelings in decision making, and supportive relationships have been much discussed.[20] Studies are conducted under the labels of leadership, power, group dynamics, task teams, social support, conflict management, political decision making, participative management, relationship development, social cognition, mentoring, and office politics. In addition, researchers use various frameworks and terms drawn from different disciplines.

This fragmentation makes appreciating and applying research difficult. Studies fail to complement each other. Leadership research is not related to work on task groups. The implications of power and conflict for participative management or leadership are rarely discussed. Findings appear contradictory. Researchers have emphasized the value of trusting and supportive relationships; others argue that power politics and conflict are inevitable and beneficial.

Attempts to summarize research findings and suggest desirable relationships have not been very successful. Writers have characterized relationships on one continuum and have argued that relationships at one end of the continuum are the ideal. They have argued that employees should trust rather than suspect each other, be open-minded rather than closed-minded, and be supportive rather than unsupportive. These classifications oversimplify organizational reality, however. Relationships vary a great deal, and theories must be able to analyze this variety.

Nor can it be unquestionably assumed that there is one best way to work with others. Managers must at times be competitive and tough, in other circumstances trusting and compassionate, and at other times indifferent and aloof. Research must identify various ways employees interact and suggest when they are the most appropriate, not propose one way as always best.

Credibility

Researchers are accused of presenting an overly socialized, optimistic view of working together.[21] The advocacy of openness and trust has appeared simplistic and without sound evidence. At times, organization members distrust each other with good reason; at other times, they must exercise power to force their own way. Studies must consider the role of self-interest, conflict, and power and base their conclusions on documented findings, not assumptions and prejudices.

Findings consistent with current views often are dismissed as mere common sense. Researchers have documented findings that surprise and contradict widely held beliefs and have argued for unpopular positions. For example, writers have argued that all kinds of conflict should be encouraged and that the use of power to win corporate battles contributes to the organization. This research grabs attention but also undermines research credibility. Counterintuitive conclusions are difficult to accept, seem contradictory and unreliable, and raise doubts about the validity of research. Research findings do at times contradict common sense, and managers should be ready to challenge and question their present views. More often, though, research refines and develops popular views rather than directly contradicts them.

Relevance

The connection between work relationships and achieving company goals seems indirect and distant to some observers. How collaboration might aid and interfere with the basic purposes of the organization has not been specified. Interaction is assumed to affect job satisfaction and employee morale more than productivity and profits. As a consequence, constructive work relationships are considered desirable but not essential. As already discussed, though, collaboration directly affects the bottom line.

Research has seemed removed from the setting of organizational life. Employees do not just relate; they work together to accomplish concrete tasks under important constraints. Work assignments, roles, authority, bosses, and organizational norms and values all affect how employees work together.

Mutual Dependence

Researchers with a psychological perspective tend to investigate interaction without clearly recognizing that employees depend on each other. Leadership research, for example, focuses on the effects of leader behavior on employees, sometimes on employees' influence on their boss, but seldom on how leaders and employees are mutually dependent.[22] Researchers with a sociological background have examined mutual dependence but tend to assume that it directly and simply affects coordination. For example, technology is thought to determine coordination between departments by stipulating the flow of work among them.[23] Employees depend on each other very much, and the role of mutual dependence must be investigated.

There is a large gap between research and practice. Despite the skepticism of researchers, managers and consultants are very interested in teamwork. Articles, books, and training programs concentrate on the importance of people skills. These writings, while often informative, seldom are based on systematic research. At last, years of empirical research are bearing fruit. Progress has been made in developing ideas and theories, combining findings, and drawing implications for organizational practice. This book develops an integrated, empirically developed approach to understand how people work with each other and to help employees work as a team.

Research Base for the Book

This book synthesizes research and develops an empirically based approach to cooperation in organizations. Chapters review major propositions and findings of organizational research and then discuss the research and implications of the model developed. The book does not review all relevant research, nor does it critique the methods used in the research. It does cite studies and reviews of literature that readers interested in a more thorough treatment of the research can consult.

The theories, procedures, and suggestions are based on considerable empirical evidence using a wide range of research methods. Rather than base the major premises on one set of studies conducted using one research method, the propositions have been tested through laboratory experiments, field experiments, and field studies using surveys, interviews, and observations conducted in many settings with different samples.

These research methods complement each other. Experiments typically have internal validity, as the causal link between variables are documented.

Field studies are useful for external validity because the results are found to occur in actual organizations. Consistent evidence using different methods and samples is much more convincing than evidence using only one method.

The book bridges the macro sociological perspective to structure, design, technology, roles, size, and corporate philosophy and the micro psychological view of individual differences, attitudes, leadership, and group dynamics. Both perspectives are needed to understand interaction. Personalities affect how employees work together; persons collaborate in the context of an organization's structure and technology. Social psychological research on mutual dependence integrates the psychological and sociological perspectives on coordination and connects structure and attitudes with interpersonal behavior.

Within organizational studies, many researchers have become disenchanted with the outcomes of traditional empirical research. They doubt that these studies have much payoff and are impatient with the slow accumulation of evidence. They want bold new theories and ways to develop them. The research reported in this book is the result of the slow development of ideas and theories through years of empirical work carried out by many different social scientists. I trust that the book reaffirms the value of empirical research to understand organizations and improve managerial practice.

The reliance on systematic, empirical research contrasts with widely read books such as *In Search of Excellence* and *Theory Z*. These books rely on observation to draw conclusions, a method that has substantial shortcomings. For example, it is not clear that all the excellent companies can be so categorized or that they are effective for the reasons asserted.[24] The evidence presented in such books often is telling, however, and offers informative glimpses into effective organizational work. The research presented here does not contradict the conclusions of these books as much as it develops them further and suggest major ways to achieve teamwork and organizational productivity.

Overview of Chapters

The book has four parts. Part I discusses the significance of working as a team for organizations. Chapter 2 describes the approach to understanding alternative ways in which people work with each other that is used throughout the book. Attitudes, values, tasks, and rewards affect how employees perceive they depend upon each other and interact. Employees, groups, departments, and organizations can cooperate, compete, or work independently. Chapter 3 shows the effects of teamwork on motivation and productivity.

Part II suggests methods to help employees understand that they must cooperate with each other. Research shows that employees who believe that their goals are compatible work together to get tasks done and solve problems. Groups are concrete ways to establish this cooperative dependence, and chapter 4 illustrates how groups have improved collaboration and productivity. Chapter 5 continues with this theme by elaborating on major ways to establish cooperative goals. Not just individual employees must coordinate; groups, departments, divisions, and profit centers also must work together. Interdepartmental rivalries can be very costly and can even threaten an organization's survival. Chapter 6 indicates how the book's approach can be applied to integrate departments and form a cohesive company.

Setting cooperative dependence is a first step, but employees also must have the opportunities, procedures, and skills to collaborate. Part III identifies constructive ways for employees to work together. Probably no organizational phenomenon is as misunderstood as power. Power need not disrupt coordination, however, and chapter 7 indicates how cooperation helps managers to recognize and develop employee abilities and to manage power positively. Organizations require problem solving and decision making; chapter 8 reviews research indicating that decision makers who discuss opposing views constructively create more effective solutions. Chapter 9 shows that conflict is compatible with cooperation; indeed conflict is part of teamwork and can be very productive. Employees must, of course, learn skills and procedures to manage conflict.

Organizations must take advantage of changes and opportunities to innovate. Chapter 10 describes organizational innovation and the employee interaction that promotes it. Chapter 11 presents a fresh view of leadership. Leaders are at the center of their groups; they must develop effective relationships with employees and help them work with each other. The ideas, procedures, and skills described in the previous chapters are all relevant to managerial leadership.

The last part shows that working collaboratively helps employees make use of their experiences to acquire technical and interpersonal skills and to develop more successful teamwork. The last chapter reviews major themes and summarizes the book's implications for developing a productive, humane organization.

2
Alternative Ways to Work with People

Everyone has to work together; if we can't get everybody working toward common goals, nothing is going to happen.
—*Harold K. Sperlich, President, Chrysler Corporation*

How can the teamwork so vital to organizational productivity be understood? When do employees work with and not against each other? What can managers do to get employees to work as a team to achieve company goals?

Managers need powerful methods to improve coordination and build work relationships. They are advised to demonstrate that they care for their employees and want them to care for and trust each other. They should create a common vision that binds all employees together. Managers also have been told to change procedures and designs; the benefits of profit sharing, task forces, liaison officers, and other changes have been advocated. Calls for greater cooperation have been loud and persistent. Training in communication and conflict skills also have been popular.

But simultaneous, reinforcing changes in values, design, and skills are needed to get employees to work together. New attitudes, values, and procedures do not inevitably lead to new behavior; employees may not have the skills or opportunity to express their new values. Teamwork results only when attitudes, design, procedures, and skills are changed systematically. Employees who value teamwork and show support, have group assignments and rewards, believe that they are positively dependent on each other, and use appropriate procedures and interpersonal skills work together successfully.

People work with each other in three fundamentally different ways. They may work together for cooperative goals; they compete and work against each other's interests; they feel independent and work alone. Let us first examine the major components that determine how people work with each other and then take a closer look at the three ways of working.

The Model

Attitudes and values have long been used to understand how persons work with each other. Positive attitudes and common values are thought to underlie teamwork. But the design and requirements of the organization also play a role. For instance, some organizations reward employees for competing. It is important to remember, however, that an organization's culture or design combine with values and attitudes, tasks and rewards, and mutual dependence to determine collaboration. Figure 2–1 shows how these components reinforce each other to influence how employees work with each other.

Attitudes and Values

Attitudes of support and trust contribute to productive teamwork.[1] Shared values about relationships and people in the organization help forge a cohesive organization out of its diverse groups and individuals.[2] Openness and cooperation contribute mightily to a productive organizational climate.[3] Successful companies develop a corporate philosophy that conveys to members that the company values them as persons, wants them to develop trusting, personal relationships with each other, and believes that company goals are valuable to employees and society. People who feel distant and doubt that the company or their co-workers value them have difficulties working as a team.

Tasks and Rewards

Employees work within the assignments, expectations, and opportunities of the organization. They are responsible for tasks, use a given technology, fulfill specific roles, are evaluated by standards, and seek rewards. Assigned tasks greatly affect interaction.[4] Employees who have the information and resources to complete their jobs can work independently and rely on rules and procedures to coordinate their efforts. Complex tasks that demand more knowledge require direct discussion and exchange among employees to coordinate their work.[5]

Roles stipulate how employees are expected to act toward others. Roles indicate that persons are to work alone or give them complementary and overlapping responsibilities. Although attention has been directed toward how persons come to learn their roles and the effects of roles on individual behavior, research has not elaborated on the impact of roles on working with others.[6]

The standards by which employees are rewarded and evaluated affect interaction. Rewards given for group success rather than individual success, for example, induce employees to exchange information and assistance.[7] Profit-sharing plans also may improve coordination among units in a company.[8] Unfortunately, organizational researchers have concentrated on the impact of rewards on the motivation and performance of individuals.[9]

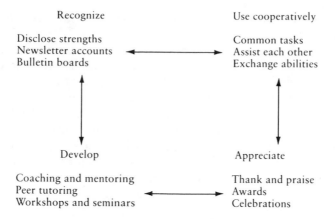

Figure 7–1. Positive Power

associated with unequal relationships. But power differences unconfounded by competition are still apt to influence collaboration. Powerful persons have been found to be relatively disinterested in taking the perspective and understanding the interests of the less powerful and to be less open to being influenced by the less powerful.[16] This reluctance may make establishing productive cooperation difficult.[17]

These studies suggest that cooperation depends more on the orientation and skills of the powerful than the less powerful. The powerful often can structure work to make it difficult for others to talk about problems openly, or they can emphasize cooperative goals and encourage mutually rewarding collaboration.

Positive Power

Power can be a highly constructive force within organizations, but the key to power management is that employees believe that their important goals are cooperative. To make all employees feel like winners, have them recognize each other's abilities, share knowledge, and develop each other's strengths and confidence, managers must work to establish strong, cooperative goals. Employees who believe that their goals are competitive are reluctant to appreciate abilities and share resources.

Positive power (see figure 7–1) means that employees search out each other's abilities and appreciate their contributions, negotiate and influence each other to exchange resources that will help them both be more productive, and encourage each other to develop and enhance their strengths. This positive power pattern occurs as employees work on a common task with cooperative goals.

As they begin, employees can identify previous experiences, achievements, and strengths that are relevant to their task. Shared knowledge about each one's abilities makes it easier to call upon the right team member and to use all the resources available to the group. Throughout their joint assignment, employees can continue to identify abilities. Giving thanks, praise, and compliments conveys appreciation as well as recognizes abilities. Working together also is critical for developing skills. Coaching, on-the-job training, peer tutoring, and mentoring are important ways for employees to learn and grow on the job. These are discussed in chapter 12.

Power and Recognition in a Growing Company

North American Tool & Die, Inc., had experienced the troubles of many small manufacturers—marginal profitability, an unenthusiastic work force, and lots of competition.[1] But in the three years beginning with 1980, company sales went from $1.8 million to $6 million, profits were increased by six times, the customer reject rate declined from 5 to 0.3 percent, and turnover dropped from 27 to 6 percent.

The co-owners, Thomas H. Melohn and Garner Beckett, Jr., realized that to compete successfully and grow they had to provide both quality and service. Competitors were run largely by technically skilled entrepreneurs who were only semiskilled managers. Melohn and Beckett wanted to build a well-managed company to supply computer manufacturers with timely, quality products, many of which have a tolerance of 19.001 of an inch. That's about a fourth of the size of a human hair.

They believed that people would be the difference between them and their competitors. Employees received shares provided that they met basic requirements. Meetings also informed employees of where the company had been and where it was going. Employees recognized that the company's success and profits were their success and profits.

Melohn and Beckett worked hard to recognize the abilities of all employees. At monthly plantwide meetings, they gave the "Super Person of the Month" plaque and a check to the employee who had produced excellent quality. The employee's name was engraved and the plaque was prominently and permanently displayed in the plant. Every employee who had an anniversary of working with the company that month got a silver dollar. Customer's compliments were announced and the employees responsible honored. The award the company won as the best supplier of a customer was given to the department heads who had earned it.

Throughout the month and every day, the company complimented employees. Two or three times a week, Melohn and Beckett went through the plant chatting and complimenting those who had worked well. They also showed concern for employees as people. When a Korean worker had trouble conveying his symptoms to his doctor, they found a physician who spoke Korean. Employees were allowed to borrow a week's pay with no interest. The

What Makes Someone Powerful?

Employees in three companies were asked in interviews to identify the abilities they needed from each other in specific situations.[8] Although the companies were quite different—one provided computer services for a large retailer, another was a municipal engineering office, and the third provided services for mentally handicapped persons—employees valued similar abilities in all of them. Knowledge, assistance, and emotional support were mentioned often in all three organizations. Funding, evaluation, and authority were infrequently mentioned.

Employees greatly valued information and knowledge; to make decisions, plan how to proceed, and perform a host of other tasks requires others' advice and data. They also frequently cited willingness to give assistance to complete tasks as important; many tasks cannot be accomplished by one person working alone. Perhaps surprisingly, emotional support also was seen in nearly half the situations as an important, valued resource, even among groups such as computer specialists, people not typically thought to have strong emotional needs. Even when working with their boss, employees thought that knowledge, effort, and emotional support were more important than official approval. Although rewards of bonuses and evaluations were cited infrequently, persons who control these also have power.

Employees understand that they need others' abilities to get their jobs done. They value others' knowledge and effort and often turn to each other for support and encouragement. Job requirements and emotional needs underlie much of the power in organizations. Power is not restricted to competition but is very much a part of cooperative work.

Research Findings

Experiments and studies in companies indicate that cooperative, compared to competitive and independent, goals promote constructive power in organizations.

Cooperative Goals Foster Recognition and Appreciation of Employee Abilities. People in cooperation identify and value each other's strengths because they realize that abilities will be used for mutual benefit. It is to one's advantage that others are powerful and resourceful, for powerful others can help reach cooperative goals. Competitors, on the other hand, fear that others will use their abilities against them. Knowledge that others have different information and ideas is welcome in cooperation but threatens when goals are competitive. Collaborators help each other to be aware of their ideas, information, skills, and other abilities so that they are in a better position to reach goals and do their jobs.[9]

Cooperative Goals Encourage Mutual Influence and a Profitable Exchange of Abilities. Collaborators, even though they may be unequally powerful, are able to exchange abilities and resources for mutual benefit. Both the powerful and less powerful with cooperative goals expected to help each other, were trusting, shared their resources, and came to like each other. In contrast, those in competition suspected each other, failed to exchange resources, and intensified their mistrust and dislike. Powerful competitors felt confident, but less powerful ones were insecure.[10]

Managers who feel powerful are thought to use their power supportively.[11] Although power bestows a capacity to aid employees, cooperative goals compel managers to use their power constructively. Managers who had power and were cooperatively linked with their employees encouraged, guided, and gave tangible assistance that aided productivity.[12] Managers with or without power in competition discouraged and gave little assistance.

In another experiment, powerful managers in competition used their power to try to coerce employees.[13] Cooperatively linked managers relied less on coercion and used more collaborative influence. It has been shown that cooperative goals help managers use their power flexibly.[14] In this experiment, managers demanded more from employees who performed poorly because they failed to apply themselves but supported and encouraged those who lacked the ability to do the task. Managers in competition were punitive regardless of whether employees performed poorly because of low ability or low effort.

Studies conducted in organizations further document the positive pattern of power in cooperation.[15] Three hundred ten medical technicians employed in the laboratories of ten major hospitals in the Vancouver, British Columbia, metropolitan area, indicated that cooperative supervisors used their power to help them accomplish their tasks and become committed to the hospital.

In addition, colleagues also have been found to use their power constructively in cooperation. An analysis of the interviews of 140 employees from three organizations indicated that when they believed that their goals were cooperative, they exchanged abilities, strengthened their relationships, and accomplished their tasks.

Cooperation Encourages Learning and Development. Employees with cooperative goals want others to become more capable because that helps everyone to be effective. They initiate activities and discussions to learn. They coach each other on the job, review information and ideas that aid learning, reflect and learn from their experiences, and provide feedback to learn skills. Chapter 12 elaborates on these findings and their implications.

Unequally Powerful Persons Can Work Together Effectively, But Power Differences Can Interfere. Competition between unequally powerful persons, not power differences, account for the suspicion and difficulties traditionally

- Resources should be given so that the receiver does not feel belittled. Exchanges help members to feel confident that they have important assets and that they can rely on others for assistance.

6. As they collaborate, team members help each other to learn and develop skills.

7. The team celebrates its accomplishments and recognizes that everyone contributed to the group's success.

Comparisons

In cooperation, employees identify each other's strengths and feel reassured and motivated by them, not threatened. Inevitably, though, employees will compare themselves and at times will believe that they have much less knowledge, experience, and ideas than others. Comparisons themselves are not inevitably harmful, and they can help people learn about themselves. But invidious ones that create feelings of inferiority and competition should be avoided.[18] Recognizing employee abilities and achievement must be well managed.

Skills and Achievements are Not Confused with Personal Worth. Employees are intrinsically worthwhile and are not important just because of their knowledge and resources. Highly valued abilities do not make an employee more moral, just as having few abilities that are not valued in that situation does not make one an unimportant person.

Recognition of Abilities Is Based on Facts, Not Prejudices. Strengths and capabilities are recognized regardless of the sex, race, age, verbal skills, or physical appearance of employees. Not just attractive persons who speak fluently have abilities. Similarly, expertise in one area does not automatically confer expertise in others.

Everyone's Value Is Recognized. Differences in abilities should not obscure the fact that all employees have abilities, are important to the organization, and can contribute to its success. Employees understand that everyone must do their job well and contribute to the organization.

Identifying abilities and recognizing differences can, if properly done, avoid invidious comparisons and strengthen cooperation. Disclosure and recognition of abilities create a great deal of goodwill. People feel fulfilled and rewarded, and these good feelings lead to a desire to reciprocate, help others, and work together.[19]

Guides for Action

Positive Power

- Know your own abilities and strengths.
- Know others' abilities and accomplishments.
- Show that people's abilities help everyone to be successful.
- Discuss how people can use each other's abilities to get things done.
- Celebrate achievements to make everyone proud.

Pitfalls to Avoid

- Assume that only a few people have abilities.
- Use stereotypes to decide who has valued resources.
- Classify people as winners or losers.
- Suspect people who want to feel confident and powerful.

Concluding Comments

Power traditionally has been considered part of the dark side of social life. It is usually believed to be used for self-aggrandizement in the struggle against others. This win-lose view is only one side of the story, however, and the prevalence of competitive power probably has been exaggerated.

Power and recognizing employee abilities are very constructive for organizations. Knowledge, expertise, information, assistance, emotional support, and other abilities necessary to make decisions, solve problems, develop new products, accomplish tasks, and maintain the organization are disclosed, valued, exchanged, and further refined and developed. Positive power enhances employees and productivity.

To make all employees feel like winners requires more than handing out pins and awards. It requires highly cooperative goals in which people draw out and appreciate each other's strengths as they work together. Company practices and the way employees collaborate can help to identify, use, appreciate, and develop the abilities of employees and boost the company's collective might.

company sent flowers to every employee or spouse who was in the hospital. Each employee got a check as a wedding present. National Tool & Die continually recognized and appreciated the abilities of its employees and got them to work together for success.

Company practices reinforce positive power. Newsletters, employee rosters, award ceremonies, celebrations, and bulletin boards identify the talents, backgrounds, and achievements of employees and make them known. To facilitate the exchange of resources, the organization can use project teams, task forces, and other forums in which employees can work together and use their abilities to accomplish common objectives. The organization can provide workshops, encourage professional activities, establish mentoring programs, and subsidize tuition for courses to develop employee abilities.

Example of Positive Power

Esther wanted to build apartments for the elderly. Her experience owning a nursing home convinced her that many elderly persons need housing that helps them to live independently but with companions and without the hassles of home ownership. At a community breakfast, she sought out John, a manager of a general contractor–development firm. She told him that she liked his new condominiums and that she wanted something like them next to her nursing home. Esther knew that Bill, the administrator at the nursing home, would be excited about the project because he and his staff also wanted opportunities to work with healthy, independent elderly people. Bill agreed to arrange the first formal meeting with John.

In the first meetings, Esther, Bill, and John explored the feasibility of the project and got to know each other better. John questioned them on how the building would be different from a typical apartment complex and was reassured when he found that Esther already owned the land next to the nursing home. Bill said that the nursing home's reputation would be useful in attracting residents and that initial operating expenses could be covered by income from the nursing home. Bill asked John about his building, marketing, and financing experience. John described the projects his company had helped develop and gave Esther and Bill a tour of two apartment buildings his company had just completed. He estimated the cost of construction and his fees.

Esther and Bill were impressed with John's buildings and concluded that he had the needed expertise. John's experience in developing attractive market-rate apartments was a big plus because they wanted a residential, not an institutional, look. John concluded that Esther and Bill were serious people who had already developed one business and would work to build another, were practical enough to make reasonable decisions, had sufficient equity, and would not be too difficult, maybe even a little fun, to work with. He also knew that having a nursing home and the land were major financial assets to help them build the project. They agreed to work on the project together, pursued it steadily, and after seventeen months broke ground.

Esther, Bill, and John, like others who want to develop a business or get a job done, need power, provided it is used cooperatively. They knew they had a common goal that, if reached, would benefit each of them. Esther and Bill initially wanted to know what John could do for the project. They were delighted that what he told them and his past achievements indicated that he had the abilities to make the project a reality. John wanted to identify Esther's and Bill's abilities. If they did not have the right ones, John would have concluded that he would be wasting his time on the project. In addition to having the abilities, they wanted to be sure that they would use their abilities collaboratively.

Esther, Bill, and John used their abilities to reach their cooperative goal, and the apartments were built. They also learned. John found out about managing a nursing home and building for the elderly; Bill realized the differences between a market-oriented business and a government-regulated and reimbursed one.

Steps to Positive Power in Teams

Team members must recognize each other's abilities and exchange them to accomplish tasks and solve problems.

1. Team members together recognize, emphasize, and clearly understand that their goals are cooperative. They know that as others reach their goals, they too are successful. Important cooperative goals lay the foundation for the following activities.
2. Members indicate the abilities and resources needed to accomplish team goals and aspirations.
3. Team members identify and demonstrate their knowledge, ideas, and other strengths. They know each other's abilities.
4. Employees indicate how they can use each other's abilities to reach the team's goals, accomplish its tasks, and meet their own aspirations.
5. Aware of their cooperative goals and valued abilities, team members agree to exchange resources. These exchanges should be timely, fair, and enhancing.
   - Abilities are valued at a particular time; information useful at one time is noise at another. Employees let each other know when they need the others' abilities.
   - Fairness demands that everyone give as well as receive.

making is costly because employees' time and energy are wasted, projects are delayed, and opportunities are missed.

But there is no single way that all problems should be discussed and solved. Some decisions demand careful exploration and creation of new approaches; others are solved in quick, routine ways. Some decisions break new ground; many decisions use precedents as guides to determine what should be done. Managers and organizations must be flexible. They must make wise decisions about how they are going to make decisions.

By working cooperatively and using their power positively, managers and employees are able to dig into issues, pool their information, integrate ideas, and create useful solutions. But how exactly are they to work together to solve problems? What procedures are useful and what skills needed? Decision makers must be able to discuss their opposing ideas and information openly and constructively. Constructive controversy is the key to making the most of cooperative goals and positive power to solve problems. Avoiding controversy or trying to make one's views dominate often are disastrous. Constructive controversy is a powerful tool for solving problems and an important safeguard against fiascos.

Effective Problem Solving

Getting quality solutions is important in decision making, but it is not the only objective. Decisions are not simply puzzles and riddles to be solved; they are part of the whole stream of working and managing. A problem must be felt and understood and alternative choices created before employees can consider its solution. The decision must be implemented, its impact assessed, and new problems identified.

Problem solving is an ongoing process that is an integral part of working. To be effective, problem solving must find a solution that gets the job done, efficiently uses resources, promotes future cooperation, and fosters employee competence.

Decisions that promote all these objectives are highly effective; decisions that promote none of them are highly ineffective. Of course, these objectives are not always important; managers must be aware of the most relevant criteria. For major decisions, a high-quality solution is critical, but for a minor problem, saving time may be more important.

High-Quality Solutions

Bob Clinton and his group want to know whether and how they should seek business in neighboring states. They want a solution based on thoughtful analysis and relatively complete information, not whim and fancy. The solution should be appropriate and relatively permanent; they do not want to decide to seek the business one month only to retreat the next. The benefits of the solution should outweigh the costs to implement it.

Bob and his group will be unable to validate their solution completely, however. It might be years until they have a good picture of the benefits and costs, and there is always the possibility that another strategy would have been more successful. Although quality is usually important, it is difficult to measure and feel confident about it.

Implementation and Ownership

Bob's health-care group wants a solution that it can and will implement. It does little good to decide to make loans and then not do it. No matter how brilliant the plan, if it remains unimplemented, it cannot work. Ideally, employees should own the solution and be willing to implement it without costly supervision and monitoring. They should understand the decision, know what they must do to implement it, be internally committed to seeing the solution put into practice, and report any difficulties or unexpected consequences that occur when the solution is implemented.

Efficiency

Proper priorities and common sense about practicality are important ingredients in using the time and energy of employees wisely. Not all problems are equally important, and their relative significance must be kept in perspective. Minor problems do not deserve exhaustive consideration or million-dollar solutions. Issues that substantially affect the health of the company need careful, ongoing exploration. Although there may be benefits to having the department as a whole solve a problem, employees will have to forgo work on other tasks to coordinate schedules, attend meetings, and focus their attention. They will be annoyed and perhaps less committed if they believe that their time is not well spent.

Future Decisions

The issue of making loans in nearby states will not be the last one that Bob's group decides. Ideally, decision makers should become more informed and able to create and implement high-quality solutions. Experiences that leave them less willing to share information and difficulties, combine their ideas, and implement useful solutions bode ill for the organization.

8
Solving Problems and Making Decisions

If Doug Fraser had served on Lynn Townsend's board, maybe Chrysler wouldn't have bought up the lousiest companies in Europe. Some of those terrible moves could have been stopped by just one bold man asking, "Why are we doing this? Does it really make sense?"
— Lee Iacocca, CEO, Chrysler Corporation

The best way ever devised for seeking the truth in any given situation is advocacy: presenting the pros and cons from different, informed points of view and digging down deep into the facts.
— Harold S. Geneen, former CEO, ITT

*G*etting ready for his weekly squash match with Wilbur Oxman, Bob Clinton declared, "I found out that I'm a participative manager."

"That sounds good," Wilbur responded. "How did you find that out?"

Bob explained that he had learned at a workshop that participative managers involve people in making decisions. "I used to think that it was my job to solve all the problems, but it is a great relief to know that I can get my group together and we can work out a solution together. When Preston and Fred have very different opinions about what we should do, I don't feel as though I have to resolve it right then, but we talk the issue over. These team sessions take the pressure off me, my staff like them, and we've come up with some very good programs.

"Another thing I learned was that disagreements are important for making sound decisions. That makes a lot of sense to me. It bothers me when everyone agrees with the first suggestion. I get nervous that we aren't really involved and haven't dug into the issue."

"Apathy can certainly be a problem, but so can arguing and arguing," Wilbur interjected. "Our group always seems to drag the debate on; people get very stubborn."

"We do that sometimes, too. It's not just debating but constructive disagreement that we want. Arguments between Preston and

Fred are very useful for getting at the facts, but there is one thing that they do wrong rather regularly. They try to win and prove that they are right and the other is wrong. That's when the debate is endless and progress slow. People must disagree but should work for a solution that is good for all, not to prove they are right and that everyone must agree with them."

"You have a point there, but is it realistic? People, especially professional types, always want to be right," Wilbur asserted.

*"I think it can work," Bob answered. "Everyone does want to be right, but they must want the group to be right and make the best decision. My job as a manager is to make sure my people understand that it is **unimportant to begin with the right position,** but it is **very important that we all end up with the right one.** We need to emphasize the common objective and point out when persons get carried away and are browbeating others."*

"Maybe that's a way to stop the debate from getting out of hand and turning into an endless argument," Wilbur offered.

"I have a good way to use this idea," Bob continued. "We haven't been able to decide whether we should seek business out of state—it would be very profitable, but we have not gotten around to discussing it thoroughly. My plan is to divide the group in half, assign one the pro position and one the con position, have them research their position, and then have them debate the question. We would let the issue rest for a few days and then meet to get some consensus. I'll probably invite the boss to join us."

"Sounds interesting," Wilbur said. "Keep me informed about your experiments. If they work for you, they might work for me."

Problems challenge, invigorate, and disrupt. Every day managers confront problems that must be solved: How should the requests of Abbey Hospitals and City Health be answered? Is more information needed? Employees must make decisions to complete their tasks: Is additional collateral for the loan required? Companies face decisions to enter new markets, develop new products, and acquire businesses that very much affect the profits, even the survival, of the firm. Skills to identify problems and make decisions greatly determine the success of managers and the productivity of companies.

Problem solving is the sine qua non of successful management; no company can thrive unless it can grapple with difficulties, cope with uncertainties, and seize opportunities. Selecting efficient technologies, adapting and responding to the environment, forming a shared vision, and developing employee skills all demand identifying problems and implementing solutions.

Decision making competence pays off handsomely; the organization stays on course, handles setbacks, and remains confident. Ineffective decision

Constructive Controversy

Begin with certainties, end with uncertainties.
Begin with uncertainties, end with certainties.

—*Chinese proverb*

It is not who is right, but what is right.

—*Popular saying*

Don't find fault, find a remedy.

—*Henry Ford*

Managers and employees must know how to work together to reduce their biases, avoid closed-mindedness and simplistic thinking, dig into problems, and make successful decisions. They must discuss their opposing positions and opinions constructively to be open-minded, evaluate new information objectively, incorporate new ideas, and avoid unwarranted commitment to their position.

Not all controversy is beneficial. To be productive, differences of opinion must be discussed within cooperative goals. But we now know that skillfully discussed controversy is vital for successful problem solving.

IBM and Controversy

IBM's contention system required managers to "nonconcur" if they did not agree with a proposed plan or program.[1] The corporation wanted issues to be discussed thoroughly by those directly involved. People within and across divisions were expected to voice their opposing opinions and differences. To encourage this controversy, the company respected individual rights of free expression and provided a system to resolve controversies that the protagonists themselves could not. The top executives in the Corporate Management Committee listened to all sides of any dispute that could not be resolved at lower levels. To affirm its commitment to this contention system, the committee listened to debates even on issues that involved relatively few resources.

The Value of Controversy

Decision makers who express their opposing ideas, opinions, conclusions, theories, and information as they discuss problems are in controversy. Controversy involves differences of opinion that temporarily prevent, delay, or interfere with reaching a decision. Some managers want harmony as employees discuss problems; others want debate, even acrimony. Fortunately, recent research clarifies the role of controversy.

Suppressed controversy has resulted in major fiascos.[9] President John F. Kennedy and his advisors pressured foreign policy experts to suppress their reservations about the invasion of Cuba in the Bay of Pigs fiasco. Learning from this experience, Kennedy insisted on controversy in the Cuban missile crisis, and his actions still earn him high marks.

The inability of flight crews to discuss opposing views is thought to undermine safety and performance and to have contributed significantly to disastrous airplane crashes.[10] Suppressed controversy contributed to the tragic decision early in 1986 to launch the space shuttle that exploded one minute after takeoff. Engineers and managers apparently did not openly and constructively discuss their opposing views on the safety of flying the shuttle in cold weather. Harold S. Geneen, former CEO of ITT, argued that company boards cannot protect stockholders because directors have neither the knowledge nor the courage to disagree with the CEO and act only when the company is near ruin.[11]

Suppressed controversy is not restricted to disasters or the boardroom. The organizational development group suppresses survey results that criticize a manager's leadership style. Managers do not point out weaknesses in a colleague's proposal. Market researchers withhold information that indicates little consumer market in a new product that their boss wants to market. Every day thousands of employees fear expressing their opposing information and ideas, and the resulting ineffective solutions cost their companies a great deal of money and embarrassment.[12]

The potential of controversy for problem solving has been demonstrated. Groups composed of persons with different views and outlooks and groups whose leaders encourage expression of minority opinions have made high-quality decisions. Consensus decision making results in useful decisions by stimulating open controversy.[13] Controversy is used by executives to formulate company strategy.[14]

Controversy helps individuals to cope with their limitations and make successful decisions.[15] Decision makers in controversy were found to be open to new and opposing information. Confronting an opposing opinion created doubts that their position was adequate. People became interested in the opponent's arguments and asked questions to explore the opposing views. They demonstrated that they knew the opposing arguments and understood the reasoning the other used to develop them.

In addition to openness to new information and ideas, people in controversy were willing to take the information seriously, develop a more complex and accurate view of the problem, and incorporate the opposing position into their own thinking and decisions. Controversy resulted in the creation of new solutions not originally proposed. By combining their information and ideas,

Individual Competence

Many people seek decision-making responsibility. They enjoy the challenge to draw upon and develop their abilities to identify and overcome obstacles. They are pleased that others trust their judgment and seek their opinion. They enjoy the give and take, exploration, camaraderie, and sense of importance that often accompany decision making. The abilities and resources of individuals should be recognized and utilized.

Legitimacy

Decision making involves rights to influence and responsibilities to obey. Employees are likely to be more committed to implementing the solution and to the organization in general if they believe that the decision was reached by legitimate, just means. Although employees recognize their superiors' right to make decisions, they usually see the methods as fairer if they have participated in making the decision.

Cooperation promotes all aspects of effective problem solving. Decision makers with cooperative goals combine their ideas to create high-quality solutions, understand and become committed to the solution, make problem solving a rich experience, develop confidence and skills to make decisions, and accept the procedures used to arrive at the decision. In addition to its significance, how decision makers work together can be influenced and managed. Not all organizations can hire geniuses and the best experts, but they can improve the way employees discuss and make decisions.

Limitations of Individuals

The rational ideal holds that decision makers should agree on their goals, exhaustively search for alternatives, evaluate options thoroughly, and select the best alternative. Management researchers doubt that this rational, comprehensive decision making is realistic for the many complex problems contemporary organizations face.[1] They argue that decision makers do not have the cognitive capacity to process information necessary for this rational approach. Decision makers are unable to understand the changing vagrancies of the external and internal environments. Individuals also are thought to be self-interested and to promote their own interests rather than the common good.[2]

Studies document that individuals have limited ability to consider various information and have biases that prevent full and open consideration of ideas.[3] Many different ways of biasing processes have been identified. Simplification and biases occur in identifying the problem, analyzing it, developing alternatives, considering consequences, and selecting the decision.[4]

Decision makers have been found to be closed to considering information, especially information that is new and opposes their present position. They rely on easy-to-recall, available information to form their opinions. Decision makers often evaluate information inadequately. With a "belief in the law of small numbers," they have made unreasonable conclusions based on very small samples and have used early trends to predict final results.[5] Despite being closed to information and evaluating data inappropriately, decision makers often are confident in their conclusions, apparently oblivious to their own faulty reasoning.[6] Individuals have many ways to make bad decisions.

Potential of Team Decision Making

The speed, suddenness, and complexity of changes make great demands on decision makers. Past policies cannot be expected to be successful continuously. Decision makers must, after monitoring the company's environment and understanding its internal workings and strengths, determine its goals, plans, and procedures. But individual decision makers have limited capacity to monitor these developments and create solutions. Organizations require individuals to pool their information, explore complex issues thoroughly, and create new, appropriate measures.

Forming teams to make complex decisions does not automatically result in effective problem solving. Indeed, sometimes people working together reinforce their biases and enhance their limitations.[7] They may develop groupthink conformity that results in fiascos that severely damage the company. Alternatively, individuals use the group to push for their own self-interest at the expense of the company's welfare.[8]

To cope with the limitations of individuals, decision makers must work together successfully to solve problems. But how can a team solve complex problems effectively? Conflict-filled discussions, when conducted cooperatively, can help the team to cope with the cognitive limitations and biases of individual decision makers. It is not proposed that teams always rationally and comprehensively make decisions, that their cognitive limitations do not interfere, or that conflict always aids coping with these limitations. But *decision makers with highly cooperative goals who are able to discuss their opposing views openly and constructively can thoroughly investigate problems and create useful solutions.*

goals. They treat discussions as debates to win instead of issues to solve. In these cases, people are apt to believe that open controversy should be avoided if possible. Although competition often is assumed to stimulate conflict, co-operative goals create a willingness to discuss differences openly.[20]

People avoid controversy for fear of losing face and being thought ineffective. Organizations pressure managers to present themselves as strong and mature; they may conclude that a direct challenge of their ideas makes them look weak. Managers also are under pressure to show that they can dominate.[21] Employees may quite reasonably conclude that their manager will perceive their opposition as an attack designed to make him look weak and ineffectual and that the resulting discussion may escalate dangerously.

Controversy also is avoided because many employees do not have the skills and procedures to discuss it constructively. Skills in working with others traditionally have been underemphasized in management and vocational training. Controversy poses many challenges and is a rich and demanding experience. Decision makers must express their ideas, information, and feelings in such a way that others will be encouraged to express theirs. They must be open-minded, take the other's perspective, and be able to integrate material. They also must manage the strong feelings that controversial discussions arouse. Controversy skills and procedures require considerable effort and practice, and many employees recognize that they need more ideas and experience to disagree constructively and directly with superiors, friends, co-workers, and experts.

Establishing Constructive Controversy

Although it is difficult, controversies are discussed productively in some organizations. What is needed is to encourage open controversy together with cooperative dependence.

Initiate Controversy

Controversy can be encouraged by group membership, subgroups, leadership style, openness norms, and decision-making rules.

Group Membership. Teams composed of persons who are heterogeneous in regard to background, expertise, opinions, outlook, and organizational position are likely to disagree. Including persons from outside the department or organization and independent thinkers makes controversy more likely.

Openness Norms. All persons should be encouraged to express their opinions, doubts, uncertainties, and hunches. No idea should be dismissed quickly because it first appears to be too unusual, impractical, or undeveloped.

Individual Rights. The right to dissent must be protected; everyone is expected to voice her opinions and knows that she will not be punished.

Subgroups. Forming two smaller groups that are assigned opposing positions on the issue is a direct way to structure controversy. For example, a manager can assign one subgroup the position that the company should buy an existing plant and another that the company should build its own to decide how to expand production capacity. At Gould Electronics, senior managers form pro and con groups to debate serious possible acquisitions.[22] Alternatively, two different groups can be assigned the same problem and their solutions compared.

Devil's Advocate. Assigning one person to be a devil's advocate or everyone to take a critical evaluation role of expressing all their criticisms can reduce the chances of the group's seeking agreement too quickly.

Managerial Style. Leaders may make it easier for others to speak their minds by refraining from expressing their opinions early in the discussion. They may be active in structuring and overseeing the controversy rather than participating by taking positions. Although leaders may stimulate controversy by expressing their own views, they also must be aware that some employees might find it difficult to express opinions that oppose their boss's.

Decision-Making Rules. Requiring that the group reach a consensus rather than a majority vote or unilateral decision by the leader makes it more likely that everyone will participate and opposing views will be heard.[23]

Time. Crises orientation and an emphasis on finding a solution quickly pressure group members into suppressing their uncertainties and criticisms. Group members need time to ponder the problem, search for information, understand others' ideas, and develop their own positions. After a preliminary consensus has been reached, second-chance meetings give persons an opportunity to discover shortcomings in the proposed solution and reconsider it.

Create a Productive Discussion

Disagreement is by itself insufficient. Decision makers must argue, debate, and disagree cooperatively and skillfully.

Cooperative Dependence. Decision makers must keep focused on their common task and emphasize their cooperative dependence. They can communi-

people were more aware, appreciated the complexity of the problem, and arrived at a solution responsive to the complete situation.

These studies showed that controversy helped individuals to cope with the biases of closed-mindedness and inadequate evaluation of new information, the danger of simplifying the problem, and unwarranted confidence in initial positions. Through controversy, decision makers came to understand opposing positions, develop alternatives, and adopt high-quality solutions.

Making Controversy Constructive

Not all controversies are constructive; some controversy makes reaching a reasonable decision impossible. Opposing views must be discussed cooperatively. When adversaries maintain a strong emphasis on mutual benefit and reaching their common objectives, they exchange ideas and information and discuss their opposing positions to make effective decisions.

Cooperative dependence has been found to contribute to constructive controversy.[16] Decision makers who emphasized competition by trying to win and outdo the other were interested and understood the opposing position, but they were closed-minded to new and opposing information and ideas. They rejected the other and his ideas. Competitive managers understood but did not use employees' information and ideas to make their decisions. On the other hand, decision makers involved in a cooperative controversy incorporated opposing ideas and accepted each other as persons. Commitment to cooperative goals is important in discussing differences constructively.

Cooperative Controversy Skills

Maintaining a strong sense of cooperative goals in controversy is difficult. Many persons confuse disagreement with competition; they assume that another's opposing argument or disagreement means that the other is working against their interests. Controversy degenerates into a win-lose debate. Particularly in controversy, employees need consistent evidence that their goals are cooperative.

Decision makers usually feel competitive when threatened. They become defensive when they believe that they have appeared, or fear they may appear, weak and ineffective. Threatened decision makers have been found to remain committed to their own positions despite the costs of such intransigence and to derogate and reject others.[17]

When Fred Johnson thought Preston Cheung was trying to make him look ineffective and incompetent, Fred felt competitive, reasserted his own position, stopped listening to Preston's arguments, and criticized them as having little validity. Fred retaliated that Preston, not himself, did not know what he was talking about.

Decision makers who feel respected argue logically and rationally. They accept informed, reasonable positions. They continue to believe that their goals are cooperative, are interested in the opposing view, understand it, and are open to the other person and position.

How decision makers influence each other also affects whether they feel cooperative or competitive and discuss controversy constructively. Strong, coercive attempts to get others to accept one's views create competition and resistance.[18] Decision makers assume that the dominator wants to win and thus become competitive themselves. They retaliate by attacking and rejecting the dominator's position and become close-minded and rigid. Conversely, decision makers who are willing to be influenced feel cooperative, exchange their perspectives, and combine their ideas to develop high-quality solutions.

A recent field study documents that constructive controversy contributes substantially to decision making.[19] Experienced managers were asked to identify an important successful decision and an important unsuccessful decision. The results indicated that successful decision makers discussed their opposing opinions openly, emphasized cooperative goals, respected each other, and were open to being influenced.

Open controversy, cooperative dependence, respect, and mutual influence reinforced each other. The substantial correlation (.67) between constructive controversy and successful decision making indicates that discussing opposing views skillfully contributes significantly to effective problem solving. By discussing their opposing views constructively, employees solve problems.

Why Is Controversy Avoided?

Constructive controversy should be widely used in organizations, but often much more effort is put into avoiding and smoothing over differences than confronting them directly. Controversy often is avoided because employees do not understand the value of open controversy or do not have the skills to make controversy constructive.

Many managers and employees do not appreciate that controversy can contribute to decision making. Traditional values against conflict are giving way to more acceptance of controversy, but internalized ideas that guide behavior are much slower to change. Many organizational procedures, norms, and practices reinforce the negative values of conflict. Employees typically defer to the more powerful and prestigious; managers believe that they are expected to be decisive and end disagreements quickly. Norms to not rock the boat and be a team player reinforce controversy avoidance.

Controversy requires an emphasis on cooperative dependence to be constructive, but many decision makers take a competitive approach to discussions. They seek to advance their groups and careers rather than common

can be implemented in several ways. It refers to practices such as task forces, project teams, quality-control circles, informal meetings on the shop floor, and union membership on the board of directors. What these procedures have in common is that they involve employees by encouraging them to contribute to making decisions and solving problems.

Rather than having the CEO make the organization decisions, the vice president make the department decisions, and the supervisor make the work unit decisions, these managers seek the ideas, opinions, and views of their subordinates. Participation can be formally or informally established and carried out through representative subordinates or direct involvement. Employees may be consulted for information, asked to present ideas and suggestions, or actually make the decision.

Participation stimulates controversy because it involves persons who bring a variety of information, ideas, opinions, arguments, and perspectives to bear on problems. The controversy in participation, if handled correctly, helps employees analyze problems and create effective solutions.

Participation Research

Studies comparing decision making when employees are asked to contribute and when managers make the decisions alone are inconsistent. To resolve the mixed findings on participation, reviewers have used two major methods, neither of which has been very successful.[1] They have tried to assess the relative methodological rigor of the supportive and unsupportive studies to determine whether the more valid studies consistently support one position. Yet apparently valid studies support both positions.[2] The second method to resolve discrepant findings is to try to identify aspects—employee needs and values, the distribution of information, leaders' characteristics—that affect the success of participation. There is, however, little direct evidence to indicate how these aspects affect participation.

The consequences of how employees work together on participation have been largely neglected. Studies included in reviews have employees work together in many different ways. Participation is operationalized as group leadership and problem solving, goal setting, feelings of power, organizational change, workers councils, authoritarism, permissiveness, and codetermination. The way participation actually is carried out or measured seldom is seen as that important; much more likely to get attention is the type of research method the study used.

When researchers consider how people work together in participation, they mostly allude to group factors and the dangers of suppressed ideas.[3] They have been most impressed with the debilitating impact of process losses through dynamics such as groupthink.[4] Indeed, suspicion of groups is intense. Expert members are thought to be outvoted by less knowledgeable ones; groups are expected to be unable to combine their ideas and information to develop high-quality solutions. Interaction does not invariably harm decision making, however, and as we have seen, it can contribute greatly to it.

Participation, it is well recognized, can be carried out in various ways, but much less recognized is the fact that what actually happens in participation varies a great deal. Participation gives employees the legitimacy to discuss organizational issues and problems, usually forms a group, and provides a setting for discussion and decision making. Organizational employees can discuss their opposing views constructively or destructively; whether participation is successful depends greatly on the handling of controversy.[26]

Participation contributes greatly to the quality of the decision when constructive controversy is created. Employees incorporate their ideas and information rather than rely on one person's judgment and perspective.

Participation, when controversy is discussed constructively, improves employee morale and relationships. Participation meets needs to express oneself, feel powerful, exercise control, and feel more like a team.

Constructive controversy in participation results in the commitment to implement solutions. Employees, through an open discussion of their opposing opinions, come to understand each other, use each other's ideas to develop solutions, know the reasoning behind the ultimate decision, and believe that the solution is effective. Participative team members also support and pressure each other to carry out their assignments. Decision quality, incorporation of one's ideas into the final solution, understanding of the decision's rationale, group support, and feeling rewarded all promote implementation.

Using Participation

Deciding to Use Participation

Participation of employees in organizational decision making has great potential, but it must be skillfully and appropriately used. These general guidelines can help managers plan how to use participation.

- The problem is important and the need for an effective solution is strong enough to warrant the investment, effort, and time of many employees.

- Constructive controversy can be established. The employees have the skills, procedures, and time to discuss their opposing views openly and productively.

- Employees accept their participation as legitimate. Participation requires the active involvement of employees, and their understanding that their participation is valued can help them to use these opportunities.

- Managers and supervisors realize that participation helps them to be more

cate expectations that they and others will work for a solution that is mutually beneficial. Efforts to pursue individual objectives at the expense of others should be identified and discouraged. Statements such as "We are all in this together" and "Let's seek a solution that is good for everyone" should characterize the group rather than "I am right, and you are wrong."

Financial rewards, evaluations, and prestige should be given for group success, not for independent work, appearing better than others, or proving that one is right. Group members must not seek to find winners and losers but a successful, productive solution to the common problem. All group members must share in the rewards of success and the responsibility for failure.

Personal Acceptance. Decision makers must feel that their personal competence is accepted by others even though their ideas are disputed. They must carefully and respectfully listen to everyone's ideas. They can directly criticize another's ideas but not the other as a person. They can object to ideas while communicating respect and appreciation for others as competent persons. Insults or implications that challenge another's integrity, intelligence, and motives must be avoided. Communication of interest and acceptance should accompany disagreement with another's current position. Demonstrating understanding by paraphrasing opposing ideas accurately and warmly is a concrete way of conveying acceptance and interest in another as a person while disagreeing.

People should not confuse disagreement with their ideas as a personal rejection or rebuff. Having one's ideas challenged can be taken as a sign of interest in one's position and as a way to further one's learning. Members must separate the validity of their thinking from their competence and worth as persons.

Mutual Influence. Problem solvers must try to influence each other rather than dominate. Controversy requires persons to try to persuade, inform, convince, and in other ways influence each other. Without this influence, controversy is much less stimulating and involving and is unlikely to be productive. People should have the conviction and willingness to put forth their arguments forcefully and to persuade others, but they must avoid trying to convey that they want to dominate and coerce. Statements such as "I want you to consider this seriously" and "You will probably find this convincing" should characterize group discussion, not "You must accept this point" and "You have no choice but to agree."

Group members can indicate that they are willing to be influenced and identify how they have incorporated parts of others' perspectives into their own. Give-and-take influence, rather than dominance or passivity, facilitates productive controversy.

Guides for Action

Making Decisions

- Oversee the making of the decision.
- Assign teams to solve complex problems.
- Make sure team members see that their goals are cooperative.
- Have them identify each other's abilities.
- Initiate open controversy.
- Express your views without dominating.
- Encourage mutual respect and influence.

Pitfalls to Avoid

- Assume that you alone are responsible for solving the problem.
- Assert that you have to be right.
- Move so fast on important problems that open discussion cannot develop.
- Try to do it all yourself.

Who Should Make Decisions: The Issue of Participation

> *I believe in the principle that you should manage in an open way: Tell people what is going on and listen to what they have to offer, particularly when it concerns matters which affect them very directly. That, I hope is a view which would be shared right around the world.*
> —Sir Adrian Cadbury, Chairman, Cadbury Schweppes PLC

Whether employees should participate in making organizational decisions has sparked a lot of debate. From Lewin's leadership-styles research in the 1930s until the present, much has been written about the virtues and bane of employee participation. Proponents defend participation as a democratic right as well as a boon to organizational decision making.[24] Detractors portray proponents as guilty of wishful thinking and participation as having no serious empirical support.[25] Participation, I argue, can be very productive, in large part because it encourages controversy. But managers and employees must be able to discuss their opposing views constructively.

Participation is best considered as a general management approach that

9
Making Conflict Productive

Managers and employees with cooperative goals use power and controversy to solve problems and achieve success. They also clash, quarrel, and battle. Sandy Hamel complains that Fred Johnson barks out orders and interrupts her when she asks questions; Sandy's typographical errors drive Fred nuts. Dennis Mann is annoyed that he must first write a memo and then wait to get Duncan Foster's reply; Duncan snaps at Dennis for not having the report ready on time. Preston Cheung seethes when Dennis takes all the credit for their proposal; Jenny sulks because Bob Clinton did not recommend a raise. Fred sees red when Preston teases him about going bald; Bob is irritated that Fred and Preston bicker. Conflicts are watersheds in working with others. If handled well, they reduce frustrations, update procedures, and make employees more productive and confident. Poorly managed conflicts exacerbate difficulties, intensify anger, tear relationships apart, and undercut productivity.

Conflict is inevitable. Managers and employees must know how to manage them. There is no reasonable alternative to conflict management. Well-handled conflict is a manager's delight, for it improves the quality of work life and stimulates motivation. Traditionally, conflict has been considered at least harmful and sometimes devastating. Successful cooperation has been equated with a conflict-free environment; conflict is assumed to be antithetical to teamwork and productivity. This is absolutely not true. Cooperation and conflict are not only compatible, but much and probably most conflict occurs when employees have cooperative goals. People in cooperation argue as they set objectives, decide how to proceed, assign tasks, and distribute the rewards of their joint success. Employees must develop procedures, attitudes, and skills to manage conflict; the key to productive conflict is to maintain, and strengthen if possible, the cooperative links between protagonists.

Resolving Conflicts: Peter and Allan

Peter and Allan had worked together for nearly twelve years at Rang-Dorf Engineering. Peter's skilled, determined leadership of the division and Allan's considerable technical competence were instrumental in making the division highly productive. Over the years, they had developed a great deal of respect for and loyalty to each other. Recently, however, they had become more wary and suspicious. They avoided conflict and allowed issues to obscure their cooperative dependence; they had begun to think of each other in competitive, win-lose terms.

Peter had concluded that Allan lacked important managerial competencies, but he did not confront Allan directly. Instead he "promoted" him to head the division's major department and then brought in Dick below him to manage it. They avoided other issues. For example, Peter told Allan that the Ansett project had top priority, only to return two weeks later to find that Allan had completed other projects but not Ansett. Peter did not express his anger directly, nor did he thank Allan for the completed projects. Allan took Peter's silence as ingratitude and further evidence that he had become a tough, unreasonable taskmaster. Allan complained that Peter had begun to rely on memos to communicate problems and that memos did not give him a chance to discuss problems and learn.

Peter and Allan were no longer sure they were working together. Peter attributed Allan's behavior to a desire to satisfy others, even at Peter's expense. Allan suspected that Peter was indifferent to him, had no desire to help him feel effective and confident, and perhaps did not want to see him promoted.

Both Peter and Allan had strong reservations about an open discussion of the conflict. Peter thought that Allan would be hurt by such a discussion and would quit. Peter was able to use his superior authority to act on his beliefs without discussing them with Allan. Allan assumed that Peter had the prerogative to initiate discussion about problems. Their conflict did not disappear, and they faced a crisis. Peter anticipated a promotion, and he would have difficulty recommending Allan as a replacement.

Peter and Allan did agree to discuss their conflict with the help of a consultant. The first step was to refocus on their cooperative dependence. They reminded themselves that their basic aspirations were cooperative. They both wanted to make the division as productive and respected as possible. They also were committed to each other's welfare and development. They each wanted the other to improve his skills and gain promotions.

After several meetings, they became aware that their conflict avoidance frustrated their goals and harmed their relationship. Peter expressed his concerns about Allan as a manager and talked about his frustrations in getting Allan to focus on tasks that he, Peter, considered high priority. Allan revealed his feelings of being taken for granted and of Peter's apparent lack of interest in his learning.

Together they discussed how Allan could develop managerial skills or find a position that required his technical abilities. Through joint problem solving, they again realized how much they depended on each other and that they had each other's basic interests at heart. They were once again tuned in to each other's aspirations, better able to support each other, and more aware that they needed to discuss, rather than avoid, conflicts.

effective; it does not replace them. Managers benefit from participation because it helps them to solve pressing problems.

- Managers play a critical role. They must decide when to use participation and structure it effectively. Managers need to discuss their opposing opinions constructively. They should probe, question, challenge, and disagree with employees so that the decision is acceptable to them as well as to employees.

- Participation is practical. Sometimes participation is not reasonable because employees are on different shifts and locations. Pressing demands and deadlines can make participation impractical.

- The particular form of participation depends on the situation. Task forces, labor-management problem-solving groups, project teams, and other groups are concrete ways to implement participation. Informal discussions on the shop floor as well as formal representation on boards can be useful.

Concluding Comments

Organizations must be able to solve problems and make decisions. They must develop plans, implement them, and remove barriers to their success. A widely accepted view is that organizations are unable to analyze problems thoroughly and create new solutions. Managers are overtaxed by the demands to process information, respond to new situations, and integrate competing claims. Employees who discuss their opposing views constructively, however, can combine their ideas, information, and perspectives to make decisions. Many companies can, and do, overcome the limitations of individuals to create successful new products and strategies.

Having employees participate in decision making has great potential, for it involves employees with different and overlapping information, ideas, and perspectives. To make participation work, employees must use procedures and skills to discuss their opposing views openly and constructively.

ulcers, hypertension, and related ailments; they must try to learn to live with frustrating procedures and problems; and they feel a lack of power over their lives and commitment to their company. Avoiding conflict wastes energy, undercuts morale, and sabotages effective change.

The positive view of conflict can be carried to extremes. Some persons assume that anger is the honest emotion and that all conflicts must be discussed openly. Some theorists have argued that organizations should communicate inconsistently, assign ill-defined responsibilities, encourage employees to express all their frustrations and anger, prevent managers from decisively ending conflict, and in other ways foster conflict and stress.[3] Although the research reviewed here contributes to conflict-positive values, it is the *appropriate, skilled management of conflict*, not just conflict, that promotes healthy organizations and people.

Criteria for Productive Conflict

The choice for organizations is not between conflict and no conflict but in deciding how conflict is managed. Employees need criteria so that they can work toward making conflict productive and know when they have succeeded. There are several criteria for conflict, and their importance varies. Perhaps the ultimate standard is the extent to which the protagonists believe that they have benefited rather than lost from the conflict. They usually feel that they have benefited when:

- The underlying problem is solved, a new solution has been created and implemented, and it is unlikely that the problem will appear again in a new form.

- The relationship has been strengthened. The persons know each other better, are more responsive to each other's feelings and interests, are pleased that their relationship has withstood the rigors of conflict, and believe that they can work effectively in the future.

- The participants believe that their time and resources have been well spent and conclude that resolving the conflict was not too costly.

Conflict between individuals and groups is a common, inevitable aspect of organizations. It is neither practical nor desirable to avoid, suppress, or smooth over all conflicts. Employees need encouragement, opportunities, procedures, and skills to discuss their conflicts well. They must be able to express their feelings, uncover the underlying problem, develop solutions, and in other ways manage their conflicts productively. The ideas and procedures discussed in previous chapters are highly relevant to conflict management. Additional procedures and skills to help employees make their conflicts productive are discussed in this chapter.

Defining Conflict

In recent years, conflict has become an important issue in management research.[4] But because it is so pervasive and elicits such strong feelings, defining conflict is difficult. There is agreement that conflict characterizes a relationship rather than an individual and that it is not inevitably harmful. Conflict often is defined as opposing interests, however, and the resulting assumption that conflict is competitive interferes with understanding.

Conflict as Opposing Interests

Conflict typically is considered in terms of bargaining and negotiation. People have opposing interests and preferences in mixed-motive situations.[5] Common interests motivate them to continue to work together and reach an agreement, but their opposing interests require bargaining. Collective bargaining is a well-known conflict, but organizational members in many settings also must seek compromises and agreements on their differing interests and preferences.

A serious problem with the definition of conflict as opposing interests is that conflict is confused with competition. Cooperators, however, often have conflicts. Co-workers with the same goal of developing a new market plan may not have any opposing interests; they seek a high-quality plan that earns them all the gratitude and respect of their boss. Despite this agreement on interests, they may dispute the best way to begin, who is best equipped to do the various tasks, the type of consultants needed, and the theories they should use.

Policymakers may want a successful strategy so that they prosper with the company but disagree sharply over the actual risks and opportunities of available options. Labor and management may disagree about how certain organizational decisions should be made even if they agree upon wages, grievance handling, and fringe benefits. Contrary to the mixed-motive perspective, employees with highly overlapping interests and goals will at times disagree and conflict.

The idea that conflicts arise out of mixed-motive situations misleadingly suggests that there is a direct link between opposing interests and conflict. This link is not simple and direct. One employee may be angry at a co-worker who insists on gossiping, whereas another employee encourages the co-worker to tell more. A worker may be in conflict by blaming the union for a recent settlement; another holds management responsible. The extent to which persons experience conflict depends on their perceptions, expectations, and evalutions of the situation. People construct conflicts; they do not just appear. Perceptions and beliefs about others' behavior, standards of fairness,

Changing Values about Conflict

Company president: *"If there isn't conflict, your organization isn't going anywhere. Conflict helps us move forward."*
Plant manager: *"Conflict makes my job. I don't think I would go to work if there wasn't conflict."*

Conflict traditionally has been considered painful and harmful, a sign that something has gone terribly wrong. Because conflict engenders anger, bitterness, and revenge that disrupt coordination and productivity, managers assumed that they should handle conflict decisively. Norms told employees that if they could not avoid feeling frustrated and angry, they should at least not express such feelings. Today conflict is recognized as a natural, sometimes productive part of working with others. The contemporary perspective is that employees must learn to discuss their conflicts rather than suppress and avoid them.

Everyone experiences conflict, and many people have a conflict a day.[1] Managers have been found to spend 20 percent of their time coping with conflict.[2] Some conflicts are serious, provoking frustration and anger; some are minor and merely irritating; some conflicts are even light and comical. Employees fight over job assignments; they squabble about parking spaces; they tease the colleague who misspelled the boss's name in the last memo. Conflicts occur between two departments as well as two employees. Production accuses marketing of excessive demands, and marketing contends that production is obstinate. Conflict spills over organizational boundaries. Customers complain about late deliveries and product defects. Companies dispute terms with suppliers and contest markets with rivals. Conflict is a daily, sometimes an hourly experience in organizations.

We now know that conflict is built into us and our social lives; it is too basic to be denied. Anger and frustration come from involvement with others and a commitment to excellence and getting the job done; denying anger is denying involvement and commitment. Managers and others are beginning to recognize that productive conflict helps individuals and the company.

Conflict's Benefits

- Discussing conflict makes organizational members more aware and able to cope with problems. Knowing that others are frustrated and want change creates incentives to try to solve the underlying problem.

- Conflict promotes organizational change and adaptation. Procedures, assignments, budget allocations, and other organizational practices are challenged. Conflict draws attention to those issues that may interfere with and frustrate employees.

- Conflict strengthens relationships and heightens morale. Employees realize that their relationships are strong enough to withstand the test of conflict; they need not avoid frustrations and problems. They can release their tensions through discussion and problem solving.

- Conflict promotes awareness of self and others. Through conflict, people learn what makes them angry, frustrated, and frightened and also what is important to them. Knowing what we are willing to fight for tells us a lot about ourselves. Knowing what makes our colleagues unhappy helps us to understand them.

- Conflict enhances personal development. Managers find out how their style affects their subordinates through conflict. Workers learn what technical and interpersonal skills they need to upgrade themselves.

- Conflict encourages psychological development. Persons become more accurate and realistic in their self-appraisals. Through conflict, persons take others' perspectives and become less egocentric. Conflict helps persons to believe that they are powerful and capable of controlling their own lives. They do not simply need to endure hostility and frustration but can act to improve their lives.

- Conflict can be stimulating and fun. Persons feel aroused, involved, and alive in conflict, and it can be a welcome break from an easy-going pace. It invites employees to take another look and to appreciate the intricacies of their relationships.

The Need to Manage Conflict

Conflict-positive values and the research on which they are based have far-reaching implications. Rather than apologize for their conflicts and anger, employees need skills to express their feelings and deal with conflicts. Leadership styles that suppress conflict and norms, values, and procedures that tend to smooth them over are being questioned. Managers must try to make conflicts improve how they and employees collaborate. They also must be aware of conflicts between employees and develop approaches and procedures for open discussion.

But isn't avoidance of conflict a reasonable approach, especially when people may not have the time, energy, and skill to manage conflicts well? At times, of course, avoiding conflict is prudent. In addition to missing conflict's benefits, however, avoiding it is much more costly than is generally appreciated. Avoided conflict does not simply disappear. Employees must use time and energy to try to cope with it. They complain and gossip about their problems with others; they work to hide their feelings and anger; they suppress their tensions, which makes them more stressed and more prone to burnout,

problems, and improve the quality of work life through developing cooperative work. Experience and research both indicate that groups—when managed well and used appropriately—play a very important role in organizations. But serious shortcomings frustrate group effort. Companies need teams and the ability to use them wisely.

5
Becoming a Team: How to Develop Cooperative Goals

*S*imply put, Bob Twigs, Laverne Stern, and Howard Kaplan want *their new advertising agency to be the best, one that is totally dedicated to creativity and excellence. They want to deliver for their clients, but with integrity, and will refuse clients, even cash cows, whom they cannot help without compromise. The work is so demanding that they want to have fun doing it.*

From working in other agencies, they know what they do not want. They do not want the agency to be divided into the creative group and the account group. The writers and artists must work with, not against, research, account services, and media to combine creativity with smart marketing. Everyone including the reception ist, stat-camera operators, and secretaries—must back up the creative department and account people. Pretense and posturing are out.

But Twigs, Stern, and Kaplan are much less sure about how to make the vision a reality. They realize that having employees work together openly and productively is the key to building a successful organization. But they wonder, "How can we get everyone committed to our dream and work to make the agency as good as it can be?"

Employees pulling in the same direction are at the heart of an effective organization. They understand that they have a common fate, are part of their community, and must work toward common goals. What is good for one is good for all; success for one is success for all. They celebrate each other's victories and share each other's defeats. Cooperative dependence is critical so that employees in work groups and task forces, within and between departments and business units, exchange their information, ideas, and assistance to get things done.

But getting employees to feel like a team moving in the same direction demands managerial skill and effort. Telling them to cooperate is not enough;

employees themselves must be convinced that their own important goals and aspirations make them cooperatively dependent.

Employees often doubt that their goals are cooperative. They may believe that, to advance their careers, they must demonstrate to their boss that they are superior to colleagues; some employees try to prove to themselves that they are better than others. At times cooperation seems impractical. Pressed by deadlines, employees want to work on their own tasks, not spend time coordinating and solving additional problems. The time and effort required to work with others—to schedule another meeting into a crowded day or rearrange vacation time—often are obvious, but the rewards of jointly developing a new product, while potentially considerable, may seem distant and vague. It takes two to collaborate: Both persons must understand that they have cooperative goals and work toward them. Cooperative goals do not just happen; they must be carefully engineered.

Need for a Comprehensive Approach

> *You can go out and preach common goals and work at it. . . . But you can bring your credibility down in a second. It takes a million acts to build it up, but one act can bring it down. . . . People are suspicious because for several thousand years that suspicion was warranted. So it's fragile. And we work very hard to try not to do things that will create distrust.*
> —*Howard K. Sperlich, President, Chrysler Corporation*

Managers must use an integrated approach to develop strong feelings of pulling together. Employees need consistent guidance, cues, and information; they need to understand that by working together they can be successful.

The model of working with people outlined in chapter 2 provides managers with powerful ways to develop cooperative goals. Task assignments and rewards must be coupled with congruent company attitudes and values to convince employees that it is in their own interest—and the best interest of their department and company—to work cooperatively. When combined, developing a strong culture and values, devising the right organizational chart and procedures, and offering training in human relations are powerful ways to establish a shared sense of fate and cooperative goals.

Values and Attitudes

Employees use the company's culture to decide whether their goals are cooperative. Shared vision and support bind employees together and foster trust and cooperation. Employees who believe others like and care for them and have similar outlooks and values usually conclude that their goals are cooperative.[1] A common background leads to a sense of community, whereas separation and distinction result in competition and independence.

A corporate philosophy that espouses a feeling of trust and caring toward each other does not itself convince employees. They want to know whether this philosophy really counts and is backed up by consistent action. If managers talk about common effort but reward competitors, and if they talk about trust but do not truly trust workers, then employees are apt to conclude that the corporate philosophy is comprised of empty words intended to confuse and perhaps exploit them. The corporate philosophy must be credible, and the employees must see that it works in the company's daily operations.[2]

Tasks and Rewards

Perhaps the most direct way employees conclude that they have cooperative goals is through group tasks, complementary roles, and shared rewards: Employees know that their bonus depends on how well their team's product does in the marketplace. Often, however, companies do not give a clear message. Although the employees' bonus depends on a cooperative effort, the boss might congratulate some for being the stars of the group.

Yet even consistent rewards are not enough. Formal goals and rewards are not necessarily the goals employees are motivated to achieve. Employees bring different aspirations to work situations: They want to be promoted, to be liked, to enjoy their jobs, to get through the day, and to become friends. They also have different ideas about how they can reach these goals: They must be accommodating, assertive, or aggressive. Employees transform organizational tasks to fit their needs. They may see a new assignment as a way to increase their chances for promotion to appear aggressive, as a vehicle to be more accommodating and appreciated by their colleagues, or simply as a fun, stimulating challenge. It is not formal goals but the goals employees accept as their own that motivate.

Even employees who are confident that they know each other's goals may not know how they are related. Different goals and orientations may wrongly be assumed to be incompatible. Preston is oriented to prestige and Dennis to money, but a successful joint project could help them achieve both objectives. Sometimes a creative idea is necessary to see how goals can go together. If the work were restructured, one employee's desire to complete a task could be cooperative with another's desire to learn.

Different emphases and paths can be mistaken for competitive goals. A demanding, confrontational manager may think that his goal is incompatible with that of a manager who wants to reward outstanding performance, but they both could want a more productive plant and only disagree about how to get there. Superficial agreement on goals can hide competitiveness. Even if team members voice a desire to arrive at the best decision for all, they might be much more committed to having their solution dominate.

Constraints on communication interfere with assessing goals and how they are linked. Employees often are unaware of or think that they should not reveal their real goals; sometimes what employees say is just not to be believed. Time constraints also interfere. Employees may have minutes, even seconds to decide whether goals are cooperative or competitive. They try to know how their goals are linked with their boss's as they discuss a new proposal. Some managers pride themselves on being able to scoop out another person in a minute. Employees often make quick decisions about how their goals are linked without making a thorough assessment of the tasks and rewards.

Interpersonal Skills

How employees treat each other is important evidence in determining how goals are related. Everyone has repeated experiences with cooperation, competition, and independence, and they know the behavior associated with each. Helping and giving resources are evidence of cooperative goals; distorting information is a sign of competition. Showing respect, conveying warmth, and discussing conflicts productively develop cooperative goals.[3]

Employees need interpersonal skills, but training is not enough to develop cooperation. Employees must see that using skills is appropriate and reasonable. Learning to manage conflicts constructively does little good if the environment is highly competitive or the boss is hostile. The tasks, rewards, attitudes, and values of the company must encourage employees to use their skills.

Employees want to know whether their goals go together, go against, or are unrelated to each other so that they can plan how they will act and know what to expect. Sometimes they base their conclusions on assigned goals and rewards, but often they have incomplete, ambiguous information with no timely way to discover the goals that motivate others and how these goals are linked. Another's gestures, style, and initial behavior are used to decide whether goals are cooperative or competitive. Past behavior, attitude similarity, and group membership also are used. Employees use attitudes and values, tasks and rewards, and interaction to decide how they depend on each other. Managers must use strategies that combine attitudes and designs to give overlapping, consistent, and credible evidence that will convince employees that their important goals are cooperative.

An Integrated Approach

To establish cooperative goals, managers should develop a supportive climate and shared values, assign tasks to groups and reward them for group success, and encourage them to develop and use skills to work together, discuss problems, and manage conflicts. Employees should become actively involved in understanding how their goals are cooperative.

Attitudes and Values

Trusting, supportive attitudes, shared values on the importance of people and relationships, and morale and pride in the company contribute to a cohesive organization in which employees emphasize their cooperative dependence. They expect to help and to have others reciprocate; they take pleasure from others' success. Shared values emphasize a sense of community, common interests, and similarity in basic hopes and aspirations. In such an environment, individuals and groups discuss their goals, understand each other's needs and aspirations, conclude that their important goals are cooperative, and seek opportunities to cooperate.

But how can these attitudes and values be developed? Leaders can use anecdotes, stories, legends, symbols, and myths to encourage employees to accept company values. In highly successful companies, legends and metaphors portray employees whose commitment to productivity, a strong work ethic, and teamwork have won them honor and success.[4] Stories at 3M tell of employees who, though told not to work on a project, were so committed that they worked on their own time and are now, because the product is very successful in the marketplace, respected, wealthy vice presidents.

Bank of America has gone back to its roots to convey its vision of what it would like to be and to reach its goal of becoming "the leader among the world's financial institutions." A. Giannini, the founder of Bank of America has inspired employees to create a more customer-oriented, entrepreneurial company.

Giannini's belief that "you serve yourself best by serving others first" has become widely quoted at Bank of America. Employees have learned that he resented banks that catered only to the wealthy, so he set out to build a bank that would serve all the people. He put his banks on accessible street corners, kept them open late in the day, and thereby pioneered the modern branch banking system. Long before it was fashionable, Giannini used the open office. His own desk was not even next to a window. He wanted bank officers to work together and to be available to customers. Bank of America hopes that knowledge about Giannini can help the company break away from its bureaucratic past. The bank wants employees to take risks, experiment, and find new ways to serve customers.

Companies formulate philosophies that boldly pronounce their ideals. A successful company values its employees as individuals and seeks to promote their welfare, is united by a common purpose to serve its customers and society, and encourages its employees to care for each other and work together.[5] Formal philosophical statements as well as informal stories make explicit that the company serves employees and society, seeks a supportive interpersonal climate, and asserts that employees are cooperatively linked with each other as well as with the company and society.

Philosophies and stories must be backed up with action. Not only must leaders talk about ideals, but they also must demonstrate their commitment to these espoused attitudes and values. They show they are committed to common goals. If necessary, they work late, run the copier, and order take-out food for dinner. They also value employees. They listen to their complaints and troubles, help when family members are sick or in trouble, help employees overcome chemical addictions, and remember special birthdays and anniversaries. They show the same caring for employees as they want them to have for each other.

Tasks, Roles, and Rewards

To promote cooperation, the organization's design must be consistent with supportive attitudes and shared values. A company that says it values caring but rewards Machiavellian behavior leaves employees confused, skeptical, and wary. Its tasks, roles, and rewards must be consistent with each other.

Assigning tasks, especially complex ones, to groups of employees helps to develop cooperative goals. Project teams, work groups, task forces, and committees are asked as a group to solve various problems. Groups are particularly suited for difficult tasks; complex tasks make it clear that people must collaborate to get the job done. Faced with a task that requires varied information, different areas of expertise, and several perspectives, employees understand that they can be successful only if everyone is successful. The requirements to exchange information and ideas to solve complex tasks lead to frequent interaction and the greater use of coordination devices.[6] When tasks are simple and routine, employees, having the information to complete the tasks, can more easily rely on their own efforts and believe that they are independent.

Roles, the flow of work, and expectations also must reinforce cooperation. Employees who are clearly informed that their role is to share information, listen to each other's ideas, exchange resources, and respond to each other's requests develop positive dependence. Individuals and groups who must work together to complete their tasks use various methods to coordinate their efforts.[7]

Tangible and intangible rewards—bonuses, salary increases, awards, honors, praise, recognition, and appreciation—must be given to employees according to the performance of their department and group. Employees understand that they will be rewarded to the extent that their group is successful and that they will be held accountable for inadequate group performance.

It is not necessary that all group members share equally. The project leader might get 5 percent of the first year's cost savings of a new inventory-control plan, while the others receive only 2.5 percent. All team members must, however, recognize that they will be rewarded as the group continues to reduce inventory costs. Evidence does indicate that unequal division of rewards can make group members compete over who should get more.[8] If team members agree that the project leader deserves more, however, then unequal rewards do not cause problems. Managers cannot expect to inspire teamwork if they reward employees for their independent performances or for doing better than others.

Complex tasks assigned to a group that requires employees to exchange information and ideas are likely to convince them that their goals are cooperative. As they jointly work on the task and see that they need each other's information and ideas to be successful, they realize that all employees should contribute and all can complete the task together. They have clear evidence that as the group succeeds and accomplishes its task, they all will gain rewards.

Steps to Become a Team

Values and attitudes

- Explain that the company values employees as people and wants them to develop caring, supportive relationships to make their work more rewarding and productive.
- Work and live by these values.
- Have employees determine what these values mean for how they can work together effectively.

Tasks and rewards

- Assign tasks to groups and indicate that rewards will be given if the group is successful.
- Indicate that employees are expected to share information and ideas and aid each other.
- Provide procedures to coordinate effort.

Deciding that goals are cooperative

- After explaining the rationale and purpose of the task, have employees discuss how it can help them and the company.
- Have employees discuss the task to help them understand that their goals are cooperative.
- Encourage employees to understand each other's aspirations and objectives so that they know how they can help each other.

Working together

- Plan how to share the work efficiently and fairly.

- Develop a policy urging employees to show respect and acceptance of each other.

- Encourage employees to improve their abilities to solve problems, manage conflicts, and work together.

Employee Involvement

Managers can develop the values and structure that foster a team feeling, but employees must decide that their goals are cooperative and be motivated to reach them. Employees must be actively involved in discussing the company's culture and their tasks and roles.

To shape their company's philosophy, employees can discuss attitudes and values that would be useful to them and how they could put these ideas into practice. Work groups identify company values, decide what they mean for how they work together, discuss how these values help them and the company, and publicly commit themselves to abide by the values. Employees are influenced by listening to stories and legends that show the values at work in the organization, but they may be more convinced when they tell others. Actively playing out stories also can inspire commitment.[9] For example, employees might take part in skits at company parties that dramatize basic organizational values. Through direct participation, employees can better understand company attitudes and values, see their implications for how they and others should act, and realize how they are useful for themselves and others.

By discussing their tasks and roles, employees also realize that they have cooperative goals. Their cooperative dependence should be made concrete: All group members will receive an award if they win the contract. The company should specify how all team members will benefit if the group is successful.

Ideally, employees not only believe that their goals are cooperative, but they also are highly motivated to reach them. They are willing to persist and are not easily distracted by other objectives. But assigning a task to employees does not make them committed to it. They must believe that the task is valuable in the sense that it helps them satisfy their needs, attain their own aspirations, and promote their values.

After the manager explains a task's rationale and its importance, employees can discuss how the assigned task is important to them and the company and why their contributions will be useful. Often it is helpful to have employees reveal their personal aspirations and needs and to discuss how they can meet them by working on the common task. If possible, employees should be able to modify the task so that it facilitates the organization's objectives but is more meaningful to them. In this way, the organization benefits from more meaningful work. Employees' public agreement that the common task has high priority and that they will pursue it together further strengthens motivation.

Interaction

How people actually work with each other also determines whether they see their goals as cooperative or not. Despite a strong company philosophy and group task, people may treat each other in such a way that they doubt they are working together and can even come to see each other as enemies. Employees who believe that they can and will work together successfully maintain a strong sense of cooperative dependence. The following chapters describe many useful skills and procedures, including coordination plans, taking each other's perspective, and respecting each other as people.

Employees should plan and agree to an efficient, fair way to share the tasks. Cooperative goals can be undercut if employees believe that the work is not fairly distributed or that it is difficult to coordinate. They begin to doubt that others are committed to the common task and that they will get the job done.

Sometimes cooperation is obscured when employees feel that they are not allowed to complete their part of the task; they feel frustrated with a boss or colleague who does not let them do their part. Discussion that specifies the responsibilities and expectations of each individual can reduce coordination problems. Scheduling group meetings, having a common meeting space, bunching offices together, establishing times for consultation, sharing secretaries, appointing a recognized coordinator, and having a respected leader can help coordination.

Employees should try to understand each other's perspective, ideas, objectives, feelings, and motives. If they know each member's priorities, they can determine how to assist each other. Sharing aspirations allows employees to understand each other's actions and demands.

Employees who do not understand a colleague's goals and purposes may consider him unpredictable and frenetic and treat his demands as unreasonable nuisances. Colleagues, managers, and employees may appear to be crazy without reasonable purpose but seldom are.

Employees must be sensitive to each person's need to be respected and accepted; they should help each other feel valuable and worthwhile. Employees who feel insulted, unfairly blamed, or unduly pressured may be defensive and doubt that their goals are positively linked. As employees plan to coordinate their efforts, they must develop norms and procedures that help them convey the ways in which they value each other. For example, they should avoid accusations and personal attacks, make requests rather than demands, avoid arbitrary deadlines, and give each other sufficient time to respond to requests. Showing respect, acting politely, and demonstrating warmth strengthen positively linked goals. Harsh, brusque, and ill-mannered behavior indicates a general hostility toward others and their goals.[10]

Managers need a highly comprehensive approach to develop cooperative goals. Developing strong corporate values and norms, using the formal structure to provide common tasks and shared rewards, and discussing these values and tasks with employees to help them realize and become committed to working together give employees a sense of community and of the importance of working together.

After understanding the importance of cooperative goals, Bob Twigs, Laverne Stern, and Howard Kaplan are prepared to build their agency as an organization and make their vision a reality. To develop a shared vision and values, they talk openly with potential employees and clients. They want to be creative, maintain their integrity, and try "to make the needle move" for each client. Everyone soon hears stories about how the agency was founded on Twigs's and Stern's offbeat and wild free-lance work. To show their dedication, the partners work until 2 A.M. if necessary and expect others to join them. They are accessible to staff and take a personal interest in them. They talk to staff about personal problems and try to help them. Staff are valued as people and for their work; their marital status, handicaps, and sexual orientations are not used against them.

The agencies' tasks and roles support cooperation. Writers, artists, account executives, and media specialists are expected to produce as a group for a client. Teams within the agency are given autonomy and support and are held responsible for success or failure. To prevent cliques, which are common in most advertising agencies, new teams are formed for each client; everyone soon works with everyone else. Exchange and debate are encouraged. Copywriters are free to suggest approaches to artwork, and art directors propose copy ideas. To facilitate this give and take, offices are arranged in a circular floor plan, with no doors and lots of glass, and are not grouped by function or department. The partners themselves set an unpretentious, open example.

Both financial and intangible rewards are important. The agency pays bonuses to groups that have helped increase the market share or in some other way have served their clients superbly. Although professional awards such as the Clio are given to an individual, the company recognizes the whole group, for it knows that a successful ad is not just clever copy or stylish art. Employees also participate in a 15 percent profit-sharing plan that makes their cooperative goals concrete and highlights that everyone needs to move in the same direction.

The agency wants all employees to strengthen their abilities to work and live with each other. Groups meet regularly to examine how they are working together, make sure everyone is pitching in and doing his or her share, identify frustrations, and work out solutions. They exchange articles and books on management, teamwork, and conflict, and they discuss how they can work together better. Finally, the agency has a yearly weekend retreat to review progress, make plans for the future, and have fun.

6
Forming One Company: How to Integrate Groups into an Organization

> *How we work together [needs the most attention at Ford]. The whole concept of employee involvement—particularly in a management team effort as opposed to individual effort—has many elements that are still quite fragile. . . . It's going to take time for everyone to become accustomed to participating together.*
> —*Donald E. Peterson, CEO, Ford Motor Company*

> *The failure of synergy [in the 1960s and 1970s] stemmed from the inability of companies to understand and implement it, not because of some basic flaw in the concept. . . . Compelling forces are at work, however, that mean that firms must reexamine their attitude toward synergy.*
> —*Michael E. Porter,* Competitive Advantage

Strong corporate culture companies, recent books have told us, have forged a work force bound by a shared vision where everyone wants to do what needs to be done to make the company a leader. What makes these companies noteworthy is that everyone throughout the organization works hard together. Not only do people within groups collaborate, but departments, divisions, and business units work together. Cooperation among teams, departments, and units is essential because it is not just a quality product, brilliant marketing strategy, the right market niche, or favorable financing, but all of them together that makes a company successful. Technical, manufacturing, engineering, and marketing expertise all must be brought to bear to deliver successful products and services.

Top management wants a team approach. Savvy executives realize that cooperation among the company's departments and business units is more than nice to have; it is increasingly needed for corporate survival.[1] Companies must use their total abilities to win market share, use emerging technologies, make progress in research and development, and adapt to political and trade changes. To meet these challenges, groups within a company must work together. Departments, divisions, and business units cannot just do their own thing; they must work for the company's health. Confronted with intense competition and challenges and inspired by accounts of strong corporate culture companies, many managers are experimenting with ways to develop a corporate family.

Corporate history is replete with failed companies whose groups did not work together. They had the right niche and the right product but did not have adequate marketing. Others concentrated on marketing and lost control of production and costs. Some companies survive but are plagued by inter-group hostilities. Departments protect turf rather than reach out to collaborate; divisions fight each other, not the competition.

Managers at TRW realized that its business units had few incentives to collaborate, and the company has suffered because its full abilities have not been brought to bear to solve problems and deliver new products.[2] TRW is not alone; most companies never capitalize on all the knowledge and energy distributed throughout various groups.

The prevalence of troubled relationships between departments has led some theorists to conclude that competition is built into organizations.[3] They argue that groups invariably suspect and blame each other but are slow to assist and encourage; they use their power to pursue their own particular ends, not the common good. But competition is not inevitable; some companies not only overcome it, but forge a united work force.

Why is cooperation between units so difficult to achieve? It is not because CEOs and executives do not work hard to get groups to work together. They talk of the importance of working together, cajole and plead with departments to collaborate, assign a manager to act as liaison, organize meetings, and have conference telephone calls to improve communication. They continually fight fires and resolve disputes.

The fact is that executive pressure and procedures to work together are ineffective when groups believe that their goals are competitive. Competitive departments press managers to be tough and uncompromising and to be sure to get more than they give up. Managers are expected to fight and win the battle for larger budgets and more influence for their groups. If they accommodate others, they risk being considered weak leaders, even traitors. Managers, pressured by their groups to compete and by corporate officers to cooperate, are unsure about how to pursue both group and company interests. Corporate management feels frustrated and powerless to improve collaboration.

What executives should do, but often fail to do, is help groups commit themselves to cooperative goals. It is not enough that executives know that departments will be better off working together; the groups themselves must be convinced.

Executives need systematic, powerful ways to convince groups that it is in their interest as well as the company's to collaborate. They often establish new committees and other procedures to improve communication and might restructure the organization if bolder action is required. Researchers have identified several devices useful in coordinating groups in a company. However, the company's structure and procedures must be combined with cooperative goals to get groups to work together to form a cohesive, productive enterprise.

Procedures to Coordinate

Managers are experimenting with various ways to coordinate departments and business units.[4] Common devices, listed in the order of increasingly thorough ways to coordinate, are as follows:

Direct contact: Managers informally discuss common concerns directly, circumventing channels and the hierarchy.

Liaison positions: Managers and employees are assigned to facilitate the flow of information between groups. An engineer is placed in the production department to keep the engineering department informed of production problems and to translate engineering ideas into practical production procedures. Integrating managers help groups to discuss problems and come to a mutually advantageous solution. Sometimes they control budgets for intergroup tasks to give them more power.

Task forces: Employees from the groups involved in a problem form one group with the assignment to develop a solution and oversee its implementation.

Permanent teams: Members meet to discuss recurring interdepartmental problems.

Management committees: The CEO meets regularly with leaders of departments and business units to discuss companywide issues and advise the CEO.

Market groups: McGraw-Hill recently reorganized from divisions such as publications, books, and statistical services into market focus groups. People who serve the same market are now in one group to encourage synergy.

Matrix management: Employees are members of two units. They may belong to a functional department, such as engineering, marketing, and research, and an interdepartmental project team. They may be responsible to the head of the engineering department and to the project manager building a dam. Or they may be part of both market-oriented and production groups, belonging to the aviation industry market group and the computer services division.

The more groups are expected to collaborate closely, the more they need thorough, but costly, procedures to coordinate. To exchange a lot of information, make complex decisions, plan how to distribute work, and discuss problems, groups must supplement direct contact with task forces, project teams, integrating managers, and possibly even a matrix organization. But coordination procedures are insufficient; they must be managed and used properly. Liaison managers, for example, must develop goodwill, be able to take different perspectives, facilitate communication, solve problems, and manage conflict.[5] Cooperative goals are essential in making procedures work. Interpersonal skills discussed in future chapters also are necessary.

Cooperative and Competitive Goals

How groups believe they depend on each other determines their use of coordination procedures. Studies demonstrate that the model of working with people described in chapter 2 is valid for groups as well as individuals. The way in which groups see their goals as related greatly affects their expectations, behavior, emotions, attitudes, and productivity.[6]

Groups with cooperative goals want each other to be effective because then they can all be successful. Groups in competition are threatened and frustrated by others' success. They pursue their self-interest at the expense of others. These different orientations result in much different ways of working:

Groups with cooperative goals are optimistic and expect that they will work together; they trust that they can rely on each other. They communicate openly and use their abilities to help each other.

Cooperative goals do not eliminate conflict, for these groups, like individuals, conflict over how to reach their shared goals. They disagree about how to use their resources and how to distribute both the burdens and rewards of their joint effort. Cooperative groups are able to discuss their difficulties openly, however, and are able to integrate their ideas and information to create high-quality, accepted solutions to problems. They negotiate their differences so that they feel fairly treated.

Cooperative groups, as they exchange information and assist and support each other, are productive in many situations. Having cooperative group goals is more productive in making decisions, solving problems, combining ideas from different perspectives, using several resources, or coordinating effort. In contrast to the popular belief that competition makes groups productive, studies taken together indicate that groups are generally more productive in intergroup cooperation than in competition.[7]

Cooperative goals help group members overcome biases toward each other. Through cooperative experiences, people from different ethnic, economic, sexual, and handicapped groups get to know and accept each other and reduce their prejudices.[8]

Managers from groups that have cooperative goals respond to each other's ideas and interests rather than defend their positions. Intergroup competition pressures department leaders to resist influence and compromises for fear of being accused of selling out.

Cooperative goals improve communication, coordination, and productivity and are critical for groups and their leaders to use coordination procedures. My argument is not that all groups in all circumstances must have cooperative goals. At times, competitive and independent goals are useful. With independent goals, a group can complete many tasks effectively without the bother of coordinating. Companies have experimented with competition between groups. Departments compete over sales volume, new customers, and quality service. Teams compete to see which one can develop the most promising new product. Competition can be a stimulating and challenging device to test a group's ability, and it can increase group camaraderie and pride, at least for the winners.[9] Executives cannot, however, establish serious competition and then realistically expect groups to exchange resources and manage conflicts productively. To promote the collaboration needed to complete many important, complex tasks, cooperative goals must be created.

What Is Needed to Bind Groups?

- Cooperative goals that convince them it is in their best interests to work together.
- Procedures for groups and their managers to discuss issues and work together.
- Skills to solve problems and manage conflicts.

Obstacles to Cooperative Goals

Getting groups to compete is much easier than getting them to cooperate. They compete without any explicit competitive goals.[10] In many companies, groups find their cooperative goals weak, vague, and unmotivating. They have no concrete common task, are not rewarded for collective success, and do not know each other as people.

Groups do have the cooperative goal of promoting the company's productivity and profitability. They need a successful company for job security, compensation, and prestige. But company goals to make profits or provide a fair share of return often are too abstract and distant to be highly motivating. These general aspirations have few specific implications for how groups should collaborate. Many groups have little concrete feedback on whether they are cooperating and reaching company goals. The consequences of failure to pursue these common goals, although potentially substantial, usually are perceived as being at a distance and are salient only during crises.

Competitive goals, in contrast, are specific and motivating. Budgets, promotions, and other resources are limited; allotments to one department mean less for others. Although groups have the cooperative goal of a budget that promotes the overall productivity of the firm, they easily cast their goals in terms of getting plentiful resources for themselves and conclude that they have competitive interests.

Another major obstacle is that top management, while wishing for cooperation, rewards competition. Company officers remark that one department is superior to others or sponsor contests to determine the best department. They often make budget, promotion, and bonus decisions on the basis of which group has outperformed the others. Although this competition can be exciting and involving at times, serious competition undermines coordination. Groups come to believe that they must strive to outdo each other and that giving assistance harms their own interests.

Employees usually feel more a part of and important to their group than to the company. The members of one group may not know those in others and have little opportunity to develop a sense that they are dependable, reliable allies. People from different groups often have no forum in which to meet face to face, iron out problems, and manage conflicts. Conflicts are avoided or handled through channels that are neither understood nor accepted. There is the temptation to direct the group's internal tensions against other groups. Rather than examine its own problems, the group blames others for its frustrations.

Groups do not automatically or even easily understand that they have cooperative goals and that everyone wins through cooperation. Indeed, the incentives for cooperation often are weak, and groups find many reasons to compete. Executives must work systematically to establish cooperative goals.

Cooperative Goals and Procedures

To integrate teams and units into one company, managers must develop cooperative goals and design useful, appropriate procedures. Company goals, shared rewards, personal relationships, project teams, and problem-solving groups are major ways to make one company out of many groups.

Company Goals

Commitment of groups to companywide goals makes them cooperatively dependent. But traditional ways of defining company goals—by profitability and market share and as an industry leader—often seem unrelated to employee needs and group objectives. Companies such as 3M and Dayton-Hudson define their goals as serving the important needs of customers, providing high-quality products and services, developing a company that deserves employee pride, improving society, and providing a return on shareholders' investments.

These companies consider profits to be their rewards for helping customers and society solve problems, work effectively, and live fully. Profits are tangible signs of the gratitude of their customers. Involving employees in discussing and writing corporate goals and philosophy helps employees become committed to them and understand that these goals bind employees cooperatively.[11]

Symbols and slogans dramatize and communicate that the company is a community. Hewlett-Packard people talk warmly about "The H-P Way" and the company's faith in people. The J.C. Penney Company has "The Penney Idea" that embodies its ideals of service, value to the customer, return to the company, training and employee participation, and justice. All practices should "square with what is right and just." Ray Kroc, the founder of McDonald's, is said to have revoked a franchise because it did not live up to his "Quality, Service, Cleanliness, and Value" standard. IBM wants everyone to know that IBM is service; its people aim to answer every customer complaint within twenty-four hours. At 3M, the eleventh commandment is "Thou shalt not kill a new product idea." Delta Airlines develops the "Delta-Family Feeling." Under Harold Geneen, ITT embodied financial discipline through total dedication.

Shared Rewards

Profit and productivity-gain sharing plans make the cooperative dependence of groups on company success concrete. These plans should be structured so that employees realize that they will be rewarded for the performance of all groups. They have a positive stake in the success of other groups; they help themselves by assisting others.

Sharing information about the company supplements shared rewards. Groups get feedback to understand what is needed to reach their common goals and their progress toward success. Profit and information sharing create incentives to collaborate and reach company objectives.

Versatec, a Xerox subsidiary that makes computer printers, had a dramatic way to let everyone know that through profit-sharing, the employees had enjoyed an exceptional year.[12] Executives told the eight hundred employees at a special gathering, "We can't say how big the numbers are, so let's *see* how big they really are." The doors opened and the president of the company rode in on an elephant accompanied by the Stanford University marching band!

Cost and profit centers decentralize and give divisions more autonomy, feedback, and incentives, but they can make collaboration difficult. The centers and their managers are evaluated on the basis of maximizing their returns; they have no positive stake in other centers' performance. They may even compete when they believe top management will compare their financial performance with other centers.

Many corporate managers complain, however, that they must try to mediate conflicts over transfer prices and other issues that centers seem unable to resolve. They also lament their inability to get the centers to exchange their abilities and to assist each other.[13] Given the independent and competitive goals, it should come as no surprise that they are unmotivated to share information and resources. Performance criteria should give centers cooperative goals. A center's performance should be judged in part on the profitability and costs of other centers.

Personal Relationships

People who know each other personally and feel that they can rely on each other use procedures to work together. Company cultures that emphasize the fact that all employees are important and that they should know and value each other as individuals encourage cooperation. Job rotation in which employees take positions in other departments helps them to understand their strengths and perspectives as well as form friendships. Company dinners, bowling leagues, softball games, fitness classes, picnics, and community projects provide opportunities for informal, personal talk.

Having offices close together and norms of openness increase communication and the chance that emerging conflicts will be discussed and resolved. In a campus setting, persons from all parts of the company get to know each other and recognize and use opportunities to collaborate. 3M, for example, has a campus at its corporate headquarters and sponsors a variety of clubs and activities to increase the chances of communication.

Project Teams

Project teams give employees specific, cooperative goals and a forum to collaborate. Members from engineering, production, research, marketing, and consumer affairs departments form a team to develop and market a new product, devise a new accounting system, or implement performance appraisal. These teams should have challenging, motivating tasks and know that they all will be rewarded to the extent the group is successful. Task teams at Litton Microwave (described in chapter 4) illustrate the use of intergroup project teams.

Problem-Solving Groups

Even groups that have appropriate coordination procedures and cooperative goals inevitably have problems and conflicts. Groups should discuss and solve them so that they can continue to coordinate. Groups need encouragement and settings to confront their difficulties. Intergroup meetings in which both departments have a chance to identify the problems that are interfering with collaboration and plan ways to resolve them are useful. Unfortunately, such meetings tend to be planned only after the conflicts have escalated.[14] Task forces composed of persons from affected departments should be appointed to analyze conflicts and propose solutions.

IBM, General Electric, and other companies use management committees to advise CEOs on company policies and problems.[15] In addition to keeping the CEO informed and the organization informed about the CEO, these committees bind executives to the management team. They form personal links, develop a shared understanding of companywide issues, and become committed to solving problems.

Teams can link management and labor. The Ford Motor Company and United Automobile Workers (UAW) established regularly scheduled problem-solving groups.[16] The groups were designed to be forums for ongoing discussion and resolution of conflicts before such conflicts could fester and grow.

Case Studies

Three cases illustrate the need to develop both the appropriate procedures and cooperative dependence. The first case indicates that sharing rewards without the appropriate procedures undercuts collaboration. In the second case, cooperative and competitive goals affected how IBM and GE used their corporate management committees. The third case shows how managers formed a cooperative team to learn management skills and improve coordination among their divisions.

Profit Sharing without Coordination Procedures

Bender Box Company supplies corrugated containers that are designed, die-cut, and printed to the specifications of customers who use them for shipping, display, and packaging. Bender has twenty-five employees, sales of more than $4 million annually, and reasonable profits and growth. Donald Weiss, the owner and chief officer, was excited about the success other companies had with profit sharing. He wanted his company to be more like a family and to have the departments work together to improve the long-term stability and profitability of the firm. The managers agreed, and with the help of accountants developed a plan whereby once sales exceeded a standard based on previous years, all employees would share in the benefits of increased productivity.

Although profit sharing created the cooperative goal to improve productivity and sales, employees within and across departments had no effective forum in which to work together. Workers were expected to develop productivity improvements alone or in spontaneous groups. Nor was there a way for management, marketing, and production to develop ways to improve sales and productivity. Employees did not have concrete ways to discuss how to improve profits.

The profit-sharing plan did not motivate, improve coordination, or develop a family atmosphere but instead heightened Donald Weiss's suspicions about his employees. The lack of success was due to the company's failure to create appropriate procedures, however, and not to the fact that employees were lazy.

Management Committees

IBM and General Electric both had management committees to advise the CEO on important corporate issues through the 1970s.[17] These committees helped link the CEO and the organization so that both were informed and involved. They tackled the large questions of how the company should respond to current and future conditions and hammered out budgets. IBM was able to develop highly cooperative goals that made the committee very effective and influential. But at GE, competitive and independent goals limited the committee's usefulness.

IBM's Corporate Management Committee (CMC) was very active and touched on a broad range of issues. Three to five official members, including the company's chairman and president, formed the committee and met several times a week for the total of thirty to forty hours per month. IBM considered itself in one business, and the CMC saw itself as part of the process of developing a consensus of what the company should do. It encouraged full discussion and settlement of issues at the lowest possible level. If groups could not agree, the problem was discussed at higher levels until it reached the CMC.

The CMC discussed and decided programs. It examined the merits of new products and coordinated new offerings across the various divisions within IBM. Even after budget decisions were made, the CMC reviewed new and revised programs all year. Before issues came to them and later in their deliberations, the CMC encouraged open, constructive conflict. Through their discussions, CMC members became very familiar with each division, as well as with the overall company thrust. The CMC contributed to the strong sense of unity and respect for individuals within IBM.

GE used the Corporate Policy Board (CPB) supported by the Corporate Executive Council to review budgets, planning, and operations of its forty different businesses. While important, the CPB met only for sixteen half-days in 1980, and the Corporate Executive Council met nine times. In contrast to IBM's CMC, the CPB funded businesses and discussed finances more than ideas.

The strategic business units (SBUs) within GE had the cooperative goal of creating a healthy company but also had competitive and independent goals. They realized that GE could not fund all requests, so they sought to make as strong a case as they could for their own proposals and businesses. They competed over funds. SBU managers rarely discussed each other's proposals. Nor did the CPB have enough knowledge to discuss the businesses. It decided on the basis of past and predicted returns on investments. It made budget decisions on the basis of presentations and each SBU's track record.

The strongly cooperative goals within IBM encouraged full discussion and debate about programs. Groups disputed the merits of specific ideas, and the CMC would hear these arguments if groups were unable to agree what was best for the company. The CMC worked for consensus decisions and reinforced that IBM was a large family. The competitive and independent goals of the SBUs at GE limited discussion and made consensus decisions difficult. The CPC helped link the SBUs at GE, but they still remained quite independent.

Management Learning and Coordination

Margaret Quillan, the chief administrator of Northwest Services, a diversified health-care company with divisions that provided care and services to different client groups, wanted to improve links between the divisions and upgrade the management skills of administrators. She formed a management-development group of the top two administrators from each of three divisions. They had concrete, cooperative and specific ways to work together.

The administrators met regularly for half a year to study management ideas, become more aware of the strengths and weaknesses of their management style, discuss common problems, learn skills, give each other feedback, and in other ways help each other become more effective. They visited each other's divisions to get another perspective on difficulties. In this way, they learned more about the overall company and were better prepared to replace each other if necessary.

In addition to learning together, they discussed how they and others in their divisions might work together. They found ways to share information and avoid duplication of effort. Administrators with similar responsibilities met outside the meetings to discuss specific management problems. Task forces of employees from the various divisions were formed to solve specific problems. The administrators worked as a team, not only to help themselves learn, but also to heighten the cooperative goals and improve the procedures for divisions to work together more effectively.

Concluding Comments

Direct contact, project teams, management committees, and other procedures must be combined with cooperative goals to integrate groups. Procedures are insufficient because groups easily compete for limited resources and the favor of corporate officers. As with individuals, groups must have multiple, overlapping incentives that their goals are cooperative and have practical opportunities to combine their ideas and information. A corporate vision that is related to employee aspirations, shared rewards, personal relationships, and interdepartment task teams convinces groups that they have cooperative goals.

Part III
Making Cooperation Work

7
Power and Recognition

Power, when appropriately applied, is a company's strength, even its salvation. Despite its dark and often sinister reputation, power can, in enlightened hands, be the force by which management can recognize employees, encourage them to collaborate, and develop their abilities. Managers and workers, because they depend on each other for information, assistance, and support to get their jobs done, have power and are subject to it. Power cannot be denied and should not be minimized. Companies must know how to manage power to make it highly useful.

Power is a positive force in many organizations. To make their employees feel powerful and like winners, companies recognize their achievements and contributions in newsletters, bulletin boards, and award presentations. Public recognition empowers, invigorates, and mobilizes employees to be productive and fulfilled. Powerful managers have the self-confidence and resources to support and encourage others; managers who feel powerless are easily threatened, hesitate to provide needed resources, and may even undermine employees to protect themselves.[1] Power's very positive face must be appreciated to encourage capable persons to seek leadership and use power constructively.[2]

But thoughtful managers also worry about power and recognition. Recognizing one employee might make others feel slighted. Is it really possible to make everyone feel like a winner? Might not empowered employees be self-centered and arrogant? Powerful bosses can be nasty autocrats. Power has long been suspected. Lord Acton's admonition that power corrupts and absolute power corrupts absolutely is still widely believed. Since the American Revolution, power has been portrayed as alive and evil; it consumes even good persons and destroys anything in its path to domination.

Many researchers also are wary of power.[3] Power differences are thought to distort communication and conflict management. Power results in domineering, aloof superiors and deflated, ingratiating subordinates. Researchers and managers have tried to find methods to neutralize the ill effects of power. Companies use participative decision making and other procedures to equalize power.

Conflicting attitudes toward power make understanding and managing power in organizations difficult. On one hand, power is constructive, and employees should be empowered; on the other hand, power corrupts and should be minimized. Because of the importance of power and changes in values toward it, there is a great need to document the role of power in organizations. Exasperated with the diverse discussions about power, however, some researchers have argued that power is too ideological and confused an idea to be of much use.

What is important to recognize is that whether power occurs in cooperation or competition greatly affects its consequences. Ambiguity toward power reflects that it has a much different character in cooperation than in competition. When employees believe that their goals are compatible, they appreciate each other's abilities, work out arrangements to exchange resources, and encourage each other to develop their strengths. Recognition, exchange, and development of abilities are handled much differently in competition. Competitors are threatened by others' achievements and capabilities, try to coerce them to be helpful, and do not encourage them to become more able.

Power is analyzed here as people depend on and work with each other. Power can be used to understand the extent of that dependence and thus complements cooperative and competitive goals. Distinguishing power in cooperation and competition strengthens research, contributes to the contemporary rehabilitation of power, and suggests how organizations can successfully manage power. As we shall see next, managers who have both power and strong needs to compete can create turmoil.

Power and Competition: The Case of Ward Himmel

Ward Himmel managed twenty-five professionals in a department that for years experienced high turnover, moderate productivity, and low morale. Young professionals left for other opportunities; long-term employees worked without enthusiasm. One said, "After working here thirty-three years, I have no loyalty whatsoever to this place." Departmental personnel were polite in public but privately talked of their frustrations and suspicions. Ward Himmel also was frustrated. With a half-laugh and smile, he would lament that he must be crazy to work so hard when no one else bothered. But his self-mockery conveyed too much hostility to be funny. Although he worked hard as a professional and gained recognition, he failed as a manager because department employees were frustrated and unproductive.

The driving force behind this unfortunate state was Himmel's competition with his employees and how they came to feel competitive toward him. Himmel could see the potential of cooperation and wanted a highly productive department of which he could be proud, but even more he wanted to be considered the department's most able member. His employees saw this competition very clearly.

Himmel downplayed others' contributions and was skeptical of their plans and projects. He defended such actions as necessary to be a strong, candid, productivity-oriented boss. Employees considered him ungrateful and punitive, saw his demanding style as repeated attempts to feel superior, and became suspicious and competitive themselves.

It was Himmel's competitive orientation, not his power, that created these unhappy events. His superior power, however, interfered with recognizing and resolving the problem and left his competitiveness unchallenged. Department members assumed that, if confronted, he would be defensive, hostile, and revengeful. He could bite them, but they could not bite back.

They tried to accommodate themselves to Himmel's style. They avoided discussing difficulties directly with him, privately complained to each other, and put their energies and hopes in nondepartmental activities. The competition created an arrogance by the boss and submissiveness and withdrawal by employees.

The irony, which is no less tragic because it is common, was that Ward Himmel's superior power worked against him as well as his department. He remained blind to the impact of his behavior, felt isolated and unappreciated, and did not gain the rewards of a successful manager.

Many writers and managers have thought that power disrupts communication and joint action and have pointed to the difficulties that managers and workers face. But power itself does not undermine coordination. Many unequally powerful persons believe that their goals are cooperative and develop enriching, productive collaboration. Power differences can make establishing such a relationship much more difficult, however, when they are coupled with a competition that interferes with solving problems.

Power in Competition

Organizational theorists have labored over how to define power. There is a loose consensus that power should be defined in terms of the capacity of one person to get another to do what he or she would not otherwise do. It is being able to produce effects on others despite their opposition.[4] This definition assumes that persons with power and those subject to it have competitive goals. Persons subject to power, realizing that compliance is not in their self-interest, do not freely comply with the powerful's request. What helps the powerful persons reach their goals does not help those subject to power reach theirs.

The assumption that power occurs in competition shapes our thinking.

People are thought to use power when they are in conflict over resources and are competitively linked in the sense that as one gets more, the others must get less. Empirical studies have focused on allocation of budgets and other scarce resources. There are winners and losers in the contests of power.[5]

It could be argued that restricting power to competition is reasonable and useful. But a boss still has the power of promotions, raises, and assignments over subordinates even when they pursue cooperative goals. A loyal worker and chief executive officer may chat, laugh, and share common goals, but it is doubtful that they will be unaware of or uninfluenced by their power differences. As the model of working with people suggests, competitive goals greatly affect the dynamics and consequences of power and make managing power more difficult.

Power in Cooperation

How can power be considered so that it does not assume competition and sheds light on cooperation? Power is defined as the control over valued abilities or, equivalently, as the capacity to affect another's rewards and costs.[6] Abilities themselves do not bestow power; they must be known and valued by others.

Fred Johnson has power over Jenny McCollough when she believes that Fred has abililties she values. Jenny values these abilities because she believes that they affect her goals. Power depends on a goal-resource correspondence; the powerful has a resource that can facilitate or frustrate the dependent person's goal.

How much power Fred has depends on how committed Jenny is to the goal that Fred can affect and on whether Jenny believes she can get Fred's ability elsewhere.[7] Fred's control of information and acceptance into the group do not give him power. Only when Jenny believes that these abilities can help her and that she cannot, or at least not easily, obtain them elsewhere does Fred have power. Jenny can reduce her dependence by lowering her desire for information and respect or by believing that she can obtain them from someone else.

It is possible that only one person has power over another, but typically employees have power with each other. Managers have power vis-a-vis subordinates, but most managers value the efforts, ideas, and respect of subordinates. The extent of dependence varies a great deal. A CEO has the capacity to make decisions and distribute rewards that are highly valued by a vice president, but the CEO might not see the vice president's information and knowledge as very important or may believe that these abilities can be easily obtained elsewhere.

What Makes Someone Powerful?

Employees in three companies were asked in interviews to identify the abilities they needed from each other in specific situations.[8] Although the companies were quite different—one provided computer services for a large retailer, another was a municipal engineering office, and the third provided services for mentally handicapped persons—employees valued similar abilities in all of them. Knowledge, assistance, and emotional support were mentioned often in all three organizations. Funding, evaluation, and authority were infrequently mentioned.

Employees greatly valued information and knowledge; to make decisions, plan how to proceed, and perform a host of other tasks requires others' advice and data. They also frequently cited willingness to give assistance to complete tasks as important; many tasks cannot be accomplished by one person working alone. Perhaps surprisingly, emotional support also was seen in nearly half the situations as an important, valued resource, even among groups such as computer specialists, people not typically thought to have strong emotional needs. Even when working with their boss, employees thought that knowledge, effort, and emotional support were more important than official approval. Although rewards of bonuses and evaluations were cited infrequently, persons who control these also have power.

Employees understand that they need others' abilities to get their jobs done. They value others' knowledge and effort and often turn to each other for support and encouragement. Job requirements and emotional needs underlie much of the power in organizations. Power is not restricted to competition but is very much a part of cooperative work.

Research Findings

Experiments and studies in companies indicate that cooperative, compared to competitive and independent, goals promote constructive power in organizations.

Cooperative Goals Foster Recognition and Appreciation of Employee Abilities. People in cooperation identify and value each other's strengths because they realize that abilities will be used for mutual benefit. It is to one's advantage that others are powerful and resourceful, for powerful others can help reach cooperative goals. Competitors, on the other hand, fear that others will use their abilities against them. Knowledge that others have different information and ideas is welcome in cooperation but threatens when goals are competitive. Collaborators help each other to be aware of their ideas, information, skills, and other abilities so that they are in a better position to reach goals and do their jobs.[9]

Cooperative Goals Encourage Mutual Influence and a Profitable Exchange of Abilities. Collaborators, even though they may be unequally powerful, are able to exchange abilities and resources for mutual benefit. Both the powerful and less powerful with cooperative goals expected to help each other, were trusting, shared their resources, and came to like each other. In contrast, those in competition suspected each other, failed to exchange resources, and intensified their mistrust and dislike. Powerful competitors felt confident, but less powerful ones were insecure.[10]

Managers who feel powerful are thought to use their power supportively.[11] Although power bestows a capacity to aid employees, cooperative goals compel managers to use their power constructively. Managers who had power and were cooperatively linked with their employees encouraged, guided, and gave tangible assistance that aided productivity.[12] Managers with or without power in competition discouraged and gave little assistance.

In another experiment, powerful managers in competition used their power to try to coerce employees.[13] Cooperatively linked managers relied less on coercion and used more collaborative influence. It has been shown that cooperative goals help managers use their power flexibly.[14] In this experiment, managers demanded more from employees who performed poorly because they failed to apply themselves but supported and encouraged those who lacked the ability to do the task. Managers in competition were punitive regardless of whether employees performed poorly because of low ability or low effort.

Studies conducted in organizations further document the positive pattern of power in cooperation.[15] Three hundred ten medical technicians employed in the laboratories of ten major hospitals in the Vancouver, British Columbia, metropolitan area, indicated that cooperative supervisors used their power to help them accomplish their tasks and become committed to the hospital.

In addition, colleagues also have been found to use their power constructively in cooperation. An analysis of the interviews of 140 employees from three organizations indicated that when they believed that their goals were cooperative, they exchanged abilities, strengthened their relationships, and accomplished their tasks.

Cooperation Encourages Learning and Development. Employees with cooperative goals want others to become more capable because that helps everyone to be effective. They initiate activities and discussions to learn. They coach each other on the job, review information and ideas that aid learning, reflect and learn from their experiences, and provide feedback to learn skills. Chapter 12 elaborates on these findings and their implications.

Unequally Powerful Persons Can Work Together Effectively, But Power Differences Can Interfere. Competition between unequally powerful persons, not power differences, account for the suspicion and difficulties traditionally

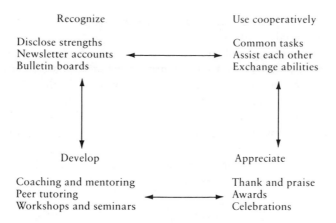

Recognize

Disclose strengths
Newsletter accounts
Bulletin boards

Use cooperatively

Common tasks
Assist each other
Exchange abilities

Develop

Coaching and mentoring
Peer tutoring
Workshops and seminars

Appreciate

Thank and praise
Awards
Celebrations

Figure 7–1. Positive Power

associated with unequal relationships. But power differences unconfounded by competition are still apt to influence collaboration. Powerful persons have been found to be relatively disinterested in taking the perspective and understanding the interests of the less powerful and to be less open to being influenced by the less powerful.[16] This reluctance may make establishing productive cooperation difficult.[17]

These studies suggest that cooperation depends more on the orientation and skills of the powerful than the less powerful. The powerful often can structure work to make it difficult for others to talk about problems openly, or they can emphasize cooperative goals and encourage mutually rewarding collaboration.

Positive Power

Power can be a highly constructive force within organizations, but the key to power management is that employees believe that their important goals are cooperative. To make all employees feel like winners, have them recognize each other's abilities, share knowledge, and develop each other's strengths and confidence, managers must work to establish strong, cooperative goals. Employees who believe that their goals are competitive are reluctant to appreciate abilities and share resources.

Positive power (see figure 7–1) means that employees search out each other's abilities and appreciate their contributions, negotiate and influence each other to exchange resources that will help them both be more productive, and encourage each other to develop and enhance their strengths. This positive power pattern occurs as employees work on a common task with cooperative goals.

As they begin, employees can identify previous experiences, achievements, and strengths that are relevant to their task. Shared knowledge about each one's abilities makes it easier to call upon the right team member and to use all the resources available to the group. Throughout their joint assignment, employees can continue to identify abilities. Giving thanks, praise, and compliments conveys appreciation as well as recognizes abilities. Working together also is critical for developing skills. Coaching, on-the-job training, peer tutoring, and mentoring are important ways for employees to learn and grow on the job. These are discussed in chapter 12.

Power and Recognition in a Growing Company

North American Tool & Die, Inc., had experienced the troubles of many small manufacturers—marginal profitability, an unenthusiastic work force, and lots of competition.[1] But in the three years beginning with 1980, company sales went from $1.8 million to $6 million, profits were increased by six times, the customer reject rate declined from 5 to 0.3 percent, and turnover dropped from 27 to 6 percent.

The co-owners, Thomas H. Melohn and Garner Beckett, Jr., realized that to compete successfully and grow they had to provide both quality and service. Competitors were run largely by technically skilled entrepreneurs who were only semiskilled managers. Melohn and Beckett wanted to build a well-managed company to supply computer manufacturers with timely, quality products, many of which have a tolerance of 19.001 of an inch. That's about a fourth of the size of a human hair.

They believed that people would be the difference between them and their competitors. Employees received shares provided that they met basic requirements. Meetings also informed employees of where the company had been and where it was going. Employees recognized that the company's success and profits were their success and profits.

Melohn and Beckett worked hard to recognize the abilities of all employees. At monthly plantwide meetings, they gave the "Super Person of the Month" plaque and a check to the employee who had produced excellent quality. The employee's name was engraved and the plaque was prominently and permanently displayed in the plant. Every employee who had an anniversary of working with the company that month got a silver dollar. Customer's compliments were announced and the employees responsible honored. The award the company won as the best supplier of a customer was given to the department heads who had earned it.

Throughout the month and every day, the company complimented employees. Two or three times a week, Melohn and Beckett went through the plant chatting and complimenting those who had worked well. They also showed concern for employees as people. When a Korean worker had trouble conveying his symptoms to his doctor, they found a physician who spoke Korean. Employees were allowed to borrow a week's pay with no interest. The company sent flowers to every employee or spouse who was in the hospital. Each employee got a check as a wedding present. National Tool & Die continually recognized and appreciated the abilities of its employees and got them to work together for success.

Company practices reinforce positive power. Newsletters, employee rosters, award ceremonies, celebrations, and bulletin boards identify the talents, backgrounds, and achievements of employees and make them known. To facilitate the exchange of resources, the organization can use project teams, task forces, and other forums in which employees can work together and use their abilities to accomplish common objectives. The organization can provide workshops, encourage professional activities, establish mentoring programs, and subsidize tuition for courses to develop employee abilities.

Example of Positive Power

Esther wanted to build apartments for the elderly. Her experience owning a nursing home convinced her that many elderly persons need housing that helps them to live independently but with companions and without the hassles of home ownership. At a community breakfast, she sought out John, a manager of a general contractor–development firm. She told him that she liked his new condominiums and that she wanted something like them next to her nursing home. Esther knew that Bill, the administrator at the nursing home, would be excited about the project because he and his staff also wanted opportunities to work with healthy, independent elderly people. Bill agreed to arrange the first formal meeting with John.

In the first meetings, Esther, Bill, and John explored the feasibility of the project and got to know each other better. John questioned them on how the building would be different from a typical apartment complex and was reassured when he found that Esther already owned the land next to the nursing home. Bill said that the nursing home's reputation would be useful in attracting residents and that initial operating expenses could be covered by income from the nursing home. Bill asked John about his building, marketing, and financing experience. John described the projects his company had helped develop and gave Esther and Bill a tour of two apartment buildings his company had just completed. He estimated the cost of construction and his fees.

Esther and Bill were impressed with John's buildings and concluded that he had the needed expertise. John's experience in developing attractive market-rate apartments was a big plus because they wanted a residential, not an institutional, look. John concluded that Esther and Bill were serious people who had already developed one business and would work to build another, were practical enough to make reasonable decisions, had sufficient equity, and would not be too difficult, maybe even a little fun, to work with. He also knew that having a nursing home and the land were major financial assets to help them build the project. They agreed to work on the project together, pursued it steadily, and after seventeen months broke ground.

Esther, Bill, and John, like others who want to develop a business or get a job done, need power, provided it is used cooperatively. They knew they had a common goal that, if reached, would benefit each of them. Esther and Bill initially wanted to know what John could do for the project. They were delighted that what he told them and his past achievements indicated that he had the abilities to make the project a reality. John wanted to identify Esther's and Bill's abilities. If they did not have the right ones, John would have concluded that he would be wasting his time on the project. In addition to having the abilities, they wanted to be sure that they would use their abilities collaboratively.

Esther, Bill, and John used their abilities to reach their cooperative goal, and the apartments were built. They also learned. John found out about managing a nursing home and building for the elderly; Bill realized the differences between a market-oriented business and a government-regulated and reimbursed one.

Steps to Positive Power in Teams

Team members must recognize each other's abilities and exchange them to accomplish tasks and solve problems.

1. Team members together recognize, emphasize, and clearly understand that their goals are cooperative. They know that as others reach their goals, they too are successful. Important cooperative goals lay the foundation for the following activities.
2. Members indicate the abilities and resources needed to accomplish team goals and aspirations.
3. Team members identify and demonstrate their knowledge, ideas, and other strengths. They know each other's abilities.
4. Employees indicate how they can use each other's abilities to reach the team's goals, accomplish its tasks, and meet their own aspirations.
5. Aware of their cooperative goals and valued abilities, team members agree to exchange resources. These exchanges should be timely, fair, and enhancing.
   - Abilities are valued at a particular time; information useful at one time is noise at another. Employees let each other know when they need the others' abilities.
   - Fairness demands that everyone give as well as receive.

- Resources should be given so that the receiver does not feel belittled. Exchanges help members to feel confident that they have important assets and that they can rely on others for assistance.

6. As they collaborate, team members help each other to learn and develop skills.

7. The team celebrates its accomplishments and recognizes that everyone contributed to the group's success.

Comparisons

In cooperation, employees identify each other's strengths and feel reassured and motivated by them, not threatened. Inevitably, though, employees will compare themselves and at times will believe that they have much less knowledge, experience, and ideas than others. Comparisons themselves are not inevitably harmful, and they can help people learn about themselves. But invidious ones that create feelings of inferiority and competition should be avoided.[18] Recognizing employee abilities and achievement must be well managed.

Skills and Achievements are Not Confused with Personal Worth. Employees are intrinsically worthwhile and are not important just because of their knowledge and resources. Highly valued abilities do not make an employee more moral, just as having few abilities that are not valued in that situation does not make one an unimportant person.

Recognition of Abilities Is Based on Facts, Not Prejudices. Strengths and capabilities are recognized regardless of the sex, race, age, verbal skills, or physical appearance of employees. Not just attractive persons who speak fluently have abilities. Similarly, expertise in one area does not automatically confer expertise in others.

Everyone's Value Is Recognized. Differences in abilities should not obscure the fact that all employees have abilities, are important to the organization, and can contribute to its success. Employees understand that everyone must do their job well and contribute to the organization.

Identifying abilities and recognizing differences can, if properly done, avoid invidious comparisons and strengthen cooperation. Disclosure and recognition of abilities create a great deal of goodwill. People feel fulfilled and rewarded, and these good feelings lead to a desire to reciprocate, help others, and work together.[19]

Guides for Action

Positive Power

- Know your own abilities and strengths.
- Know others' abilities and accomplishments.
- Show that people's abilities help everyone to be successful.
- Discuss how people can use each other's abilities to get things done.
- Celebrate achievements to make everyone proud.

Pitfalls to Avoid

- Assume that only a few people have abilities.
- Use stereotypes to decide who has valued resources.
- Classify people as winners or losers.
- Suspect people who want to feel confident and powerful.

Concluding Comments

Power traditionally has been considered part of the dark side of social life. It is usually believed to be used for self-aggrandizement in the struggle against others. This win-lose view is only one side of the story, however, and the prevalence of competitive power probably has been exaggerated.

Power and recognizing employee abilities are very constructive for organizations. Knowledge, expertise, information, assistance, emotional support, and other abilities necessary to make decisions, solve problems, develop new products, accomplish tasks, and maintain the organization are disclosed, valued, exchanged, and further refined and developed. Positive power enhances employees and productivity.

To make all employees feel like winners requires more than handing out pins and awards. It requires highly cooperative goals in which people draw out and appreciate each other's strengths as they work together. Company practices and the way employees collaborate can help to identify, use, appreciate, and develop the abilities of employees and boost the company's collective might.

8
Solving Problems and Making Decisions

If Doug Fraser had served on Lynn Townsend's board, maybe Chrysler wouldn't have bought up the lousiest companies in Europe. Some of those terrible moves could have been stopped by just one bold man asking, "Why are we doing this? Does it really make sense?"
—Lee Iacocca, CEO, Chrysler Corporation

The best way ever devised for seeking the truth in any given situation is advocacy: presenting the pros and cons from different, informed points of view and digging down deep into the facts.
—Harold S. Geneen, former CEO, ITT

*G*etting ready for his weekly squash match with Wilbur Oxman, Bob Clinton declared, "I found out that I'm a participative manager."

"That sounds good," Wilbur responded. "How did you find that out?"

Bob explained that he had learned at a workshop that participative managers involve people in making decisions. "I used to think that it was my job to solve all the problems, but it is a great relief to know that I can get my group together and we can work out a solution together. When Preston and Fred have very different opinions about what we should do, I don't feel as though I have to resolve it right then, but we talk the issue over. These team sessions take the pressure off me, my staff like them, and we've come up with some very good programs.

"Another thing I learned was that disagreements are important for making sound decisions. That makes a lot of sense to me. It bothers me when everyone agrees with the first suggestion. I get nervous that we aren't really involved and haven't dug into the issue."

"Apathy can certainly be a problem, but so can arguing and arguing," Wilbur interjected. "Our group always seems to drag the debate on; people get very stubborn."

"We do that sometimes, too. It's not just debating but constructive disagreement that we want. Arguments between Preston and

Fred are very useful for getting at the facts, but there is one thing that they do wrong rather regularly. They try to win and prove that they are right and the other is wrong. That's when the debate is endless and progress slow. People must disagree but should work for a solution that is good for all, not to prove they are right and that everyone must agree with them."

"You have a point there, but is it realistic? People, especially professional types, always want to be right," Wilbur asserted.

*"I think it can work," Bob answered. "Everyone does want to be right, but they must want the group to be right and make the best decision. My job as a manager is to make sure my people understand that it is **unimportant to begin with the right position,** but it is **very important that we all end up with the right one.** We need to emphasize the common objective and point out when persons get carried away and are browbeating others."*

"Maybe that's a way to stop the debate from getting out of hand and turning into an endless argument," Wilbur offered.

"I have a good way to use this idea," Bob continued. "We haven't been able to decide whether we should seek business out of state—it would be very profitable, but we have not gotten around to discussing it thoroughly. My plan is to divide the group in half, assign one the pro position and one the con position, have them research their position, and then have them debate the question. We would let the issue rest for a few days and then meet to get some consensus. I'll probably invite the boss to join us."

"Sounds interesting," Wilbur said. "Keep me informed about your experiments. If they work for you, they might work for me."

Problems challenge, invigorate, and disrupt. Every day managers confront problems that must be solved: How should the requests of Abbey Hospitals and City Health be answered? Is more information needed? Employees must make decisions to complete their tasks: Is additional collateral for the loan required? Companies face decisions to enter new markets, develop new products, and acquire businesses that very much affect the profits, even the survival, of the firm. Skills to identify problems and make decisions greatly determine the success of managers and the productivity of companies.

Problem solving is the sine qua non of successful management; no company can thrive unless it can grapple with difficulties, cope with uncertainties, and seize opportunities. Selecting efficient technologies, adapting and responding to the environment, forming a shared vision, and developing employee skills all demand identifying problems and implementing solutions.

Decision making competence pays off handsomely; the organization stays on course, handles setbacks, and remains confident. Ineffective decision making is costly because employees' time and energy are wasted, projects are delayed, and opportunities are missed.

But there is no single way that all problems should be discussed and solved. Some decisions demand careful exploration and creation of new approaches; others are solved in quick, routine ways. Some decisions break new ground; many decisions use precedents as guides to determine what should be done. Managers and organizations must be flexible. They must make wise decisions about how they are going to make decisions.

By working cooperatively and using their power positively, managers and employees are able to dig into issues, pool their information, integrate ideas, and create useful solutions. But how exactly are they to work together to solve problems? What procedures are useful and what skills needed? Decision makers must be able to discuss their opposing ideas and information openly and constructively. Constructive controversy is the key to making the most of cooperative goals and positive power to solve problems. Avoiding controversy or trying to make one's views dominate often are disastrous. Constructive controversy is a powerful tool for solving problems and an important safeguard against fiascos.

Effective Problem Solving

Getting quality solutions is important in decision making, but it is not the only objective. Decisions are not simply puzzles and riddles to be solved; they are part of the whole stream of working and managing. A problem must be felt and understood and alternative choices created before employees can consider its solution. The decision must be implemented, its impact assessed, and new problems identified.

Problem solving is an ongoing process that is an integral part of working. To be effective, problem solving must find a solution that gets the job done, efficiently uses resources, promotes future cooperation, and fosters employee competence.

Decisions that promote all these objectives are highly effective; decisions that promote none of them are highly ineffective. Of course, these objectives are not always important; managers must be aware of the most relevant criteria. For major decisions, a high-quality solution is critical, but for a minor problem, saving time may be more important.

High-Quality Solutions

Bob Clinton and his group want to know whether and how they should seek business in neighboring states. They want a solution based on thoughtful analysis and relatively complete information, not whim and fancy. The solution should be appropriate and relatively permanent; they do not want to decide to seek the business one month only to retreat the next. The benefits of the solution should outweigh the costs to implement it.

Bob and his group will be unable to validate their solution completely, however. It might be years until they have a good picture of the benefits and costs, and there is always the possibility that another strategy would have been more successful. Although quality is usually important, it is difficult to measure and feel confident about it.

Implementation and Ownership

Bob's health-care group wants a solution that it can and will implement. It does little good to decide to make loans and then not do it. No matter how brilliant the plan, if it remains unimplemented, it cannot work. Ideally, employees should own the solution and be willing to implement it without costly supervision and monitoring. They should understand the decision, know what they must do to implement it, be internally committed to seeing the solution put into practice, and report any difficulties or unexpected consequences that occur when the solution is implemented.

Efficiency

Proper priorities and common sense about practicality are important ingredients in using the time and energy of employees wisely. Not all problems are equally important, and their relative significance must be kept in perspective. Minor problems do not deserve exhaustive consideration or million-dollar solutions. Issues that substantially affect the health of the company need careful, ongoing exploration. Although there may be benefits to having the department as a whole solve a problem, employees will have to forgo work on other tasks to coordinate schedules, attend meetings, and focus their attention. They will be annoyed and perhaps less committed if they believe that their time is not well spent.

Future Decisions

The issue of making loans in nearby states will not be the last one that Bob's group decides. Ideally, decision makers should become more informed and able to create and implement high-quality solutions. Experiences that leave them less willing to share information and difficulties, combine their ideas, and implement useful solutions bode ill for the organization.

Individual Competence

Many people seek decision-making responsibility. They enjoy the challenge to draw upon and develop their abilities to identify and overcome obstacles. They are pleased that others trust their judgment and seek their opinion. They enjoy the give and take, exploration, camaraderie, and sense of importance that often accompany decision making. The abilities and resources of individuals should be recognized and utilized.

Legitimacy

Decision making involves rights to influence and responsibilities to obey. Employees are likely to be more committed to implementing the solution and to the organization in general if they believe that the decision was reached by legitimate, just means. Although employees recognize their superiors' right to make decisions, they usually see the methods as fairer if they have participated in making the decision.

Cooperation promotes all aspects of effective problem solving. Decision makers with cooperative goals combine their ideas to create high-quality solutions, understand and become committed to the solution, make problem solving a rich experience, develop confidence and skills to make decisions, and accept the procedures used to arrive at the decision. In addition to its significance, how decision makers work together can be influenced and managed. Not all organizations can hire geniuses and the best experts, but they can improve the way employees discuss and make decisions.

Limitations of Individuals

The rational ideal holds that decision makers should agree on their goals, exhaustively search for alternatives, evaluate options thoroughly, and select the best alternative. Management researchers doubt that this rational, comprehensive decision making is realistic for the many complex problems contemporary organizations face.[1] They argue that decision makers do not have the cognitive capacity to process information necessary for this rational approach. Decision makers are unable to understand the changing vagrancies of the external and internal environments. Individuals also are thought to be self-interested and to promote their own interests rather than the common good.[2]

Studies document that individuals have limited ability to consider various information and have biases that prevent full and open consideration of ideas.[3] Many different ways of biasing processes have been identified. Simplification and biases occur in identifying the problem, analyzing it, developing alternatives, considering consequences, and selecting the decision.[4]

Decision makers have been found to be closed to considering information, especially information that is new and opposes their present position. They rely on easy-to-recall, available information to form their opinions. Decision makers often evaluate information inadequately. With a "belief in the law of small numbers," they have made unreasonable conclusions based on very small samples and have used early trends to predict final results.[5] Despite being closed to information and evaluating data inappropriately, decision makers often are confident in their conclusions, apparently oblivious to their own faulty reasoning.[6] Individuals have many ways to make bad decisions.

Potential of Team Decision Making

The speed, suddenness, and complexity of changes make great demands on decision makers. Past policies cannot be expected to be successful continuously. Decision makers must, after monitoring the company's environment and understanding its internal workings and strengths, determine its goals, plans, and procedures. But individual decision makers have limited capacity to monitor these developments and create solutions. Organizations require individuals to pool their information, explore complex issues thoroughly, and create new, appropriate measures.

Forming teams to make complex decisions does not automatically result in effective problem solving. Indeed, sometimes people working together reinforce their biases and enhance their limitations.[7] They may develop group-think conformity that results in fiascos that severely damage the company. Alternatively, individuals use the group to push for their own self-interest at the expense of the company's welfare.[8]

To cope with the limitations of individuals, decision makers must work together successfully to solve problems. But how can a team solve complex problems effectively? Conflict-filled discussions, when conducted cooperatively, can help the team to cope with the cognitive limitations and biases of individual decision makers. It is not proposed that teams always rationally and comprehensively make decisions, that their cognitive limitations do not interfere, or that conflict always aids coping with these limitations. But *decision makers with highly cooperative goals who are able to discuss their opposing views openly and constructively can thoroughly investigate problems and create useful solutions.*

Constructive Controversy

> *Begin with certainties, end with uncertainties.*
> *Begin with uncertainties, end with certainties.*
>
> —*Chinese proverb*

> *It is not who is right, but what is right.*
>
> —*Popular saying*

> *Don't find fault, find a remedy.*
>
> —*Henry Ford*

Managers and employees must know how to work together to reduce their biases, avoid closed-mindedness and simplistic thinking, dig into problems, and make successful decisions. They must discuss their opposing positions and opinions constructively to be open-minded, evaluate new information objectively, incorporate new ideas, and avoid unwarranted commitment to their position.

Not all controversy is beneficial. To be productive, differences of opinion must be discussed within cooperative goals. But we now know that skillfully discussed controversy is vital for successful problem solving.

IBM and Controversy

IBM's contention system required managers to "nonconcur" if they did not agree with a proposed plan or program.[1] The corporation wanted issues to be discussed thoroughly by those directly involved. People within and across divisions were expected to voice their opposing opinions and differences. To encourage this controversy, the company respected individual rights of free expression and provided a system to resolve controversies that the protagonists themselves could not. The top executives in the Corporate Management Committee listened to all sides of any dispute that could not be resolved at lower levels. To affirm its commitment to this contention system, the committee listened to debates even on issues that involved relatively few resources.

The Value of Controversy

Decision makers who express their opposing ideas, opinions, conclusions, theories, and information as they discuss problems are in controversy. Controversy involves differences of opinion that temporarily prevent, delay, or interfere with reaching a decision. Some managers want harmony as employees discuss problems; others want debate, even acrimony. Fortunately, recent research clarifies the role of controversy.

Suppressed controversy has resulted in major fiascos.[9] President John F. Kennedy and his advisors pressured foreign policy experts to suppress their reservations about the invasion of Cuba in the Bay of Pigs fiasco. Learning from this experience, Kennedy insisted on controversy in the Cuban missile crisis, and his actions still earn him high marks.

The inability of flight crews to discuss opposing views is thought to undermine safety and performance and to have contributed significantly to disastrous airplane crashes.[10] Suppressed controversy contributed to the tragic decision early in 1986 to launch the space shuttle that exploded one minute after takeoff. Engineers and managers apparently did not openly and constructively discuss their opposing views on the safety of flying the shuttle in cold weather. Harold S. Geneen, former CEO of ITT, argued that company boards cannot protect stockholders because directors have neither the knowledge nor the courage to disagree with the CEO and act only when the company is near ruin.[11]

Suppressed controversy is not restricted to disasters or the boardroom. The organizational development group suppresses survey results that criticize a manager's leadership style. Managers do not point out weaknesses in a colleague's proposal. Market researchers withhold information that indicates little consumer market in a new product that their boss wants to market. Every day thousands of employees fear expressing their opposing information and ideas, and the resulting ineffective solutions cost their companies a great deal of money and embarrassment.[12]

The potential of controversy for problem solving has been demonstrated. Groups composed of persons with different views and outlooks and groups whose leaders encourage expression of minority opinions have made high-quality decisions. Consensus decision making results in useful decisions by stimulating open controversy.[13] Controversy is used by executives to formulate company strategy.[14]

Controversy helps individuals to cope with their limitations and make successful decisions.[15] Decision makers in controversy were found to be open to new and opposing information. Confronting an opposing opinion created doubts that their position was adequate. People became interested in the opponent's arguments and asked questions to explore the opposing views. They demonstrated that they knew the opposing arguments and understood the reasoning the other used to develop them.

In addition to openness to new information and ideas, people in controversy were willing to take the information seriously, develop a more complex and accurate view of the problem, and incorporate the opposing position into their own thinking and decisions. Controversy resulted in the creation of new solutions not originally proposed. By combining their information and ideas, people were more aware, appreciated the complexity of the problem, and arrived at a solution responsive to the complete situation.

These studies showed that controversy helped individuals to cope with the biases of closed-mindedness and inadequate evaluation of new information, the danger of simplifying the problem, and unwarranted confidence in initial positions. Through controversy, decision makers came to understand opposing positions, develop alternatives, and adopt high-quality solutions.

Making Controversy Constructive

Not all controversies are constructive; some controversy makes reaching a reasonable decision impossible. Opposing views must be discussed cooperatively. When adversaries maintain a strong emphasis on mutual benefit and reaching their common objectives, they exchange ideas and information and discuss their opposing positions to make effective decisions.

Cooperative dependence has been found to contribute to constructive controversy.[16] Decision makers who emphasized competition by trying to win and outdo the other were interested and understood the opposing position, but they were closed-minded to new and opposing information and ideas. They rejected the other and his ideas. Competitive managers understood but did not use employees' information and ideas to make their decisions. On the other hand, decision makers involved in a cooperative controversy incorporated opposing ideas and accepted each other as persons. Commitment to cooperative goals is important in discussing differences constructively.

Cooperative Controversy Skills

Maintaining a strong sense of cooperative goals in controversy is difficult. Many persons confuse disagreement with competition; they assume that another's opposing argument or disagreement means that the other is working against their interests. Controversy degenerates into a win-lose debate. Particularly in controversy, employees need consistent evidence that their goals are cooperative.

Decision makers usually feel competitive when threatened. They become defensive when they believe that they have appeared, or fear they may appear, weak and ineffective. Threatened decision makers have been found to remain committed to their own positions despite the costs of such intransigence and to derogate and reject others.[17]

When Fred Johnson thought Preston Cheung was trying to make him look ineffective and incompetent, Fred felt competitive, reasserted his own position, stopped listening to Preston's arguments, and criticized them as having little validity. Fred retaliated that Preston, not himself, did not know what he was talking about.

Decision makers who feel respected argue logically and rationally. They accept informed, reasonable positions. They continue to believe that their goals are cooperative, are interested in the opposing view, understand it, and are open to the other person and position.

How decision makers influence each other also affects whether they feel cooperative or competitive and discuss controversy constructively. Strong, coercive attempts to get others to accept one's views create competition and resistance.[18] Decision makers assume that the dominator wants to win and thus become competitive themselves. They retaliate by attacking and rejecting the dominator's position and become close-minded and rigid. Conversely, decision makers who are willing to be influenced feel cooperative, exchange their perspectives, and combine their ideas to develop high-quality solutions.

A recent field study documents that constructive controversy contributes substantially to decision making.[19] Experienced managers were asked to identify an important successful decision and an important unsuccessful decision. The results indicated that successful decision makers discussed their opposing opinions openly, emphasized cooperative goals, respected each other, and were open to being influenced.

Open controversy, cooperative dependence, respect, and mutual influence reinforced each other. The substantial correlation (.67) between constructive controversy and successful decision making indicates that discussing opposing views skillfully contributes significantly to effective problem solving. By discussing their opposing views constructively, employees solve problems.

Why Is Controversy Avoided?

Constructive controversy should be widely used in organizations, but often much more effort is put into avoiding and smoothing over differences than confronting them directly. Controversy often is avoided because employees do not understand the value of open controversy or do not have the skills to make controversy constructive.

Many managers and employees do not appreciate that controversy can contribute to decision making. Traditional values against conflict are giving way to more acceptance of controversy, but internalized ideas that guide behavior are much slower to change. Many organizational procedures, norms, and practices reinforce the negative values of conflict. Employees typically defer to the more powerful and prestigious; managers believe that they are expected to be decisive and end disagreements quickly. Norms to not rock the boat and be a team player reinforce controversy avoidance.

Controversy requires an emphasis on cooperative dependence to be constructive, but many decision makers take a competitive approach to discussions. They seek to advance their groups and careers rather than common goals. They treat discussions as debates to win instead of issues to solve. In these cases, people are apt to believe that open controversy should be avoided if possible. Although competition often is assumed to stimulate conflict, cooperative goals create a willingness to discuss differences openly.[20]

People avoid controversy for fear of losing face and being thought ineffective. Organizations pressure managers to present themselves as strong and mature; they may conclude that a direct challenge of their ideas makes them look weak. Managers also are under pressure to show that they can dominate.[21] Employees may quite reasonably conclude that their manager will perceive their opposition as an attack designed to make him look weak and ineffectual and that the resulting discussion may escalate dangerously.

Controversy also is avoided because many employees do not have the skills and procedures to discuss it constructively. Skills in working with others traditionally have been underemphasized in management and vocational training. Controversy poses many challenges and is a rich and demanding experience. Decision makers must express their ideas, information, and feelings in such a way that others will be encouraged to express theirs. They must be open-minded, take the other's perspective, and be able to integrate material. They also must manage the strong feelings that controversial discussions arouse. Controversy skills and procedures require considerable effort and practice, and many employees recognize that they need more ideas and experience to disagree constructively and directly with superiors, friends, coworkers, and experts.

Establishing Constructive Controversy

Although it is difficult, controversies are discussed productively in some organizations. What is needed is to encourage open controversy together with cooperative dependence.

Initiate Controversy

Controversy can be encouraged by group membership, subgroups, leadership style, openness norms, and decision-making rules.

Group Membership. Teams composed of persons who are heterogeneous in regard to background, expertise, opinions, outlook, and organizational position are likely to disagree. Including persons from outside the department or organization and independent thinkers makes controversy more likely.

Openness Norms. All persons should be encouraged to express their opinions, doubts, uncertainties, and hunches. No idea should be dismissed quickly because it first appears to be too unusual, impractical, or undeveloped.

Individual Rights. The right to dissent must be protected; everyone is expected to voice her opinions and knows that she will not be punished.

Subgroups. Forming two smaller groups that are assigned opposing positions on the issue is a direct way to structure controversy. For example, a manager can assign one subgroup the position that the company should buy an existing plant and another that the company should build its own to decide how to expand production capacity. At Gould Electronics, senior managers form pro and con groups to debate serious possible acquisitions.[22] Alternatively, two different groups can be assigned the same problem and their solutions compared.

Devil's Advocate. Assigning one person to be a devil's advocate or everyone to take a critical evaluation role of expressing all their criticisms can reduce the chances of the group's seeking agreement too quickly.

Managerial Style. Leaders may make it easier for others to speak their minds by refraining from expressing their opinions early in the discussion. They may be active in structuring and overseeing the controversy rather than participating by taking positions. Although leaders may stimulate controversy by expressing their own views, they also must be aware that some employees might find it difficult to express opinions that oppose their boss's.

Decision-Making Rules. Requiring that the group reach a consensus rather than a majority vote or unilateral decision by the leader makes it more likely that everyone will participate and opposing views will be heard.[23]

Time. Crises orientation and an emphasis on finding a solution quickly pressure group members into suppressing their uncertainties and criticisms. Group members need time to ponder the problem, search for information, understand others' ideas, and develop their own positions. After a preliminary consensus has been reached, second-chance meetings give persons an opportunity to discover shortcomings in the proposed solution and reconsider it.

Create a Productive Discussion

Disagreement is by itself insufficient. Decision makers must argue, debate, and disagree cooperatively and skillfully.

Cooperative Dependence. Decision makers must keep focused on their common task and emphasize their cooperative dependence. They can communicate expectations that they and others will work for a solution that is mutually beneficial. Efforts to pursue individual objectives at the expense of others should be identified and discouraged. Statements such as "We are all in this together" and "Let's seek a solution that is good for everyone" should characterize the group rather than "I am right, and you are wrong."

Financial rewards, evaluations, and prestige should be given for group success, not for independent work, appearing better than others, or proving that one is right. Group members must not seek to find winners and losers but a successful, productive solution to the common problem. All group members must share in the rewards of success and the responsibility for failure.

Personal Acceptance. Decision makers must feel that their personal competence is accepted by others even though their ideas are disputed. They must carefully and respectfully listen to everyone's ideas. They can directly criticize another's ideas but not the other as a person. They can object to ideas while communicating respect and appreciation for others as competent persons. Insults or implications that challenge another's integrity, intelligence, and motives must be avoided. Communication of interest and acceptance should accompany disagreement with another's current position. Demonstrating understanding by paraphrasing opposing ideas accurately and warmly is a concrete way of conveying acceptance and interest in another as a person while disagreeing.

People should not confuse disagreement with their ideas as a personal rejection or rebuff. Having one's ideas challenged can be taken as a sign of interest in one's position and as a way to further one's learning. Members must separate the validity of their thinking from their competence and worth as persons.

Mutual Influence. Problem solvers must try to influence each other rather than dominate. Controversy requires persons to try to persuade, inform, convince, and in other ways influence each other. Without this influence, controversy is much less stimulating and involving and is unlikely to be productive. People should have the conviction and willingness to put forth their arguments forcefully and to persuade others, but they must avoid trying to convey that they want to dominate and coerce. Statements such as "I want you to consider this seriously" and "You will probably find this convincing" should characterize group discussion, not "You must accept this point" and "You have no choice but to agree."

Group members can indicate that they are willing to be influenced and identify how they have incorporated parts of others' perspectives into their own. Give-and-take influence, rather than dominance or passivity, facilitates productive controversy.

Guides for Action

Making Decisions

- Oversee the making of the decision.
- Assign teams to solve complex problems.
- Make sure team members see that their goals are cooperative.
- Have them identify each other's abilities.
- Initiate open controversy.
- Express your views without dominating.
- Encourage mutual respect and influence.

Pitfalls to Avoid

- Assume that you alone are responsible for solving the problem.
- Assert that you have to be right.
- Move so fast on important problems that open discussion cannot develop.
- Try to do it all yourself.

Who Should Make Decisions: The Issue of Participation

> *I believe in the principle that you should manage in an open way: Tell people what is going on and listen to what they have to offer, particularly when it concerns matters which affect them very directly. That, I hope is a view which would be shared right around the world.*
> —*Sir Adrian Cadbury, Chairman, Cadbury Schweppes PLC*

Whether employees should participate in making organizational decisions has sparked a lot of debate. From Lewin's leadership-styles research in the 1930s until the present, much has been written about the virtues and bane of employee participation. Proponents defend participation as a democratic right as well as a boon to organizational decision making.[24] Detractors portray proponents as guilty of wishful thinking and participation as having no serious empirical support.[25] Participation, I argue, can be very productive, in large part because it encourages controversy. But managers and employees must be able to discuss their opposing views constructively.

Participation is best considered as a general management approach that can be implemented in several ways. It refers to practices such as task forces, project teams, quality-control circles, informal meetings on the shop floor, and union membership on the board of directors. What these procedures have in common is that they involve employees by encouraging them to contribute to making decisions and solving problems.

Rather than having the CEO make the organization decisions, the vice president make the department decisions, and the supervisor make the work unit decisions, these managers seek the ideas, opinions, and views of their subordinates. Participation can be formally or informally established and carried out through representative subordinates or direct involvement. Employees may be consulted for information, asked to present ideas and suggestions, or actually make the decision.

Participation stimulates controversy because it involves persons who bring a variety of information, ideas, opinions, arguments, and perspectives to bear on problems. The controversy in participation, if handled correctly, helps employees analyze problems and create effective solutions.

Participation Research

Studies comparing decision making when employees are asked to contribute and when managers make the decisions alone are inconsistent. To resolve the mixed findings on participation, reviewers have used two major methods, neither of which has been very successful.[1] They have tried to assess the relative methodological rigor of the supportive and unsupportive studies to determine whether the more valid studies consistently support one position. Yet apparently valid studies support both positions.[2] The second method to resolve discrepant findings is to try to identify aspects—employee needs and values, the distribution of information, leaders' characteristics—that affect the success of participation. There is, however, little direct evidence to indicate how these aspects affect participation.

The consequences of how employees work together on participation have been largely neglected. Studies included in reviews have employees work together in many different ways. Participation is operationalized as group leadership and problem solving, goal setting, feelings of power, organizational change, workers councils, authoritarianism, permissiveness, and codetermination. The way participation actually is carried out or measured seldom is seen as that important; much more likely to get attention is the type of research method the study used.

When researchers consider how people work together in participation, they mostly allude to group factors and the dangers of suppressed ideas.[3] They have been most impressed with the debilitating impact of process losses through dynamics such as groupthink.[4] Indeed, suspicion of groups is intense. Expert members are thought to be outvoted by less knowledgeable ones; groups are expected to be unable to combine their ideas and information to develop high-quality solutions. Interaction does not invariably harm decision making, however, and as we have seen, it can contribute greatly to it.

Participation, it is well recognized, can be carried out in various ways, but much less recognized is the fact that what actually happens in participation varies a great deal. Participation gives employees the legitimacy to discuss organizational issues and problems, usually forms a group, and provides a setting for discussion and decision making. Organizational employees can discuss their opposing views constructively or destructively; whether participation is successful depends greatly on the handling of controversy.[26]

> Participation contributes greatly to the quality of the decision when constructive controversy is created. Employees incorporate their ideas and information rather than rely on one person's judgment and perspective.

> Participation, when controversy is discussed constructively, improves employee morale and relationships. Participation meets needs to express oneself, feel powerful, exercise control, and feel more like a team.

> Constructive controversy in participation results in the commitment to implement solutions. Employees, through an open discussion of their opposing opinions, come to understand each other, use each other's ideas to develop solutions, know the reasoning behind the ultimate decision, and believe that the solution is effective. Participative team members also support and pressure each other to carry out their assignments. Decision quality, incorporation of one's ideas into the final solution, understanding of the decision's rationale, group support, and feeling rewarded all promote implementation.

Using Participation

Deciding to Use Participation

Participation of employees in organizational decision making has great potential, but it must be skillfully and appropriately used. These general guidelines can help managers plan how to use participation.

- The problem is important and the need for an effective solution is strong enough to warrant the investment, effort, and time of many employees.

- Constructive controversy can be established. The employees have the skills, procedures, and time to discuss their opposing views openly and productively.

- Employees accept their participation as legitimate. Participation requires the active involvement of employees, and their understanding that their participation is valued can help them to use these opportunities.

- Managers and supervisors realize that participation helps them to be more effective; it does not replace them. Managers benefit from participation because it helps them to solve pressing problems.

- Managers play a critical role. They must decide when to use participation and structure it effectively. Managers need to discuss their opposing opinions constructively. They should probe, question, challenge, and disagree with employees so that the decision is acceptable to them as well as to employees.

- Participation is practical. Sometimes participation is not reasonable because employees are on different shifts and locations. Pressing demands and deadlines can make participation impractical.

- The particular form of participation depends on the situation. Task forces, labor-management problem-solving groups, project teams, and other groups are concrete ways to implement participation. Informal discussions on the shop floor as well as formal representation on boards can be useful.

Concluding Comments

Organizations must be able to solve problems and make decisions. They must develop plans, implement them, and remove barriers to their success. A widely accepted view is that organizations are unable to analyze problems thoroughly and create new solutions. Managers are overtaxed by the demands to process information, respond to new situations, and integrate competing claims. Employees who discuss their opposing views constructively, however, can combine their ideas, information, and perspectives to make decisions. Many companies can, and do, overcome the limitations of individuals to create successful new products and strategies.

Having employees participate in decision making has great potential, for it involves employees with different and overlapping information, ideas, and perspectives. To make participation work, employees must use procedures and skills to discuss their opposing views openly and constructively.

9
Making Conflict Productive

Managers and employees with cooperative goals use power and controversy to solve problems and achieve success. They also clash, quarrel, and battle. Sandy Hamel complains that Fred Johnson barks out orders and interrupts her when she asks questions; Sandy's typographical errors drive Fred nuts. Dennis Mann is annoyed that he must first write a memo and then wait to get Duncan Foster's reply; Duncan snaps at Dennis for not having the report ready on time. Preston Cheung seethes when Dennis takes all the credit for their proposal; Jenny sulks because Bob Clinton did not recommend a raise. Fred sees red when Preston teases him about going bald; Bob is irritated that Fred and Preston bicker. Conflicts are watersheds in working with others. If handled well, they reduce frustrations, update procedures, and make employees more productive and confident. Poorly managed conflicts exacerbate difficulties, intensify anger, tear relationships apart, and undercut productivity.

Conflict is inevitable. Managers and employees must know how to manage them. There is no reasonable alternative to conflict management. Well-handled conflict is a manager's delight, for it improves the quality of work life and stimulates motivation. Traditionally, conflict has been considered at least harmful and sometimes devastating. Successful cooperation has been equated with a conflict-free environment; conflict is assumed to be antithetical to teamwork and productivity. This is absolutely not true. Cooperation and conflict are not only compatible, but much and probably most conflict occurs when employees have cooperative goals. People in cooperation argue as they set objectives, decide how to proceed, assign tasks, and distribute the rewards of their joint success. Employees must develop procedures, attitudes, and skills to manage conflict; the key to productive conflict is to maintain, and strengthen if possible, the cooperative links between protagonists.

Resolving Conflicts: Peter and Allan

Peter and Allan had worked together for nearly twelve years at Rang-Dorf Engineering. Peter's skilled, determined leadership of the division and Allan's considerable technical competence were instrumental in making the division highly productive. Over the years, they had developed a great deal of respect for and loyalty to each other. Recently, however, they had become more wary and suspicious. They avoided conflict and allowed issues to obscure their cooperative dependence; they had begun to think of each other in competitive, win-lose terms.

Peter had concluded that Allan lacked important managerial competencies, but he did not confront Allan directly. Instead he "promoted" him to head the division's major department and then brought in Dick below him to manage it. They avoided other issues. For example, Peter told Allan that the Ansett project had top priority, only to return two weeks later to find that Allan had completed other projects but not Ansett. Peter did not express his anger directly, nor did he thank Allan for the completed projects. Allan took Peter's silence as ingratitude and further evidence that he had become a tough, unreasonable taskmaster. Allan complained that Peter had begun to rely on memos to communicate problems and that memos did not give him a chance to discuss problems and learn.

Peter and Allan were no longer sure they were working together. Peter attributed Allan's behavior to a desire to satisfy others, even at Peter's expense. Allan suspected that Peter was indifferent to him, had no desire to help him feel effective and confident, and perhaps did not want to see him promoted.

Both Peter and Allan had strong reservations about an open discussion of the conflict. Peter thought that Allan would be hurt by such a discussion and would quit. Peter was able to use his superior authority to act on his beliefs without discussing them with Allan. Allan assumed that Peter had the prerogative to initiate discussion about problems. Their conflict did not disappear, and they faced a crisis. Peter anticipated a promotion, and he would have difficulty recommending Allan as a replacement.

Peter and Allan did agree to discuss their conflict with the help of a consultant. The first step was to refocus on their cooperative dependence. They reminded themselves that their basic aspirations were cooperative. They both wanted to make the division as productive and respected as possible. They also were committed to each other's welfare and development. They each wanted the other to improve his skills and gain promotions.

After several meetings, they became aware that their conflict avoidance frustrated their goals and harmed their relationship. Peter expressed his concerns about Allan as a manager and talked about his frustrations in getting Allan to focus on tasks that he, Peter, considered high priority. Allan revealed his feelings of being taken for granted and of Peter's apparent lack of interest in his learning.

Together they discussed how Allan could develop managerial skills or find a position that required his technical abilities. Through joint problem solving, they again realized how much they depended on each other and that they had each other's basic interests at heart. They were once again tuned in to each other's aspirations, better able to support each other, and more aware that they needed to discuss, rather than avoid, conflicts.

Changing Values about Conflict

> Company president: *"If there isn't conflict, your organization isn't going any-where. Conflict helps us move forward."*
> Plant manager: *"Conflict makes my job. I don't think I would go to work if there wasn't conflict."*

Conflict traditionally has been considered painful and harmful, a sign that something has gone terribly wrong. Because conflict engenders anger, bitterness, and revenge that disrupt coordination and productivity, managers assumed that they should handle conflict decisively. Norms told employees that if they could not avoid feeling frustrated and angry, they should at least not express such feelings. Today conflict is recognized as a natural, sometimes productive part of working with others. The contemporary perspective is that employees must learn to discuss their conflicts rather than suppress and avoid them.

Everyone experiences conflict, and many people have a conflict a day.[1] Managers have been found to spend 20 percent of their time coping with conflict.[2] Some conflicts are serious, provoking frustration and anger; some are minor and merely irritating; some conflicts are even light and comical. Employees fight over job assignments; they squabble about parking spaces; they tease the colleague who misspelled the boss's name in the last memo. Conflicts occur between two departments as well as two employees. Production accuses marketing of excessive demands, and marketing contends that production is obstinate. Conflict spills over organizational boundaries. Customers complain about late deliveries and product defects. Companies dispute terms with suppliers and contest markets with rivals. Conflict is a daily, sometimes an hourly experience in organizations.

We now know that conflict is built into us and our social lives; it is too basic to be denied. Anger and frustration come from involvement with others and a commitment to excellence and getting the job done; denying anger is denying involvement and commitment. Managers and others are beginning to recognize that productive conflict helps individuals and the company.

Conflict's Benefits

- Discussing conflict makes organizational members more aware and able to cope with problems. Knowing that others are frustrated and want change creates incentives to try to solve the underlying problem.
- Conflict promotes organizational change and adaptation. Procedures, assignments, budget allocations, and other organizational practices are chal-

lenged. Conflict draws attention to those issues that may interfere with and frustrate employees.

- Conflict strengthens relationships and heightens morale. Employees realize that their relationships are strong enough to withstand the test of conflict; they need not avoid frustrations and problems. They can release their tensions through discussion and problem solving.

- Conflict promotes awareness of self and others. Through conflict, people learn what makes them angry, frustrated, and frightened and also what is important to them. Knowing what we are willing to fight for tells us a lot about ourselves. Knowing what makes our colleagues unhappy helps us to understand them.

- Conflict enhances personal development. Managers find out how their style affects their subordinates through conflict. Workers learn what technical and interpersonal skills they need to upgrade themselves.

- Conflict encourages psychological development. Persons become more accurate and realistic in their self-appraisals. Through conflict, persons take others' perspectives and become less egocentric. Conflict helps persons to believe that they are powerful and capable of controlling their own lives. They do not simply need to endure hostility and frustration but can act to improve their lives.

- Conflict can be stimulating and fun. Persons feel aroused, involved, and alive in conflict, and it can be a welcome break from an easy-going pace. It invites employees to take another look and to appreciate the intricacies of their relationships.

The Need to Manage Conflict

Conflict-positive values and the research on which they are based have far-reaching implications. Rather than apologize for their conflicts and anger, employees need skills to express their feelings and deal with conflicts. Leadership styles that suppress conflict and norms, values, and procedures that tend to smooth them over are being questioned. Managers must try to make conflicts improve how they and employees collaborate. They also must be aware of conflicts between employees and develop approaches and procedures for open discussion.

But isn't avoidance of conflict a reasonable approach, especially when people may not have the time, energy, and skill to manage conflicts well? At times, of course, avoiding conflict is prudent. In addition to missing conflict's benefits, however, avoiding it is much more costly than is generally appreciated. Avoided conflict does not simply disappear. Employees must use time and energy to try to cope with it. They complain and gossip about their problems with others; they work to hide their feelings and anger; they suppress their tensions, which makes them more stressed and more prone to burnout, ulcers, hypertension, and related ailments; they must try to learn to live with frustrating procedures and problems; and they feel a lack of power over their lives and commitment to their company. Avoiding conflict wastes energy, undercuts morale, and sabotages effective change.

The positive view of conflict can be carried to extremes. Some persons assume that anger is the honest emotion and that all conflicts must be discussed openly. Some theorists have argued that organizations should communicate inconsistently, assign ill-defined responsibilities, encourage employees to express all their frustrations and anger, prevent managers from decisively ending conflict, and in other ways foster conflict and stress.[3] Although the research reviewed here contributes to conflict-positive values, it is the *appropriate, skilled management of conflict,* not just conflict, that promotes healthy organizations and people.

Criteria for Productive Conflict

The choice for organizations is not between conflict and no conflict but in deciding how conflict is managed. Employees need criteria so that they can work toward making conflict productive and know when they have succeeded. There are several criteria for conflict, and their importance varies. Perhaps the ultimate standard is the extent to which the protagonists believe that they have benefited rather than lost from the conflict. They usually feel that they have benefited when:

- The underlying problem is solved, a new solution has been created and implemented, and it is unlikely that the problem will appear again in a new form.

- The relationship has been strengthened. The persons know each other better, are more responsive to each other's feelings and interests, are pleased that their relationship has withstood the rigors of conflict, and believe that they can work effectively in the future.

- The participants believe that their time and resources have been well spent and conclude that resolving the conflict was not too costly.

Conflict between individuals and groups is a common, inevitable aspect of organizations. It is neither practical nor desirable to avoid, suppress, or smooth over all conflicts. Employees need encouragement, opportunities, procedures, and skills to discuss their conflicts well. They must be able to express their feelings, uncover the underlying problem, develop solutions, and in other ways manage their conflicts productively. The ideas and procedures discussed in previous chapters are highly relevant to conflict management. Additional procedures and skills to help employees make their conflicts productive are discussed in this chapter.

Defining Conflict

In recent years, conflict has become an important issue in management research.[4] But because it is so pervasive and elicits such strong feelings, defining conflict is difficult. There is agreement that conflict characterizes a relationship rather than an individual and that it is not inevitably harmful. Conflict often is defined as opposing interests, however, and the resulting assumption that conflict is competitive interferes with understanding.

Conflict as Opposing Interests

Conflict typically is considered in terms of bargaining and negotiation. People have opposing interests and preferences in mixed-motive situations.[5] Common interests motivate them to continue to work together and reach an agreement, but their opposing interests require bargaining. Collective bargaining is a well-known conflict, but organizational members in many settings also must seek compromises and agreements on their differing interests and preferences.

A serious problem with the definition of conflict as opposing interests is that conflict is confused with competition. Cooperators, however, often have conflicts. Co-workers with the same goal of developing a new market plan may not have any opposing interests; they seek a high-quality plan that earns them all the gratitude and respect of their boss. Despite this agreement on interests, they may dispute the best way to begin, who is best equipped to do the various tasks, the type of consultants needed, and the theories they should use.

Policymakers may want a successful strategy so that they prosper with the company but disagree sharply over the actual risks and opportunities of available options. Labor and management may disagree about how certain organizational decisions should be made even if they agree upon wages, grievance handling, and fringe benefits. Contrary to the mixed-motive perspective, employees with highly overlapping interests and goals will at times disagree and conflict.

The idea that conflicts arise out of mixed-motive situations misleadingly suggests that there is a direct link between opposing interests and conflict. This link is not simple and direct. One employee may be angry at a co-worker who insists on gossiping, whereas another employee encourages the co-worker to tell more. A worker may be in conflict by blaming the union for a recent settlement; another holds management responsible. The extent to which persons experience conflict depends on their perceptions, expectations, and evalutions of the situation. People construct conflicts; they do not just appear. Perceptions and beliefs about others' behavior, standards of fairness, expectations, and evaluations all determine whether persons experience conflict.

Conflict as Incompatible Activities

When defined as incompatible activities, conflict is distinct from competition. Conflict occurs when one person's behavior obstructs, interferes with, blocks, or in some other way makes another's behavior less effective.[6] Conflict can occur without any recognition, but only when people conclude that the other's actions are incompatible with their own do they experience conflict and begin to react to it. Persons who believe that the incompatible behavior is highly important, unjustified, and unexpected intensify their feelings of anger and their conclusions that they are in conflict.[7] We will discuss perceived incompatibility and experienced conflict because they directly affect how employees respond and manage conflict.

Approaches to Managing Conflict

There are many ways to deal with conflict. People shout, cry, demand, plead, praise, insult, threaten, promise, disclose, scheme, and connive. They may be warm, tough, or cold. The variety of strategies has made determining their effects difficult. In addition, the impact of any strategy appears to depend very much on the circumstances.[8] The often-discussed approaches of smoothing, compromise, forcing, and confrontation have been subject to few experimental tests.

The ideas of cooperation and competition summarize considerable experimental and organizational research on conflict and help us to understand how conflicts can be successfully managed. Research identifies three major ways to manage conflict. One approach emphasizes cooperative dependence, the second competition, and the third avoidance and smoothing over differences. This section and figure 9–1 summarize major findings; interested readers can consult references for details.[9]

Cooperative Conflict

What happens when employees discuss their frustrations openly and recognize and work for cooperative goals? These people, confronted with opposing ideas and interests, often feel resisted and challenged. They are unsure that their own ideas are adequate and that their interests can be fully met. They are motivated to explore and understand opposing views and needs to satisfy their curiosity and resolve their uncertainty about whether their own position

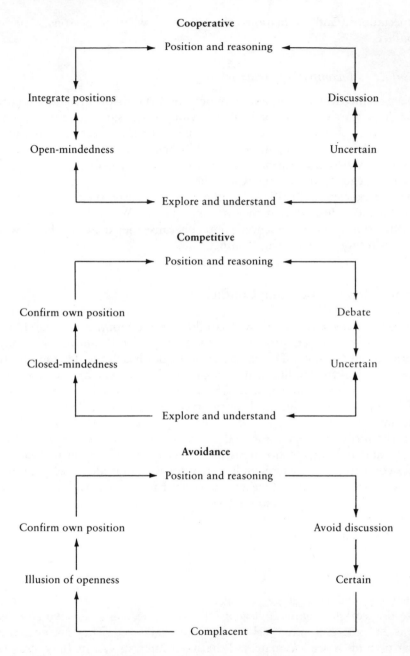

Figure 9–1. Approaches to Conflict

is adequate. After explaining their position and exploring opposing views and interests, they understand the shortcomings in their own perspective, appreciate the desires and requirements of others, try to integrate other ideas and aspirations, and develop a fresh viewpoint that responds to the reasoning, perspective, and needs of others. Then they can reach mutually satisfactory decisions based on the ideas and interests of several people. Their relationships also are strengthened, and they are confident that they can resolve conflicts in the future. Throughout the conflict, people emphasize their cooperative dependence. They consider the problem a mutual one and seek a mutually advantageous solution.

Competitive Conflict

Conflicts discussed openly in an attempt to outdo and win have been found to proceed much differently. Confronted with opposing views and interests, people feel unsure about their own positions and try to understand the other's arguments. They defend their own position vigorously, however, and try to win over others. They become locked into position bargaining in which they try to assert their conclusions. They try to understand the other to find weaknesses in his arguments, not to modify their own conclusions. They want to counterattack, undercut other positions, and make their own views and interests dominate. They may conclude that they must use superior authority or other means to impose their solutions. In this way, conflict results in a failure to reach an agreement or a solution imposed by the more powerful, along with personal ill will and little confidence that future problems can be solved.

In competitive conflict, persons convey that they are trying to pursue their own interests even at the expense of others. If necessary, they will force their position on others. They want to win and are willing, even eager, to have the other lose.

Avoiding Conflict

The third approach to conflict is to avoid expressing one's frustrations and to smooth over and deemphasize any disagreement. People remain unaware of opposing needs, interests, and ideas. They assume that others agree with their position and ideas and see little reason to explore and understand the others' interests and opinions. Why should they bother to doubt and question their own position when those around them apparently are in agreement? Avoidance of conflict often results in solutions that are not fully examined and reflect only the needs of one side. Avoidance can give a false sense of confidence in the work relationship, but it undermines the capacity to identify and solve problems.

Avoiding conflict not only fails to clear the air and begin to solve problems, but it also conveys an ambiguous message about the relationship. Avoiding conflict commonly is thought to be cooperative and supportive; people avoid the conflict out of consideration and concern for each other. But avoidance at times conveys competition: Allan was beginning to say to himself, "Peter does not talk about what he thinks of my performance because he wants me to look bad." Indeed, silence often is used competitively.

In most circumstances, when employees emphasize their cooperative dependence throughout the conflict, the benefits of conflict are realized and its costs minimized. When discussed collaboratively, conflict can be highly productive. People understand each other's issues and aspirations and reach solutions that are mutually advantageous; they are confident that they can solve future difficulties; and they have goodwill toward each other and the company

Guides for Action

Managing Conflict

- Develop a climate in which it is okay to conflict.
- Emphasize cooperative goals and dependence.
- Indicate that everyone benefits from a resolution.
- Demonstrate that you understand others.
- Ask others to show that they understand you.
- Identify and solve the underlying problem.
- Celebrate your joint success.

Pitfalls to Avoid

- Blame others for the problem.
- Prove that you are right and others are wrong.
- Make others look weak and incompetent.
- Concentrate on another's weaknesses.
- Hold out for a solution that will benefit only yourself.
- Brag that you outwitted others.

Conflict Management

It is common to advocate that people should talk about conflicts, share feelings and ideas freely, and keep communication channels open. Employees are urged to disclose their feelings and discuss their conflicts openly and are told that smoothing over conflict usually is undesirable. But communication channels can be used to fight and intensify conflict.[10] Discussion provides opportunities for people to clarify their perceptions, discover the underlying problem, and strengthen their relationships, but they must approach the discussion collaboratively.

Open Discussion

Through discussion, employees let each other know how they experience the conflict. They express their feelings and the beliefs, assumptions, and information that lie behind these feelings. Discussing their feelings and reasoning helps people to understand the specific problem, how the conflict began, and what actions contributed to the conflict. Knowing the problem well, the participants can then solve it successfully.

Yet discussing conflict can be useful even when the problem is not solved; just talking can reduce hostility. In open discussion, persons learn more information that can cause them to reevaluate their positions and feelings. They may discover, for example, that the other person did not mean to interrupt them and has no plans to do so in the future. The other may not have been able to finish the report as planned because his son was ill.

To make these modifications, people should explore the completeness of their information and the logic of their reasoning. It should be noted, however, that discussion does not automatically moderate feelings. Persons who learn that the other wanted to frustrate them, purposefully interfered with their goals and aspirations, and plans to continue are likely to be more angry and retaliatory.

Cooperative Discussion

Protagonists who clearly understand that their goals are cooperative are able to discuss their conflict productively. The key to making discussion constructive is to maintain, emphasize, and strengthen cooperative dependence.

As they discuss, people have several ways of emphasizing their cooperative dependence. They can remind each other that they both have much more to gain by working together than against each other. They can reiterate that they plan to collaborate and expect the other to reciprocate. Exchanging information and ideas, listening to each other, and working toward a mutually advantageous solution strongly convey a desire to work together.

They should fully reveal their information, positions, and feelings, along with the ideas, conclusions, and rationale that lie behind them. They must, however, avoid position bargaining in which they argue the virtues of their own position and the shortcomings of others.[11] Listening carefully and fully understanding the issues and feelings are critical. After listening to each other, they can aim to combine the best ideas and views to create a solution that works for all.

Employees can maintain cooperation by showing respect and acceptance of each other; all believe that they have appeared strong and competent and have not lost face. People who fear that they may appear weak have been found to feel competitive, to become tough and intransigent, and to escalate conflict.[12] They must avoid trying to dominate and control others by being open to being influenced as well as trying to influence.[13]

After reaching an agreement, the participants should responsibly implement their part of the solution. They can meet and reassure each other that the solution is being implemented, and they can reevaluate whether the solution is having the intended effect and works for them all. If appropriate, they can together recognize that the conflict has helped them to accomplish their task and has improved their work relationship. They should celebrate their success.

Before, during, and after their conflict, employees should avoid concluding that their incompatible behavior means that their goals are competitive or that their competence has been questioned and challenged. Instead, they should recognize the conflict as a mutual problem to be solved together for joint benefit.

Coping with Labor-Management Conflict

> *All of these examples are great, but the most dramatic change is in the atmosphere. It was hard to cooperate when you were in a war.*
> —Richard McGraw, Communications Vice President, Eastern Air Lines

Labor-management conflict can be handled cooperatively or competitively. In 1983, Eastern Air Lines had high labor costs and was at the edge of bankruptcy. Two years later, it had record profits, and employees were working to raise productivity and reduce costs. Critical to this dramatic turnaround was moving the conflict between labor and management from competitive to cooperative.[1]

Before 1983, Eastern had a fractious relationship with its unions, especially the International Association of Machinists (IAM). Eastern's management alternated between attempts to undercut the union and buying labor peace with high wages. The result was high labor costs and a suspicious union. Eastern could not compete successfully in the newly deregulated airline market and lost millions from 1980 to 1982. The union suspected that management had tinkered with the books so that it could avoid paying money in a profit-sharing plan begun in 1975.

Frank Borman, chairman of Eastern, announced in 1983 that the company would either have to go out of business, file for bankruptcy, or reduce labor costs drastically. If concessions were not agreed upon by October, the company would begin bankruptcy proceedings.

The union suspected that the company was crying wolf, but management agreed to let the union see its books. Management and union began to work together by examining Eastern's situation and reaching a joint understanding of their common problem. Management and union did agree that Eastern's position was dire, but they also agreed that the company had been poorly managed.

The crisis helped management and labor see their cooperative dependence and need to work together. The union agreed to concessions but wanted company stock, seats on the board, a new profit-sharing scheme, continuous flow of management information, and a program to increase union responsibility on the shop floor. Management agreed.

The new contract made the cooperative dependence between union and management even more clear and concrete. Union now controlled stock and would benefit directly from Eastern's dividends and stock price. Improved productivity also were translated directly into increased wages. Union and management shared information and discussed ways to improve their common lot.

Their working together had far-reaching effects. Lead machinists were given more responsibility. They assigned jobs, directed work, and signed time cards. Machinists filled out flight forms, certified flight weight, and performed many other routine but important tasks. Because of these new duties, the supervisory work force was reduced by more than a hundred people, and workers became more flexible. Flights were no longer delayed so that Eastern could find an electrician to change a light bulb or a ramp attendant to load a stray piece of luggage.

Workers helped in many small ways that added up. An IAM member found that Eastern was paying too much for an anticorrosive hydraulic fluid; his phone call saved the company $177,000. Another employee collected worn-out fan blades for jet engines. By rewelding and remachining these blades at a net cost of $19.20 a blade rather than paying $163.80 for new ones, the company saved $306,000.

Eastern had contracted out work to circumvent its unions; after the contract, unions and management formed a task force to "contract in" work. The unions wanted the work back to prove that they could save the company, and themselves, money. They rebuilt their own jet engines rather than sending them to United Airlines. Machinists also maintained ticketing systems. The IAM convinced the company to print all its forms for an annual savings of $250,000. Machinists fixed air conditioners. Stock clerks organized to find out what clerks in other cities were charged to make sure that they were not overcharged and to terminate sweetheart contracts with vendors. Workers liked saving the company money and took pride in their enhanced abilities.

The new relationships between unions and management made Eastern much more profitable. It saved hundreds of millions in wage reductions. By the first quarter of 1985, Eastern had operating profits of $107.4 million and a net profit of $24.3 million; the second quarter netted a profit of $25.5 million. For that half year, each employee enjoyed profit sharing averaging nearly $2,000.

Formal grievances went from one thousand to four hundred a year. They talked and solved problems more and took punitive action less.

Their relationship was challenged late in 1984, when Borman surprised the union by asking for a continuation of the wage concessions for another year. When the union balked, Borman unilaterally imposed wage cuts and again threatened bankruptcy. Eastern's business plunged. Eastern finally relented, rescinded its wage cuts, resumed negotiations, and stopped talking about bankruptcy. Union and management signed a contract similar to the 1983 one but returned part of the wage cuts. Although management's abrupt actions aroused old union suspicions, their relationship withstood the shock.

In 1986, Borman again faced a financial crisis, met union resistance, and sold Eastern to Frank Lorenzo's Texas Air. The cooperative handling of conflict between management and union was critical for the progress Eastern did make. The new management and unions can resolve their conflicts cooperatively or competitively. How successfully they work together will very much affect their ability to cope with the turbulence in the highly competitive airline marketplace.

Confronting Inadequate Performance

In some conflicts, the responsibility for a problem lies with only one person. The purpose of the discussion is not so much give and take and mutual adjustment but changing that person's behavior. Managers conflict with a worker who repeatedly is late for his shift or is rude to customers. Project team members are angry with a colleague who fails to pull her weight and do her share of the work. Managers and team members are frustrated, and not feeling much at fault, they are apt to be unwilling to accept a compromise solution.

Yet these conflicts can be discussed cooperatively. Even in their demands, managers and colleagues can still convey the feeling that they want the person to perform more effectively for his interest as well as theirs. An employee who believes that his manager or colleagues are working for his betterment is likely to accept responsibility for the problem and try to change. Managers and team members also can profit from an open-minded discussion by finding out the barriers that make it difficult for the person to be effective.

Coping with Competitive Conflict

Conflicts require skill, effort, and persistence to be managed well, but some conflicts are particularly challenging. Conflict is part of competition as well as collaboroation. Employees compete over limited budgets, promotions, and office space. Those conflicts can be handled well or poorly.

Richard J. Boyle, head of Honeywell Defense and Marine Systems Group, faced a competitive conflict.[14] Two rival groups had to collaborate to win a large contract. To make it particularly difficult, the project, although it required the skills of both units, would give production to only one. This unit would receive very large revenues and capital improvement funds that would give it an edge for years.

Instead of deciding alone, Boyle met with the people from both units to discuss the project and the consequences of winning and losing. He wanted the units to work together as much as possible despite their competition. The units heard each other argue its case. They decided that the winning unit should subsidize the losing unit for some time. People from both units also more clearly understood and were more committed to corporate goals. Still, both units wanted the production.

When Boyle made the decision, the losing group was not outraged, and the winning group did not gloat. They understood the reasons for the decision. They also had anticipated many of the potential snags, so the project went quite smoothly. Indeed, the groups established a good relationship. Without informing the head office, one voluntarily relinquished control over a project to the other.

Conflict over promotions also can be managed productively. Dale, the city attorney, and Al, the city planner, were in a win-lose conflict because they both wanted to be promoted to economic development officer. Yet they still benefited from a cooperative approach to the conflict. They agreed that they should continue to do their jobs as well as they could and show their abilities to the city manager, mayor, and council, but they also agreed not to discuss each other in public. They continued to work for high-quality development for the city and to play squash after work. Thus, they did not allow the conflict to interfere with their working together. One did not have to worry that the other would try to harm his reputation or sabotage his promotion chances, nor did he have to work directly against his own or his friend's self-interest. After Dale was selected, they worked together well and were both respected.

The great variety of conflict in organizations makes it impossible for one approach or set of procedures to be effective in all cases. Managers and employees must remain flexible and use the approach that is suitable for the situation. At times they must fight and try to win. First they must get everyone to agree; they can pick up the pieces later. At times they will choose to avoid and smooth over differences. Perhaps the boss is too stressed and preoccupied to talk about the problem that day. Cooperative problem solving most often captures the potential benefits of conflict, however, and all employees should have the attitudes, skills, and procedures necessary to discuss their conflicts collaboratively.

Steps to Manage Conflict Cooperatively

Resolving conflicts cooperatively requires persistence, skill, and ingenuity.

Develop Productive Conflict Climate

People must recognize that conflict is both inevitable and potentially constructive. Their norms and values should support talking about conflict openly and managing it cooperatively. In their work groups, employees can study conflict and learn how to discuss it productively. Together they agree upon the strategies that are useful to managing and those that are unacceptable.

Team members also should strengthen their bonds with each other and develop relationships characterized by friendliness, mutual concern, and respect. Doing so helps them to be more prepared to discuss conflict and to believe that it can be resolved for mutual benefit. They should support each other and try to improve each other's confidence and skills in handling conflict. When everyone is strong psychologically, conflict can be managed well.

Confront the Problem

People must openly confront their difficulties and differences. By expressing their own views of the conflict, they invite others to do the same. They let each other know their positions, ideas, and feelings, and they identify specific issues, highlight the importance of the conflict, and release tension. They include the facts, information, conclusions, and rationale that lie behind their positions and feelings.

People should be prepared to discuss conflict. Catching people off guard can make them defensive. Try to select a situation when both persons have the energy, time, and openness to discuss the problem; avoid surprises. Approaching someone at the end of a meeting or as she is trying to catch a flight out of town is not recommended.

Jointly Define the Problem

Define the problem as specifically as possible to everyone's satisfaction. Specific problems are more easily resolved than grand principles. Fight over issues, not personalities. Identify the specific behaviors that interfere and frustrate rather than use general labels. You feel frustrated because you are unsure whether your boss wants you to pursue new accounts, not because your boss is "indecisive and isn't doing his job."

Stick to the issue and main problem. Avoid diversions to side issues or bringing up new, unrelated items that diffuse your efforts. Keep focused on the problem and do not get sidelined by taking the discussion too personally, feeling indignant, or trying to save face.

Put Yourself in the Other's Shoes

Conflict should be seen as an opportunity to understand another's feelings, views, and thinking. In conflict, however, people often misunderstand the other's interests, needs, and motivation. People must know each other's perspective so that they appreciate the problem fully, understand all sides, and are in a better position to develop solutions that work for all. They must be willing to stop defending their own views and listen carefully to what others are saying.

Demonstrating that you are trying and actually do understand another's arguments and feelings is important in resolving conflict. When others believe that you know what they are saying, they become more open to your position and more convinced that you are trying to resolve the conflict cooperatively. Accurately paraphrasing or actually putting yourself in the other's position and arguing from that standpoint can be useful in resolving conflict.

Show Respect and Acceptance

People often are sensitive in conflict. They are upset and may wonder whether others really value and care for them. Many people assume that disagreeing with their positions is the same as rejecting them as people. Throughout the discussion, people should show respect and acceptance of each other. Avoid insults and challenges that question another's competence and morality. Avoid taking disagreement as a challenge to your competence.

Motivation to Resolve

Not everyone is equally motivated to discuss a conflict. Some people experience the costs of the conflict much more fully, and some can quickly appreciate the benefits of resolving the conflict. When everyone realizes the costs and the benefits, discussion is apt to be fruitful.

People can discuss the costs and gains for continuing versus resolving the conflict. Many persons underestimate the costs of fighting and deny future difficulties. For example, Fred may feel little need to release a secretary to Preston to complete a special assignment. Preston can remind Fred, however, that he may need a favor in the future or that Fred might look bad if their boss has to get involved to solve this problem.

Cooperative Dependence

Protagonists easily forget that their goals are cooperative. Trying to blame and find fault intensifies competition. At times one person is solely responsible, but more often everyone has contributed to the problem. They should focus on working together to manage the conflict, not find fault. The problem should be defined as a mutual problem for everyone to solve, not a struggle to see who will win. The emphasis is on win-win solutions in which everyone gains rather than on winning and losing.

Reaching an Agreement

Conflict is an opportunity to get new information and to understand issues more completely. By examining the problem from different perspectives, people create solutions. They should not assume that the choice is simply between the position favored by one person and the position favored by the other. They should avoid arguing for or against one of the positions but should combine the best ideas and views to create solutions that further everyone's interests. They should select a solution that is fair to all and that everyone will be willing to implement.

Many prolonged, intense conflicts must be solved through repeated discussions. Protagonists should be prepared to repeat these procedures to deepen their understanding, know feelings and reactions, and create a workable solution.

Reaffirming the Agreement

After the agreement has been reached, people must show good faith by implementing it. They check to make sure the agreement is being implemented and that it is as effective as expected. They also reflect on the discussion and recognize that people worked and took risks to help resolve the conflict.

People should celebrate their success in discussing the conflict. Managing conflict requires considerable competence and effort, and its accomplishment should be recognized. They also should point out how resolving the conflict will help them to work more productively and humanely in the future.

Concluding Comments

The old methods of avoiding conflict and decisively suppressing it are appropriate at times but are much more costly than is commonly assumed. Avoidance wastes energy, undermines commitment, and results in stagnation. The norms and values of the organization must indicate that employees can talk about problems and issues, not pretend that they do not exist or will somehow disappear. Managers and employees should use conflict to solve problems to reduce their frustrations and enhance their productivity.

Conflict is built into living and working in an organization. Knowledge about conflict has important implications for nearly all managerial work. The ability to handle conflict is needed to be a good leader, conduct performance appraisal, make a project team effective, communicate with employees, satisfy customer demands, negotiate with suppliers, and strive for and achieve goals. To be effective, managers must themselves discuss conflict constructively and help their employees to confront it.

10
Stimulating and Managing Innovation

An established company which in an age demanding innovation is not capable of innovation is doomed to decline and extinction. . . . Managing innovation will increasingly become a challenge to management, and a touchstone of its competence.
—*Peter Drucker*, Management, *1973*

Entrepreneurs and the innovations that they put in place are transforming the U.S. economy and society in general. Entrepreneurs have revitalized established companies, created new ventures, and overhauled public service. Dramatic changes are occurring in health care and other areas that not long ago were not even considered businesses. Hospitals are joining forces to develop new services in maternity care and rehabilitation that are beyond the resources of an independent hospital. They are developing links with medical clinics and nursing homes to strengthen their patient base. Entrepreneurs have formed health-maintenance organizations, hospices for the terminally ill, diagnostic laboratories, freestanding maternity homes, geriatric physical therapy centers, walk-in medical and dental clinics, and life-care centers.

The typical image of entrepreneurship is high tech. The entrepreneur is a whiz with computers, or perhaps biotechnology, who, after two years of tinkering in his basement and selling his invention himself, now oversees a company of hundreds of wizards, most of whom are, like their boss, creative eccentrics with offbeat and now luxurious lifestyles. This image is misleading. Entrepreneurs are, foremost, sophisticated, practical managers, not brilliant inventors. They may exploit an invention or discovery, or they may use existing knowledge in new ways that create new products and services.

Dr. An Wang combined a typewriter, a display screen, and a simple computer to create the word processor, and he developed Wang Laboratories to deliver the word processor to offices that found it cost-effective. Frying hamburgers and french fries are old skills to be sure, but Ray Kroc developed the organization and procedures for serving them in ways that brought millions of hungry people worldwide to McDonald's. High tech is only a small part of the story. High-tech companies accounted for only 5 to 6 million of the 40 million plus jobs created from 1965 to 1985 in the United States. Nor were most of those jobs created by new ventures. Growth has come largely from middle-size companies that have exploited opportunities and delivered valued products and services in many different industries and markets.[1]

The contemporary view is that innovation and entrepreneurship are increasingly important for all organizations because they must cope with intense competition and rapid social, technological, and market changes. To survive and prosper, companies need creativity in product offerings, market strategies, operations and production, company policy and direction, and management style. Innovation is a necessity, not a luxury.[2] Traditional attitudes that innovation is only relevant for a few large, prosperous, high-tech companies and that it involves hiring creative, independent thinkers, putting them in a laboratory, and hoping for the best must give way to more realistic assessment and appreciation of innovation. The hardheaded, results-oriented, no-nonsense approach to productivity must be tempered and combined with exploring alternatives and reaching out for innovations so that companies continue to flourish.

Creative, independent geniuses do not drive innovation in organizations; invigorating, supportive teamwork does.[3] Several persons working together are able to realize emerging opportunities from present problems, combine a variety of ideas to create new approaches, and develop the confidence and persistence to implement these ideas. Employees working together have designed and marketed highly profitable products, implemented cost-saving new technology, painstakingly improved worker productivity, and in a great number of ways helped organizations deliver valued products and services.

Innovation tests a company's mettle. Innovation requires competence, commitment, determination, and sometimes daring. Employees must develop strong relationships in which they can solve problems, discuss opposing views productively, recognize and use each other's abilities, and manage their conflicts. Managing innovation requires considerable skill, thought, and effort. But the rewards can be tremendous. The organization gains profits, security, and prestige. Knowing that they have contributed, employees feel fulfilled and may gain fame and fortune; their success binds them closer together.

Innovation may seem chaotic and unpredictable, but it happens because companies value and encourage it. Managers cannot just hope that innovation happens; they need to structure the work so that employees have the mandate, resources, and incentives to innovate. Ideas and procedures to develop cooperative goals, positive power, problem solving, and conflict management are all relevant for innovation. This chapter specifies additional procedures and skills to stimulate and manage innovation.

Need for Organizational Innovation

Although many problems and situations require variations of familiar solutions, organizations increasingly need to develop innovative, nonroutine solutions. Innovation is necessary for continued prosperity and survival. The turbulent marketplace and environment in which most companies now operate contribute to the need for organizational change and innovation.[4] Changes in the resources the organization needs and the markets in which it sells its products and services are widely thought to be increasing in their rate and unpredictability. Companies must be alert to this uncertainty and adopt new aspirations, strategies, and practices.

Emerging values, hopes, and expectations of employees also press organizations to change. Many persons want more than jobs that pay. They want and expect their jobs to challenge them and give their lives more meaning. Their jobs should give them opportunities for close, personal relationships and recognition of their accomplishments. They want the prestige and security of feeling part of a successful, dynamic effort. Specialists and professionals, alert to advances in their fields, push their companies to innovate. Emerging employee values challenge organizations to develop jobs and climates that enhance individuals and allow them to use their specialized expertise. Companies that successfully create these meaningful jobs stand to reap the benefits of a highly involved and committed work force.

Changes in the environment and work force mean that present procedures and operating methods, management approaches, products, and market strategies are often obsolete and need to be updated periodically. Bold decisions can break away from ineffective past practices. Recent writers have portrayed large and small companies that are innovating to develop a committed work force and high-quality products.[5] These companies inspire others to innovate and suggest ways to do so. Many companies are now innovating in corporate cultures, project teams, participative management, profit sharing, computer-aided design and manufacturing, quality control, and commitment to job security. Today's companies have many opportunities and incentives to innovate.

Nature of Organizational Innovation

Innovation is the process of initiating, adopting, and implementing an idea, procedure, practice, program, or product considered new by the organization.[6] Sometimes these innovations are invented by the company itself; more often they have been invented elsewhere, and the company innovates by adopting them.

Innovations come in all types and sizes. Companies can innovate by acquiring new machinery, devising new uses for old machinery, implementing new personnel and management practices, acquiring skills to make old practices work, developing products, and finding new markets for old ones. Innovations may require a total reorientation by the organization or a slight adjustment. Innovations differ in cost, return on investment, risks they present, compatibility with the organization, scientific status, ease by which they can be terminated and reversed, degree of commitment necessary to adopt them, and extent to which they can be modified.

A common belief is that a bright insight creates innovation, but organizational innovation requires much more. Problems must be found and considered opportunities. They must be discussed and seen from new perspectives, and ideas must be combined into a new solution. The solution needs to be evaluated and tested, and persistence and commitment are required to implement it.

Finding Opportunities

We usually think that problems find us and that we would be better off if fewer did so. But especially in innovation, it is important to make efforts to identify problems and to see them as opportunities to exploit rather than threats to avoid or tolerate. Recognizing that there is a discrepancy between *what is* and *what could be* stimulates innovation.[7] If the standard way of manufacturing a product is considered ideal or if the present product line is thought to be tremendous, then there is little perceived need to improve it.

Companies have translated several kinds of opportunities into successful innovations.[8] Events that surprise stimulate innovation. The Ford Motor Company was embarrassed by the flop of the Edsel. But as it investigated this failure, Ford came to doubt the dominant assumptions developed by GM that the market was divided into low, lower-middle, upper-middle, and upper segments. Customers chose a car, it was widely thought, that expressed their economic means and standing. Ford found that consumers were interested in choosing a car that fit their lifestyle and with this insight, developed the Mustang, the greatest automotive success since the Model T.

Sometimes these unexpected events are successes. DuPont's research in polymer chemistry had no payoff for years until an assistant left a burner on over the weekend. On Monday, the mixture had turned into congealed fibers, but it still took ten more years to learn how to make nylon intentionally. It is not simply that an event was unexpected, but also that it led to a reexamination of current assumptions and the development of a new understanding that allowed more effective action.

Entrepreneurs exploit changes in markets, industries, and technology. The high inflation of the 1970s left many modest investors disenchanted with bank savings accounts. Many financial institutions are now aggressively marketing products for these investors. The breakup of AT&T has opened the doors for companies to compete for long-distant phone business, mobile phones, and private branch exchange. Knowledge and technology of silicon chips and computers have created new markets and companies to exploit them.

"Necessity is the mother of invention" has, like most old sayings, some truth. For years before 1885, newspapers were printed on high-speed printers and paper made from high-speed paper machines. Only the typesetting was done slowly, manually, and expensively. Through years of hard work and ingenuity, Ottmar Mergenthaler created the Linotype, which mechanically selected letters, adjusted them to the line, and returned them for future use. But it is not just a felt need that leads to innovation. Newspaper publishers were well aware of this need, but someone had to see it as an opportunity to be exploited and be able to apply knowledge to meet it.

Creating Solutions

Once understood, an opportunity must be followed by creating a solution to exploit it. The Mustang did not simply appear out of the ashes of the Edsel; Ford employees had to create it. Creating new approaches, strategies, products, and other ideas is not a neat one-step-at-a-time approach. There do, however, appear to be characteristic phases that encourage creativity. Original proposals usually based on modifications of previous solutions used elsewhere are discussed but are found unsatisfactory. The innovators might feel quite blocked and frustrated, conclude that there is no adequate solution to the problem, and withdraw from the problem. During this period of frustration and doubt, ideas incubate, as persons consider the problem from a different point of view. Through the clash of various ideas, persons gain greater insight and offer tentative solutions. Sometimes the insight comes as a great illumination: the "Aha!" or "I've got it!" experience. These solutions are then elaborated, and one or more is chosen for more careful evaluation.

In 1976, Manuel Villafana decided to leave the profitable company he had built, Cardiac Pacemakers, Inc., to begin St. Jude Medical, a company to design and manufacture heart valves.[9] His pacemaker customers kept telling him that the valves on the market were big and clumsy. They made already weak hearts work harder and often wore out. They also made some patients more vulnerable to strokes. He and his designers thought that pyrolitic carbon was the best material for the valves. They brainstormed for months. When they thought they had a workable design and Villafana had talked to the investors, the valve broke. They had nothing but failures. One morning Peter Gombrich, then executive vice president, woke up at 4:30 with a dream about the valve. He got up and went to the lab, and that was the beginning of the solution. A year later they began selling the new valve. By 1986, a $100 investment in St. Jude was worth more than $2,000.

Evaluation and Testing

A creative solution needs to be vigorously evaluated; its very newness means that it could be easily misused or misapplied. An idea may be creative but dangerous. Debates, shoot-outs between opposing teams, the use of a devil's advocate, and other methods must be used to evaluate new ideas. In addition to these challenges, the idea must be systematically tested. Developing a prototype, field testing a market strategy, and demonstrating a project in one plant provide additional information. An idea that has gone through this rigorous testing should have data to support it in discussions with top management; the tests also should boost the innovators' confidence to push for their project. The failure to test has led to very expensive and embarrassing flops that make the company and the innovators lose credibility.

Persistence

Well-tested ideas and insights are necessary for organizational innovation, but so is persistence. Musashi Semiconductor Works of Hitachi Corporation in Japan takes a slow, careful approach to innovation. In the second half of 1980, 360 work groups produced 112,000 improvement proposals, and the company implemented 98,000 that saved production time at work stations, lowered inventory, improved safety, and increased office and clerical efficiency.[10] Even after the accidental making of congealed fibers, DuPont's chemists worked ten years to learn how to produce nylon.

Employees must be motivated to make the effort and to bear the frustrations and tensions that usually accompany innovation. The task should be seen as challenging, deserving of their best efforts, and achievable. They need to believe that they have the power and imagination to innovate. If they consider themselves dull or without the organizational clout to develop new approaches and get them accepted, they will not be very motivated to try. Working on innovations should be exciting and rewarding.

Organizational Commitment

Many proposals for innovations have proved unsuccessful because the innovators were unable to get the concurrence of top management, the union, workers, middle management, various departments, or others. Resistance is nearly inevitable in innovation. Individuals and groups are familiar and often comfortable with the status quo. Indeed, the company has rewarded them for stable, reliable performance. They may resist if the change implies that their previous work is unappreciated or considered ineffective. They may resent being sold on the innovation. Employees may fear that the change will weaken their power and status or benefit a rival.[11]

Top management and others need good reasons to make the effort to change and learn new responsibilities. They want to be convinced that the innovation is cost-effective, has acceptable risks, does not stretch organizational resources too far, is consistent with long-range plans, supports the company's reputation, and improves cooperation among corporate units. Ideally, the conflicts the innovation engenders are managed productively so that the organization as a whole is committed to it.[12]

Teams Innovate

The coordinated work of employees has great potential to negotiate the various phases of organizational innovation. Innovation typically occurs when employees together aspire to excellence, struggle with problems that interfere with excellence, see the difficulties in a new light, develop solutions not previously tried in the organization, and implement these solutions successfully. Employees often are placed into groups with the assignment to innovate, but stimulating interaction also occurs over lunch and other informal settings as employees discuss their problems, hunches, ideas, and hopes. This section uses the term *team* to refer to officially established groups and informal interaction.

Cooperative teams find problems and dig into them. They provide a forum for persons to share their feelings, hunches, doubts, and misgivings as well as discuss new ideas and practices in their fields. These discussions help them focus on problems whose solutions would aid the organization. After one person begins to reveal doubts about present products and procedures, others can look more closely and skeptically. Groups can monitor the environment to identify new technologies, practices, and other inventions to help the company become more successful. With the support and abilities of others, problems are thought to be opportunities that challenge rather than threats that overwhelm.

Several employees working together can help explore the problem and develop fresh perspectives that lead to innovative solutions. The various suggestions and ideas within teams stimulate members to come up with other views.[13] The opinion of one gets others thinking and speculating. Group members are asked to present their ideas clearly and completely, elaborate on them, and defend their usefulness. Because reasoning is evaluated and shortcomings of approaches uncovered, persons might easily feel frustrated and stymied. But group support helps employees realize that they are not alone and that others are grappling with the issue. Temporary frustration and the apparent lack of progress lead to the search for solutions not previously considered and tried. The rich exchange among team members has made a large number of ideas public. With this background, people can devise solutions that combine ideas in unique ways.

Teams can test ideas thoroughly. Through discussion, simplistic solutions can be dismissed and the adequacy of traditional approaches challenged. Persistent skepticism by some persons in the group also can underline the need for more prototypes and field tests to collect additional information. Not all questions can be answered through intellectual debate; the group needs to experiment and collect more data.

Working together develops needed persistence. Because people have discussed and challenged the solution from several perspectives, they are confident that they can be successful. If those who have had misgivings now favor the proposal, the group can have more confidence that their ideas deserve commitment. They do not feel isolated and powerless but believe that they have the resources of the group behind them to see the idea through. Having a representative of top management as a member of the group bestows the additional confidence that their proposals will be heard.

Teams encourage a commitment to implementing the solution. Through active involvement in developing and testing an idea, members own the innovation and feel that it is part of themselves. Its success will reflect well on them, their careers, and perhaps their pocketbooks. They also understand the rationale behind the solution and have been convinced that it is sound. Knowing how the plan is supposed to work, they are more sensitive to how it must be implemented. If, during implementation, the innovation is not having the anticipated effect, they are alerted and can suggest an alternative approach so that the anticipated results are reached.

Implementation of a fresh idea is rarely a routine exercise. The production and marketing of the product, or the putting in place of a new human resource procedure, requires sensitivity, flexibility, and commitment to its success. Through membership and participation in groups responsible for the innovation, understanding and dedication are acquired.

Well-managed teams develop needed organizational commitment. Placing representatives from interested departments in the innovation group helps it to focus on the needs and sensitivities of the whole organization; representatives keep their departments informed of the group's progress and what might be expected of them.[14] Team members already should have anticipated objections from different organizational units and adapted their innovation to them.

Is there a role for the independent thinker, the creative genius? Traditionally, we have thought that these people were the innovators in products (Thomas Edison, George Washington Carver) and in knowledge (Isaac Newton, Albert Einstein). Surely, the energy and foresight of independent, progressive thinkers aid innovation. Even independent thinkers, however, need to elaborate their ideas to others, get feedback, be challenged, and hear a fresh viewpoint. Putting isolated individuals in back rooms and letting them think is likely to result in many wild ideas but few that respond to the many needs and perspectives of organizations or are presented in convincing ways.

Management must feel confident that an idea has been thoroughly tested and its implications mapped out before it commits the company's resources and credibility.

Innovation teams are powerful tools that companies can use to adapt and flourish. Research groups, task forces, product project teams, and other groups have specific assignments and disband after their innovation is in place. The organizational development unit, managers of a division, and quality-improvement groups have a continuing, ongoing commitment to innovation. Loosely formed groups and informal interaction also can be very important in stimulating innovation.

Innovation Teams at Work

Groups have demonstrated that they can innovate in organizations. Teams are used to institute a new technology and operating procedures, introduce new ventures and products, support employee learning and development, develop and monitor new organizational practices, and anticipate the future. The first case described below shows how cooperative groups facilitated the introduction of a new technology. This study is a classic in the management literature and remains one of the few field experiments on organizational innovation. It reminds us that the need to innovate, now very pressing, is not itself new. The second case describes 3M's successful contemporary, systematic approach to foster and manage innovation to bring new products to the marketplace.

Implement a Technology

Management traditionally has tried to convince workers of the need and desirability of new machinery and technology. Yet management's convictions and enthusiasm often are quite inadequate to gain worker commitment. Employees will withhold support or even work against a new technology when they do not understand its rationale or when they believe that it might harm their interests. This resistance is seen as irrational, self-serving foot-dragging by management. Considerable energy may be spent and hostility generated in the fight over the new technology. Involving teams of workers in planning how to institute a new technology is a realistic option to the unilateral announcement of change.

A textile manufacturer faced stiff competition from low-cost producers. It had decided that it must use a new technology and procedures to increase worker productivity. The difficulties encountered were substantial, however, and the benefits of new machinery and other changes were significantly below those predicted by the production engineers. Indeed, worker productivity typically would fall by as much as 50 percent before climbing back to 75 percent of the original level. The affected workers were inevitably frustrated and hostile, and worker turnover added to the manufacturer's problems.

The personnel director and a group-dynamics researcher collaborated to try to solve this practical problem and to test their theory on the role of teams in change.[15] They contrasted the traditional, management-directed implementation with group methods of change. In the traditional change condition, management explained to the workers that the new machinery and their improved productivity were necessary because of competitive pressures. The production department conducted sophisticated time and motion studies and on the basis of these studies, informed the workers of the piece rates they would be expected to reach. Management solicited and answered all the questions that workers raised.

In the group change method involving employee representatives, management also explained the competitive pressures for change and the need for improved productivity. In contrast to the traditional approach, workers were asked to select special operators who would help design the new jobs and set the new piece rates. Then representatives helped to train the other workers in their new jobs. In another group method with full participation of workers, management explained the need for change, and all workers were asked to design the new jobs and select the new piece rate.

The outcomes of the traditional and team methods contrasted sharply. In the group methods, workers quickly accepted the challenge and enthusiastically offered many good suggestions. They became committed to the accomplishments and talked about "our job" and "our rate." This enthusiasm paid off in productivity and worker commitment. They quickly learned their new jobs and became more productive than before the change. Workers in the full-participation condition regained their prechange productivity in two days, while workers in the representative-group condition reached previous productivity levels in two weeks. None of these workers quit or exhibited hostility toward supervisors.

Results were much less positive for the traditional change method. Workers immediately had a 20 percent drop in their productivity and did not recover their previous level for the full eight months in which records were kept. Nine percent of this group quit, and many expressed hostility through slowdowns, complaints, and requests for transfers.

In a follow-up study, team and traditional change methods were contrasted using the workers from the first study's traditional change condition. Results of the follow-up were similar in that the persons who worked as a team to plan the change had markedly improved productivity over those who did not.

Workers do not inevitably resist change. Forming them into teams with the task of assisting implementation of change not only can overcome resistance, but also can develop useful ways to employ new technology for the welfare of the company and the workers. These teams also give management and labor actual experiences in working together on concrete, cooperative goals. These groups give substance to calls for greater management-labor cooperation.

Product Innovation at 3M

Minnesota Mining and Manufacturing (3M) relies on groups, called venture teams, to stimulate innovation.[16] 3M has thrived. *Fortune* lists it as the forty-fifth largest American company with sales of $7.7 billion, a net income of $773 million in 1984, and the eighth best return on sales in the *Fortune* 100. It also has innovated, introducing more than one hundred new products a year and offering a total of fifty thousand products. It often reaches its goal of getting 25 percent of its sales from products that are less than five years old.

The key to 3M's success is the use of teams that act like small entrepreneurial businesses beneath the umbrella of the larger corporation. After a possible new product has been identified, a new venture team is formed with full time technical, marketing, manufacturing, sales, and finance specialists. The team stays together from product conception to maturity, and if the group fails, the company provides job security and a position similar to the one members gave up to join the team. Members volunteer for this full-time assignment to ensure commitment to the project, for 3M realizes that teams will have to struggle to overcome great odds to produce a profitable product. Rewards are given for successful team effort. The company records and celebrates groups whose products reach $1 million in sales. Promotions and salary raises are given as the product reaches the market and achieves annual sales of $1 million, $5 million, and $20 million. Rewards to individuals depend on the success of their team's product.

The culture at 3M reinforces team efforts at innovation. The company's past and present leaders are celebrated, and virtually all have been part of a highly successful venture team. These stories highlight the importance of exploring new avenues, developing even unlikely ideas, being open to new ventures, and persisting in the face of obstacles. Seldom is a product idea killed, although management may deflect it by withdrawing much of the resources behind it. A reduced team, sometimes only one person, is encouraged to continue if she believes that the idea is still viable. And there are stories of persons becoming vice presidents because they worked on their own time to develop successful products that the company had decided not to sponsor.

Groups at 3M seem to combine the best qualities of a large corporation and small team entrepreneurial effort. Team members have their own identifiable, meaningful tasks that challenge them to use their full abilities. The groups are small enough that they can focus on specific customers and their needs. They realize that they have a common task with shared outcomes. The team's success clearly reflects on them as individuals and determines their tangible rewards. They are working for themselves and their co-workers, not just for a large, impersonal company. Communication, coordination, and support are more easily achieved than in a large company. They quickly move to actual demonstrations of the product and testing it with customers. But they have the advantages of the specialized technical resources, financial backing, and job security and prestige that the company can offer. Their products also benefit from the recognition and credibility that the corporation has established in the marketplace.

Guides for Action

Innovating

- Make people aware of the importance of innovation for the company and themselves.
- Foster stimulating, supportive communication.
- Form teams with the common goal of developing specific innovations.
- Involve people who will make the innovation work.
- Create diversity and controversy.
- Combine ideas into new solutions.
- Test ideas through discussion, field tests, and prototypes.
- Reward persistence and success.

Pitfalls to Avoid

- Rest hopes for innovation on one person or group.
- Insist that innovation be done *now*.
- Isolate the innovators from the rest of the company.
- Judge new ideas quickly.
- Assume that wild ideas are automatically good or bad.

- Dismiss ideas because they come from the "wrong" person or group.
- Assume that if the person was right last time, she must be right this time.

Innovation Procedures

Managers, project leaders, and employees must know how to innovate. They should have the procedures and skills to stimulate a developmental orientation, creative thinking, open-mindedness, commitment, and links between management and innovation groups. Although no set procedure is appropriate for all situations, the following can be used to develop plans.

Common Task and Cooperative Goals

All employees should work for the common goal to develop and implement innovations that are useful for the organization. Everyone must work together for mutual benefits and avoid trying to outdo each other, win, or have his ideas dominate. Bonuses, prestige, and other rewards are given to employees according to the extent to which their group is successful. Efforts to pursue individual objectives at the expense of others are identified and discouraged. All team members share in the rewards of success and the responsibility for failure.

Incentives for Innovation

Groups will not be automatically motivated to innovate, overcome obstacles, and persist. The significance of the task should be clear. The organization prospers through innovation; stagnation threatens it. Company executives can indicate that the team's success is important to them. The team members' own psychological and tangible rewards depend on successful group effort. They can meet needs for achievement and feel challenged; they can feel connected and valued by others; they can enjoy being part of a dynamic, successful team and company. Promotions, opportunities, and bonuses are tangible rewards that motivate innovation.

Incentives and pressures should not, however, be too great. Excessive motivation can create a crisis orientation and stressed attempts to find a quick solution, a reduced ability to consider a range of alternatives, and an attempt to please organizational superiors with a solution that appears more useful than it really is.[17]

Innovation takes time and may appear at times chaotic. Employees have bootlegged innovations by using resources not officially budgeted to pursue ideas that they believe will pay off. Groups should strive for an optimal level of motivation, rather than a maximum. Managers must allow them to experiment and play with ideas without oppressive pressure to produce. Few new innovations have as high a return on investment as ongoing activities, and sometimes they need years to prove themselves.[18]

Diversity

The variety of ideas, information, and viewpoints available to the team should be as great as possible.

> Teams can be formed so that members vary in background, expertise, opinions, outlook, and organizational membership. Specialists, generalists, researchers, and practitioners from various parts of the organization and outside can be included.
>
> Team members must feel free to offer tentative ideas on which others can elaborate and to develop new positions. They should avoid censuring themselves, feel confident that their efforts will be well received, and avoid evaluating ideas too quickly. Brainstorming is a technique designed to increase diversity of ideas by withholding evaluation.
>
> It is important to illustrate new approaches and ideas. Visiting other organizations and reading research reports and case studies of change can stimulate team members and suggest how they might institute innovation.
>
> Time deadlines can stifle diversity. Group members should have the time to research and prepare their positions so that they can confidently and persuasively present them. Pressure for quick solutions stifles controversy and encourages groups to be productive by deciding on something, anything.
>
> Constructive controversy should be fostered (see chapter 8).

Explore and Integrate Ideas

Group members should make sure that they fully understand each other's arguments. Accurately paraphrasing others' reasoning, asking each other questions, and listening to elaborations result in open-minded understanding and evaluation. They should avoid either/or thinking, which assumes that the solution must be one of those originally proposed. Frequently none of the original solutions is adequate. They must struggle with the problem and the inadequacies of proposed solutions until they formulate new perspectives that help them integrate ideas in a creative way. They should focus on trying to combine the best ideas to create the final solution.

Evaluate Solutions

Although innovation groups must guard against hasty evaluation, they must also rigorously evaluate possible solutions after they have been developed. Groups often concentrate on one criteria, but there are usually several important ones. First, the innovation should solve the problem in such a way that it will not reappear in a new form. The innovation should be practical in that the organization has the resources and motivation to implement it. The organization should see that the benefits outweigh the costs. Intangible benefits also should be considered. The innovation should make the organization, customers, suppliers, and employees look good and feel proud.

Links with the Organization

Teams have several major ways to develop links with management.[19] The groups should be well versed in top management's vision and mission for the company. Teams can keep management continually informed of its progress and the alternatives it is considering. It is easy when communicating the results of the group's efforts not to convey fully the underlying perspective and rationale. If management has been briefed on an ongoing basis, it will not be caught off guard and react with caution and defensiveness. Memos and joint discussions are practical ways of maintaining links with management. Often it is advantageous for a member of top management to be on the team. This person acts as a direct link to promote two-way communication and give management a sense of participation. This membership also gives the committee's suggestions more clout.

To gain support, the team must present its work so that it is congruent with top management's values and outlook. In this way, the innovation will appear more reasonable and consistent with other organizational procedures and objectives. It is hard to convince a traditional, autocratic management to accept a far-reaching participative management proposal. Before they begin, teams might negotiate with management on its responsibility, limits, and freedom and discuss what management is prepared to support. Groups will find it easier to get the backing of a management that values planned, thoughtful change.

Steps for Managing Innovation Teams

Provide Direction

Managers identify unexpected events, important unfulfilled needs, market changes, promising technology, and other opportunities. Team members have a good understanding of the major steps and obstacles to innovation. They read case studies and visit innovative companies. Managers give the team the clear common goal if creating a solution and informing members that their rewards depend on group success.

Motivate

Managers pose the task as a challenge and opportunity for team members to demonstrate their abilities and contribute to the company. Team members should know the concrete rewards that they and the company will gain through innovation and understand that they will benefit personally to the extent to which their team is successful. Team members believe that they have the abilities and resources to innovate.

Foster Open-mindedness

Managers should reinforce and reward originality, promote the open discussion of opposing positions, and encourage exploration and understanding of various ideas. The team brainstorms and uses other techniques to generate ideas. All ideas can be recorded and used later for new inspiration. The innovators try to integrate their views into new approaches.

Teams must avoid premature closure and acceptance of a solution. Possible solutions should be discussed and debated openly and should be tested through field studies and prototypes.

Link with the Organization

The team knows top management's expectations, values, and limitations. People with a stake in the innovation should participate in developing new approaches. Top management and other departments are kept informed of developments.

Recognize and Reward Success

The innovators are recognized throughout the organization and are rewarded. Celebrations honor them and underline the value of innovation.

Concluding Comments

Innovation challenges and tests managers and employees. Can they combine their knowledge, awareness, creativity, daring, and persistence to identify problems and opportunities, develop and test fresh approaches, and persist in getting them implemented? They can take inspiration from companies that are innovating in many successful ways and have reaped considerable advantage.

Innovation does not just happen; managers and employees must work hard to innovate. They must create and take advantage of a rich, diverse environment in which employees share, discuss, challenge, and dispute their fears, aspirations, problems, and solutions and together forge ideas and programs to which they are committed. Creating this innovative climate is not simple. Cooperative goals, positive power, problem solving, constructive controversy, and conflict management all make innovations happen.

11
Managerial Leadership

I was the general in the war to save Chrysler. But I sure didn't do it alone. What I'm most proud of is the coalition I was able to put together. It shows what cooperation can do for you in hard times.

—Lee Iacocca

The test of leadership is not to put greatness into humanity, but to elicit it, for the greatness is already there.

—John Buchan

*B*ob Clinton, though apprehensive, was looking forward to his professional appraisal interview as he rode the elevator to Duncan Foster's twelfth floor office. Bob reminded himself, "I can talk with that guy. He's a little old-fashioned, but I can think of worse things to say about a boss."

"You know, Bob," Duncan began, "that Don, the chairman, and I are both pleased with the performance of the health-care group. We are a step ahead of the competition because we are more prepared to get involved in the new activities. You've got a good record and, thank God, no major problem loans."

Bob relaxed and replied. "It's been an exciting three years. The changes in the health-care business are amazing. Who would have thought that the system could change so fast?"

"Those rapid changes bother an old banker like me, but there is not much we can do but live with them," Duncan replied. He cleared his throat and continued. "You know I think you're good, and I hope you don't take me wrong. But I've been thinking about you and meaning to talk to you about a few things. Now what I'm going to say is not really a criticism, and it's just between you and me. Take what I say as food for thought from a guy who has been around for a while."

Duncan's speech quickened. "Don't you think that you would be better off if you were more of a take-charge guy? Don keeps on saying we need leadership in this bank, people who take control of situations and get things done."

Bob was taken back, although not totally surprised. He could feel his muscles tighten and his adrenaline flow. "Are you saying that I'm not a good leader?" he asked.

"Don't get me wrong. Don hasn't said anything to me about your leadership qualities. We like you and your group, but sometimes it seems that you're too close to the people who work for you. You give them all the credit for your success. Sometimes you need to take a stand and show them who's boss."

Bob reassured himself that Duncan really was interested in helping him, began thinking about himself as a leader, and saw an opportunity to talk to Duncan about some things that were on his mind. "It's interesting that you brought this up. Preston, Dennis, and I were just talking about how the group has changed during the past three years. It got me thinking about how I've changed by attending seminars, reading, talking with other managers, and trying ideas."

"What did you conclude?" Duncan asked.

"I used to think that my job was to make the tough decisions and to make sure everyone worked hard. I was trying to do my job alone. I don't know if I accomplished much, but I definitely was tired at the end of the week. That approach just didn't work for me. Then we began regular group meetings. First we used them as a dress rehearsal to practice presenting new loans to the loan committee. Gradually, we started to discuss important decisions and issues. Now we really work as a team. I see my job as helping them do their job; when they produce, I produce. It's not all chocolate and marshmallow ice cream. We have our disagreements and frustrations, but I and the loan officers like it. They really work hard together, especially when it counts. I don't run them, but I certainly feel in control of the situation."

"Don't get me wrong, Bob. I like what you are doing," Duncan replied genuinely. "Your approach probably works for you. We old bankers don't change that easily."

"But, Duncan, is your leadership style that much different from mine?" Bob offered. "You're definitely the boss, but you don't take charge in the sense of domineering. We talk things over, just as we are talking about my leadership style. I think you helped me learn that."

"Do you mean that if banks and health care can change, even an old banker can?" Duncan said with a laugh. "Let's talk again soon."

Managers are at the center of the divisions, departments, project teams, and task forces that make up organizations. They link the employees of these groups with each other and the rest of the organization. They work with individual employees, help employees work together, and connect their group to the organization. The traditional image is that leaders direct and control subordinates to make sure that they complete their tasks. Actually, though, managers spend little time giving instructions and issuing orders. Instead, they continually give and get information to help employees do their jobs.[1] *Managers are the overseers and nurturers of the organization; they are the architects of cooperation through which things get done.*

Much is expected of managerial leaders. To galvanize and inspire, they are expected to create a vision that captures employees' imaginations and makes them committed to their common objectives. Executives are expected to create corporate unity and identity, which harness the energy and expertise of all departments. Managers are there to advise, develop people, and make profits. A successful leader creates a productive department that serves the best interests of employees and the company.

Expectations for managerial leaders have been discussed and elaborated, but the strategies leaders should use to realize these aspirations have not been specified. Researchers regularly express dismay at the lack of progress and offer various recommendations.[2] Theorists have even doubted that leadership has a significant impact on organizations and have recommended that it be abandoned as a research issue.[3]

What has frustrated progress is that the traditional emphasis on how leaders should influence and control employees neglects the importance of how managers and employees depend on each other and their need to collaborate. The model of working with people can be applied to leadership. To be effective, managers must develop cooperative goals with and among employees. They also must help employees use power positively, solve problems, and make conflict productive. Viewing leaders as coordinators helps us to examine their many leadership tasks and indicates that a person needs the ideas, approaches, procedures, sensitivities, and skills discussed in previous chapters to be a successful leader.

The terms manager and leader have different images. Managers typically are thought to be bureaucrats who follow procedures and precedents, whereas leaders take charge and break new ground. A knowledgeable, loyal engineer promoted into a management position may be an ineffective leader. Although charismatic leadership appears to require special gifts, the key abilities that a successful managerial leader needs can be learned. Knowing how to work together can help managers to become effective leaders.

Misleading Expectations

> *When a few men carry the entire load the business suffers.*
> —*John H. Patterson*

Leadership conjures up strong attitudes and ideals. Managers and employees share many assumptions about what makes a leader effective. Unfortunately, some of these assumptions get in the way of understanding successful managerial leadership.

Leader as Hero

Leaders are celebrated as the source of organizational excellence; they instill the values and determination that make the difference.[4] Articles and books portray leaders as rescuing companies from bankruptcy and turning them into viable operations. Leadership is sometimes restricted to those few managers who have an important, dramatic impact on organizations.[5]

Leaders do make a difference,[6] but this heroic view of leadership is a heavy burden on managers.[7] It obscures the mutual dependence of managers and employees. The failure to appreciate this mutual dependence frustrates problem solving and conflict management. Managers who accept the heroic view of leadership feel singly responsible for their departments and believe that they should motivate and inspire. They might conclude that they have failed when an employee performs inadequately and be highly stressed because they assume responsibility for someone else's behavior, something they cannot control. Alternatively, some managers place full responsibility on employees and blame them for any inadequacy.

Leadership is a shared responsibility. Leaders alone do not make a company work; they and employees must work together for a successful organization. Managers communicate expectations, provide resources and incentives, solve problems, and articulate values to help employees be productive. Employees themselves must use these resources, however, and decide to exert effort to perform effectively. Successful leadership requires managers and employees; problems must be worked out jointly rather than blamed on one or the other.

Leader as Doer

Many managers view their job as doing tasks and completing projects. They assume that they should take on the tasks that are beyond the abilities of their subordinates, do tasks when employees fall down on the job, and be prepared to take over in a crisis. Many managers are good at these tasks—that is why they have been promoted—and take pleasure in doing them.

This managerial involvement, though useful on occasion, often gets in the way. Employees resent meddling in their work, conclude that their boss does not trust them, and take on a let-the-boss-do-it attitude. A doer manager also frustrates employees by neglecting to clarify expectations, provide resources, and facilitate their work.

Confusion of Ends and Means

Leadership methods and strategies often are confused with the purpose and role of leaders. Many managers believe that their role demands them to be decisive and dominant; they should make decisions, give instructions, and make sure these are obeyed. But this is only one way to fulfill their role, and it is not uniformly effective. Managers must have various means and approaches to inspire people to work together.

Leadership Strategies

> *I never got very far until I stopped imagining I had to do everything myself.*
> —Frank W. Woolworth

Traditionally, it was assumed that effective leaders influence subordinates to contribute to the organization,[8] and studies tried to identify the strategies leaders should use to influence employees successfully; effective leaders perform the right behavior for the situation. This book proposes that leaders must develop the right mutual dependence for each situation. In most situations, they must establish cooperative goals and collaborate with employees.

Leadership is not something that managers accomplish alone but rather what they and employees accomplish together. Employees play an active, vital role in leadership; they influence leaders as they are influenced by them. A junior clerk who persuades the CEO to give him an assignment in which he contributes more to the company has successfully influenced the CEO, but the CEO is still the leader. The CEO's leadership involved openness to being influenced.

But is working together really what managers have in mind when they talk of leadership? Don't they mean something more dramatic that characterizes a talented individual, not a relationship? Leadership defined as working together is consistent with popular managerial thinking; the ability to work with people is widely thought to be essential for effective leadership. Recent research also suggests a close link between leadership and cooperation. Despite years of work, researchers have not found that capacities such as intelligence and physical size significantly distinguish leaders from followers. From this it is commonly concluded that persons cannot consistently be leaders because the abilities needed to act effectively depend on the situation.

People with interpersonal abilities and sensitivities, however, might be leaders in various situations.[9]

Guides for Action

Leading

- Have employees understand their task and its importance.
- Develop strong, concrete cooperative dependence with employees.
- Help employees to be and feel successful.
- Make yourself accessible and approachable.
- Take a team view of problems and success.
- Resolve conflicts productively.
- Form a strong employee team.
- Share recognition and rewards.

Pitfalls to Avoid

- Do it all yourself.
- Assume that employees understand your aspirations and obstacles.
- Assume that you know employee aspirations and obstacles.
- Be decisive in all situations.
- Continually fight fires to get employees to work together.
- Blame yourself for every problem.
- Blame employees for every problem.

Barriers to Working Together

Getting managers and employees to work together is very important but elusive. Employees often complain about their bosses; managers complain about their subordinates. In a recent study, successful executives described their bosses as snakes in the grass, Attilas, heel-grinders, egotists, dodgers, business incompetents, detail drones, and slobs.[10] While these are extreme cases, many managers and employees fail to develop open, productive relationships. Why?

Many managers and employees do not talk candidly and constructively.

They communicate sparsely, do not understand each other's thinking and perspective, and do not manage conflict well. Both sides contribute to these communication failures.

Managers are at times unmotivated to listen to and understand the views of employees.[11] They dismiss employees' personal aspirations and difficulties as unimportant. They wrongly assume that it does not matter what employees think as long as they do what is expected. But employees who do not understand why a task is important and needs to be done are not very motivated or knowledgeable about how to complete the task well. Employees help managers stay ignorant. They have been found to restrict their communication to what they believe the boss wants to hear.[12]

Despite the incentive (gaining his favor) to know their manager's goals and perspective, employees may not understand their manager. They often have restricted access to the manager and an unrealistic view of their boss's life. Many employees are oblivious to the pressures and demands their manager faces from her leader, colleagues, suppliers, and customers. They do not realize that they must work to help their manager understand their aspirations and difficulties. Managers also keep employees ignorant. They have been found to be reluctant to reveal their feelings and doubts to employees.[13]

Managers and employees often do not develop a close, personal relationship in which they can express their feelings and solve problems openly.[14] Many managers believe that they must maintain a certain distance and be personally neutral with their subordinates.[15] Employees may suspect that their manager will exploit them without fear of retribution.[16]

In addition to remaining personally distant from subordinates, many managers assume that they are expected to be in charge and to control employees; the boss informs and subordinates do. They do not try to discuss tasks and understand how their goals are cooperative. This attempt to control and dominate often intensifies competition. Employees, frustrated that they cannot exercise self-control, believe that they must fight with their boss for power.[17]

Physical as well as psychological barriers interfere with communication. Managers and employees without a suitable meeting place or sufficient time find it difficult to discuss issues and easy to postpone them. Employees may be leery of entering the boss's office; the boss is reluctant to approach an employee in front of others.

Managers and employees often fail to communicate and understand each other. Although their general tasks, roles, and rewards usually are cooperative, they do not know each other's specific goals and plans, nor do they understand how they are cooperative. Unaware of the other's objectives and purposes, they do not clearly see how they can help. In addition, they cannot evaluate the other's actions properly, for they do not know what the other intends. The other's behavior may seem unpredictable and his motives questionable. In such confusion and doubt, managers and employees wonder whether they are working together for common ends.

Partial, biased communication also undermines problem solving and conflict management.[18] Managers and employees are not clearly aware of each other's frustrations, nor have they developed procedures and skills to discuss difficult issues. Employees may avoid discussing their disappointments and anger with their boss for fear of making a bad situation worse. Sometimes managers avoid dealing with such issues for fear of alienating their employees. Some managers are highly confrontational but do so in an overpowering, tough manner that leaves employees hostile and competitive.

The tasks and roles that the organization assigns managers and employees do not automatically make them conclude they have cooperative objectives. Their failure to communicate fully, understand each other's personal aspirations, and manage conflict productively frustrates coordination.

Collaborative Leadership

Because of the difficulties of communication and understanding each other's perspectives, leaders and employees need to work to strengthen their relationships. Collaborative leaders invite discussion, are willing to adjust the task to fit the needs of employees, and work with employees to develop cooperative goals.[19]

Collaboration can be carried out in many different ways. A current form is MBWA, Management By Walking Around.[20] Moving among their employees, managers listen, teach, and facilitate. They get out of their office to meet employees face to face, keep in touch, and get information firsthand. They want to know what employees are excited and frustrated about and to show that they care about them. Teaching means sharing their own hopes, feelings, and values, not telling people what to do. With such knowledge and understanding, managers are in a much better position to help employees accomplish their tasks. Knowing the barriers and annoyances that employees face, they are better able to help employees get things done.

Steps for Collaborative Leadership

The manager introduces the new project and explains its importance.

Employees discuss the project to see how it relates to their present work and own aspirations.

The manager and employees develop a team feeling. They know that they will all gain by a successful project and will share its rewards.

If necessary, the project is modified so that the team is confident it can be successful.

Tasks are distributed fairly and efficiently; needed resources are allocated.

Norms and procedures that encourage managers and employees to discuss problems productively are established.

Managers and employees get regular feedback on their group progress and confront inadequate performance.

They share their rewards and celebrate their common achievement.

Collaborative leadership should not be confused with simply being nice and operating a business like a social club. Nor is it a laissez faire approach that avoids setting expectations, determining rules, and exercising discipline. Rather, collaborative leaders actively and vigorously work to build their own and employees' commitment to common goals, establish norms and procedures to coordinate efforts and resolve problems, and share the rewards and prestige of success and the responsibility for failure.

Managing the Boss

Employees not only can manage their boss, they must.[21] Employees who do not are taking a big risk. There are many examples of managers who worked hard to accomplish what they thought their boss wanted, only to leave the boss feeling victimized and angry because the manager apparently refused to do what the boss had asked. Bosses and employees should have a clear commitment to what they both want to accomplish. Many employees also frustrate their bosses because the way in which they work with them is annoying. The boss may want to be kept informed in detail and in writing, but the subordinate might assume that informal phone conversations are fine.

Leaders and employees depend on each other for success. Employees and managers prosper with strong collaboration between them. Employees should work to make sure that both perceive their goals as cooperative and use relevant skills and procedures to develop mutually acceptable ways of working with each other.

In addition to taking advantage of leaders' collaborative approach, employees must at times take the lead. Preoccupied with other pressures and already frustrated by other demands, their boss may make only sporadic attempts to communicate, understand, and resolve conflicts with subordinates. Employees must work to know the boss's goals and priorities, convey their own aspirations, show how these are cooperative, indicate how their efforts are promoting mutual goals, and discuss what they and the boss can do to help each other in the future. Employees can show their appreciation of the fact that the boss has many demands by using her time wisely and making it convenient and rewarding for her to meet with them. On the other hand, employees who just do their own thing or try to outdo their boss run great risks.

Guides for Action

Managing Your Boss

- Recognize that your boss needs you to do his job well.
- Understand his goals and how you can further them.
- Appreciate the pressures and problems he faces.
- Tell him your aspirations and goals.
- Identify how he likes to receive information and work with subordinates.
- Keep him posted on your successes as well as your problems.
- Make his working with you efficient and enjoyable.
- Make it easy for him to bring up problems and conflicts.
- Show that you appreciate his support and effort.

Pitfalls to Avoid

- Assume that he should automatically know your aspirations, problems, and needs.
- Talk to him only when he asks.
- Assume that if there are problems, he will initiate a discussion.
- Believe that your boss gets paid so well that he does not have to be thanked.

Sometimes a boss is not just harassed, preoccupied, or unaware of the need to work together but is mean, nasty, and competitive. Getting a rigidly competitive boss is unfortunate, but it is a piece of bad luck that many others share. Three-fourths of the highly successful executives in three *Fortune* 100 corporations reported that they had had at least one intolerable boss during their careers.[22]

How they coped with that boss illustrates that there is no easy solution to the problem. Only a few executives openly defied the boss, and fewer successfully mellowed their boss or got the organization to demote him. Believing that changing him was a long shot, the majority accepted the boss as boss. They reminded themselves that the situation was temporary and tried to do their jobs and protect themselves. Rather than trying to cooperate or compete, they tried to reduce their dependence and minimize the damage.

The executives worked around the boss rather than with him. When they needed to talk with him, they did so when he was in a good mood. They learned his habits; if he did not like disagreement, they downplayed any. They also learned from the experience. Many of them said that they learned to cope with adversity and be patient with others. They also discovered the kind of boss they did not want to be.

Complaint-Handling Systems

At times employees believe that they cannot discuss problems and conflicts with their boss or that she has not responded adequately when they have tried.[1] Dr. Zimmer at a major West Coast company found a technician unconscious from exposure to toxic fumes. A month earlier, employees at a nearby lab had become ill from fumes. Zimmer approached her boss, the new lab director, and argued that company rules require reporting such incidents to the company health and safety director. Zimmer did not want to go over her boss's head but also wanted something done. She repeatedly demanded that her boss report the incidents. Within six months, the boss fired her. Zimmer's unjust discharge suit and full investigation into the incidences have embarrassed the company and might cost it dearly.

IBM, AT&T, NBC, Security Pacific, Control Data, and many other companies have developed procedures for their nonunion employees to express their concerns and get problems solved. Professional counselors at NBC, employee relations managers at Digital Equipment, and resident managers at IBM help employees voice their concerns and resolve their problems. The ombudsman at AT&T Information Systems, the personnel communications director at Anheuser-Busch, and the mediators at Carleton College work to resolve problems through fact finding and mediation. At Control Data, employees have telephone and personal access to professional, personal, and work counselors. They can use a four-step complaint procedure that ends with peer review committees. A special channel is available for discrimination complaints.

Employee complaint procedures recognize that bosses and employees have difficulties in working together and resolving their conflicts productively. Bosses can force their solutions on employees; employees are unsure how they can voice their concerns. Traditional ways of dealing with such problems are limited. Employees fear reprisal if they talk to their boss's boss; they do not want to appear to be disloyal or a troublemaker. Employees also doubt that higher-ups will have the motivation and knowledge to do something about the problem.

Perhaps as many as one-third of all U.S. employers have developed complaint systems. These systems should be accessible. Employees should have hotlines, managers on the shop floor, and ombudsmen. Attitude surveys and regular meetings with people two levels up also can improve access. The systems should be safe to use, and confidentiality should be protected and reprisals forbidden. The systems should also be credible. Employees must believe that their concerns will be taken seriously and that problems will be resolved.

Complaint systems work best when they strengthen the cooperation between managers and employees. They improve communication, create motivation to deal with employee concerns, and provide assistance to solve problems. Mediators and counselors work to have the manager and employee sit down and discuss the problem. Effective complaint systems help to move companies away from the policy of always backing up the boss, supporting the hierarchy, and viewing dissent as disloyal and toward an appreciation of the importance of conflict management, the need to solve problems, and a recognition that commitment to the company requires discussion. Successful complaint systems convince managers and employees that the company wants them to discuss and solve problems together.

An Employee Team

Managers and management literature have concentrated on the manager-employee relationship, yet this is not the only vital link for managers. Cooperation among employees is the most neglected leadership responsibility. Most managers do not fully appreciate the importance of peer relationships and use weak strategies such as telling employees to communicate, cooperate, and get along.

Managers inevitably get dragged into employee relationships even if they do not want to. When employees bicker continually, cannot agree on how to proceed, or stop talking to each other, leaders feel obligated to intervene. Employees press managers to confront a co-worker who does not do a fair share of work or gossips about them. Managers may have to intervene when employees hide each other's deficiencies or pressure each other to restrict output to a comfortable level. Managers tend to react and cope with obvious problems; they fight fires rather than systematically develop productive relationships among peers.

Managers must realize that the degree to which employees believe their goals to be linked greatly affects how they work together and the quality of work life, morale, motivation, and productivity. Managers should encourage employees to see their goals as cooperative and to recognize that they are all better off by working together. When employees believe that their goals are cooperative and have collaborative skills, they rely on each other, use each other's abilities, and encourage and support each other. Employees who can discuss their problems and conflicts productively have no need to try to convince their boss to agree with their position and impose it on others. Managers are freed from trying to cope with hostility and bickering that occurs when employees compete.

Developing cooperation among peers is a greatly underused leadership strategy. Managers should try to realize the potential of employee peer relationships. Chapters 4 and 5 detail methods of developing cooperative goals, and other chapters indicate the skills and procedures employees need for a cohesive, productive, and supportive peer team.

Concluding Comments

Managers lead with employees; they do not lead by themselves or against employees. Managerial leaders are at the center of their groups, not at the top. They facilitate and encourage more than command and reward. Effective leaders realize that as the architects of their group and organization, their role is to help individuals and their department be productive. They are flexible in their methods. They demand and issue orders, cajole and request, or plead and persuade. But they are committed to helping employees work productively together.

Part IV
Becoming More Effective

12
Learning Together

One learns by doing the thing; for though you think you know it, you have no certainty until you try.
—Sophocles

Knowing is not enough; we must apply. Willing is not enough; we must do.
—Goethe

It is only when we develop others that we permanently succeed.
—Harvey S. Firestone

Managers must be capable to have companies exploit emerging opportunities; employees need skills to operate technology. Rapid changes in products and customer preferences and the explosion of knowledge and technology make learning critical for organizational productivity. U.S. companies spend as much as $100 billion annually for seminars, simulations, interactive computer programs, video demonstrations, and other kinds of education and training.[1]

A very disturbing reason why companies must encourage learning is the United States' educational and socialization crises.[2] While there are many well-prepared students, an astonishing number of young persons are poorly equipped for the demands and requirements of contemporary organizations. It is not just a matter of inadequate academic preparation. Many young persons are alienated from schools and society. The annual repair bill for damages done to schools is more than $200 million; each month 128,000 teachers and 2.4 million students report something stolen and 5,200 teachers and 282,000 students report being physically assaulted.[3]

Companies must cope with emotionally troubled young workers who lack the skills and self-confidence to apply themselves. Psychological problems are by no means restricted to the young. Rehabilitation centers report dramatic increases in high-level executives admitted for chemical dependence; they predict the number may double annually with the rapid increase in drug abuse in business.[4]

How can organizations help managers and employees learn ideas and skills, strengthen their confidence, and enhance their emotional lives? A powerful, practical way is through working together. Recent books have portrayed successful leaders as coaches; managers must teach and develop their employees.[5] New recruits are encouraged to adopt experienced managers as mentors from whom they learn the competence and savvy to be successful.

Employees learn people skills through collaboration. They learn to trust, communicate, and manage conflicts. Support and feedback build self-aware-ness and self-confidence; working collaboratively enhances feelings of self-worth and self-control. But people learn essential problem solving and tech-nical skills as well. By digging into complex issues, checking and correcting each other's thinking, and creating new solutions, team members not only accomplish their project, but also get better at solving problems. By working with others, managers learn the techniques needed to lead. By encouraging and assisting, workers acquire the technical skills and knowledge to accom-plish tasks more efficiently.

Skills in working with others are not simply social manners that make work more gracious, nor are they appropriate only for the people side of organizational life. Instead, they are at the heart of being an effective manager and employee. Working cooperatively greatly helps persons use their experi-ences to learn the people, technical, and problem-solving skills necessary to be successful.

Understanding the cooperation ideas and procedures discussed in earlier chapters is only the first step toward using them. Bridging the gap between an idea and its application is difficult because the idea must be adapted to the specific situation. Actually maintaining cooperative goals during a lively conflict can be far from obvious and simple. Practice, experience, and more practice are needed to transform ideas and procedures into approaches that managers and employees will use to work together well.

Learning through Experience

People learn from their job even if the organization does not encourage them. Assembly-line workers discover that by doing their job very fast for a while and then covering for each other, they can make the job less routine and prolong their breaks. They may learn that they must suppress their conflicts with the supervisor or that they can discuss them productively. Some workers conclude that they have little power and control over their work and their lives; others conclude that they make their own decisions. It is not whether employees learn but what they learn and how well they learn it.

Making Use of Experience

Most people believe that they learn to work together to solve problems and complete tasks through experience. But it is not simply experience that teaches. People learn much different ideas from the same experience; they may have years of experience but learn little. People must make use of their experience to learn.

Let's take a look at how managers use experience to learn. In one study, a majority of managers thought that they had learned valuable lessons from having an intolerable boss.[6] They learned that it is important to recognize employees publicly for their accomplishments and give them enough autonomy to show what they can do. They also learned that bosses who are difficult to work with often are insecure or have other problems that are not at first apparent. Not all the managers indicated that they profited from the experience, however. Indeed, managers may have learned harmful approaches. They may have concluded that the company encourages autocratic leadership and that they too must be tough and insensitive. Managers may learn productive or negative lessons from a boss. How they understand and reflect on their boss determines their conclusions and learning. What one already knows determines what one learns.

Often learning from experience is thought to mean learning from mistakes. Frustrations and failures challenge present views and habits, initiate a reexamination, and motivate change. But reflecting on successes also teaches. People appreciate their accomplishments, resolve self-doubts, and refine and improve their abilities. They learn a great deal from success.

Not everyone is equally interested or adept at reflection and learning. Some managers and employees make good use of opportunities, whereas others seem trapped by mistakes, even oblivious to them. Employees need ideas and procedures to analyze and learn from experience.

Steps to Learning from Experience

Bob Clinton realized that the conflict between Jenny McCollough and Dennis Mann was getting in the way of the department's work. He invited them into his office, asked them to work out the problem, and tried to mediate so that the conflict would be managed productively. Bob wanted them to see that their goals were cooperative, identify the underlying problem, and create a solution.

After the discussion, Bob asked them how helpful they had found the session. Did they understand how they could work out the problem? What else might he and they do to resolve the conflict? Jenny said that she better understood what made Dennis upset. Dennis indicated that he thought Bob had pushed them to develop a solution before he had a chance to make sure Jenny understood the problem. Bob, Jenny, and Dennis were learning from experience. They applied their knowledge about conflict and then reflected on experience to develop and modify their ideas.

The three major phases of learning from experience are ideas and theories, experience to apply the ideas, and reflection on the experience to draw conclusions.[7] These steps form a continuing cycle; present ideas lead to action, the reflection on the action leads to refined ideas, these refined ideas lead to action, and so on.

The first phase includes the ideas, theories, conclusions, and values used to organize, observe, analyze, and suggest action. Ideas can be general and loosely related to each other. For instance, we value genuineness but also want politeness. Some ideas are closely related and form an action theory.[8] These theories are normative and indicate action needed to achieve a specific end. They have an If . . . then form. If we smile at our boss, then she will think well of us. If we reprimand a tardy employee, then he will be on time in the future.

The ideas are applied in the second step to learning from experience. People use their present framework to plan and prepare themselves, understand the situation, and act. Two colleagues use their ideas to define and approach a conflict. If they conclude that it is competitive, they behave much differently than if they believe it is cooperative.

The third, critical phase is to reflect on the experience. People gather information on what happened to test the effectiveness of their ideas and strategies. Actual results are compared to the desired and anticipated consequences. Ideas and strategies that result in benefits become more accepted and incorporated. Unwanted consequences call for refining ideas and actions, and persistently negative results indicate that the idea and strategy should be rejected. In this way, experience, and reflection form a reinforcing cycle.

Learning with Others

Not everyone learns useful lessons from experience; such learning demands intellectual abilities and emotional strength. People must be willing to test their ideas, receive feedback, consider the consequences of their present style, adopt more useful ideas and approaches, and subject these new ideas to further testing. They must become aware of the strengths and weaknesses of their present assumptions and ideas, understand how more useful ideas can be applied in different settings, and be willing to practice using these ideas. People by themselves can learn from experience, but it is much more likely that several employees together are able to learn. Cooperative teams help people test their ideas and adopt more useful approaches.

Teams Encourage Self-Examination. People working together can better test their present ideas and approaches. They must examine their behavior and open-mindedly consider alternatives. Employees working cooperatively provide psychological support for self-disclosure and self-examination. They reveal their present views to those who they trust will not rebuke them. They are supported to evaluate their ideas and skills honestly and plan how to improve.

Teams Provide Feedback to Enhance Self-Understanding. People need help to overcome intellectual and psychological barriers and to understand how they affect others. Managers are especially vulnerable because employees feel obligated to protect themselves and their boss from information that may make the boss look bad. The boss often is the last one to know that her actions intimidate her subordinates. But bosses are not alone; employees misread their boss, and peers misread each other. Managers and employees need others' feedback to realize the consequences of their actions and to begin to assess the usefulness of their ideas and strategies.

Teams Provide Emotional Support Needed to Accept Feedback. Many ideas and beliefs about working with others are rooted deeply in personality and self-image. They have been adopted over the years and have become an integral part of the person. Reflecting on experience may challenge these basic beliefs. A person may be faced with the feedback that he has not been reasonable, fair, and appropriate. Without adequate support, he may deny the validity of the feedback, blame the messenger, and in other ways defend himself.[9]

Many managers appear to be unaware of the ideas that guide their behavior and the negative effects of their style on subordinates. Indeed, they espouse ideals about collaboration without realizing that they compete. They are not by themselves able to evaluate how they manage or gauge the actual impact their style has on others. Managers in learning teams, however, give each other the feedback and emotional support needed to understand their behavior and its impact.[10]

Teams Cope with the Emotional Side of Change. Ideas, values, and attitudes are grounded in relationships; they are learned from and with the support of others. Changing attitudes raises concerns about giving up old attitudes and implicitly challenging the persons from whom one learned them. Change also arouses fears about whether the new outlooks are correct and useful; their very newness makes them suspect. Knowing that others accept the new approaches and believe that they are useful reassures us that the new ideas and behaviors are valid and that it is reasonable to embrace them.

Teams Help People Plan How to Be More Effective. People who have tested their ideas and understand feedback on how they affect others are motivated to consider change and improve their approaches. But to adopt new ways of working is intellectually demanding. Interactions are varied and complex, and recognizing the implications of ideas in many settings and cases is not simple. In conflict, for example, the issues involved, intensity, manner of expression, seriousness, number of persons, and previous interaction all vary. The strong feelings and emotions often provoked during interaction can make planning difficult. Analyzing the situation and deciding how to use an idea to act in it demand insight and sensitivity. For example, managers and employees can jointly decide how to incorporate positive power and constructive controversy in their own department.

To learn from experience, managers and employees must review their present assumptions and approaches, understand how their actions affect others and receive their feedback, incorporate new approaches into their style, and test these new ideas and strategies. Cooperative groups are very useful, for they help individuals cope with the intellectual and emotional demands needed to make productive use of experience.

Guides for Action

Learning Together

- Recognize that learning is for everyone.
- Reinforce that everyone benefits from learning.
- Listen and accept feedback.
- Orient teams to learn as they do their job.
- Learn from successes as well as mistakes.

Pitfalls to Avoid

- Assume that learning is only for junior employees.
- Concentrate on short-term productivity and forget learning.
- Rush, rush, hurry, hurry, and keep making the same mistakes.
- Blame people rather than learn from mistakes.

Cooperative Learning at Work

How is the great potential of collegial teams used for training and learning from experience? Informal discussions among co-workers, team meetings, mentoring programs, and explicit learning groups all can help employees help each other to use their experiences, apply ideas from this and other books, give feedback, encourage, and persist in experimenting and learning to apply ideas and skills at work.

Informal Discussions

Employees want to talk about how they work with each other. They are exhilarated by another's kindness and affection and want to share their good feelings. They are irritated that a colleague dimissed their idea; these feelings churn inside and push for expression. They are unsure whether they bullied their employee or challenged him to work better. Talking about frustrations, problems, and experiences are very human needs. People typically feel relieved, optimistic, and more confident when they have talked to others.

It is not surprising then that employees informally share their feelings, frustrations, and hopes. They will find office mates, friends, colleagues, spouses, or someone to turn to discuss their relationships. Colleagues exchange information, give each other feedback, plan how to enhance their careers, and provide emotional support and confirmation that allows them to withstand the rigors of their job and to learn.[11]

A danger with these informal groups is that employees may learn that they must protect each other from the boss, slow their productivity, avoid disagreeing with their superiors, and take other harmful approaches. Companies and employees are better off if employees are explicitly encouraged to discuss and learn valid, useful ideas about how to work effectively with others.

Work Teams

Project teams, task forces, worker groups, and other teams established to get jobs done simultaneously promote learning. As they get their job done, they also identify the members' abilities and reinforce and develop them. They engage in peer teaching to help everyone become more effective. They also can discuss how they are working together to identify weaknesses and strengths and to improve their skills. Work teams may use special sessions such as weekend retreats, have learning as an ongoing agenda topic, or informally help each other learn.

Mentoring

Junior managers develop mentoring relationships with senior members of the company both informally and in established programs. Young managers must navigate in the world of work to be successful in the company. Mentors guide and counsel younger workers through this difficult task.[12] Mentors teach by sharing information, experiences, and advice. They guide by welcoming the young adults into the organization and showing them its values, customs, and people. Mentors sponsor newcomers by facilitating their assignment to challenging, rewarding projects and promoting career advancement.

At Jewel Companies, chief executives have for decades served as mentors for their successors.[13] Incoming employees with M.B.A. degrees are now assigned to members of top management. Recently, AT&T's Bell Labs, the Internal Revenue Service, Hughes Aircraft, and Merrill Lynch have developed formal mentoring programs.[14] The company matches mentors and younger volunteers and suggests useful activities.

Simulations

IBM, AT&T, Monsanto, and other companies have sent managers to the Looking Glass, Inc., training exercise that simulates corporate life with a hierarchy of commands, overflowing in-boxes, and pressing deadlines.[15] Participants read the company history, are assigned roles, and report for work in the morning. They usually become highly involved and take their tasks and roles seriously. Simulations and structured experiences have been used for decades in training.

Learning comes through reflection on the simulation experience. Participants usually meet as a group to share their impressions, provide feedback, and help people understand the impact of their management style. For the Looking Glass, Inc., simulation, each participant is evaluated by others and trainers in a series of feedback sessions. The participants share their impressions and indicate how they experienced each other's management style. They identify what helped and got in their way of working effectively as a team. Ideally, participants become more aware of their own strengths and weaknesses in working with others, and they become more knowledgeable about effective management and what is needed to make a successful management team.

Developmental Groups

Staff members of an organization that provides residential care and treatment for handicapped children were trained and conscientious. They took pride in the fact that their children were becoming more competent and more independent. When the facility expanded and accepted very severely handicapped children, however, many staff members became disillusioned and began to doubt their own effectiveness. They received few indications that the new children were learning and becoming more independent. They were at a loss for what might have a more positive impact. Simply working harder did not seem to be the answer.

Staff members felt supported by the administrator but rarely by each other. The administrator and the staff decided that those who worked with the same children and at overlapping times would form staff development teams. In these groups, they discussed the problems of specific children and provided feedback to each other about their work. They had opportunities to learn more about their approaches and together designed new programs. They held regular sessions to strengthen how they worked together and to help each other work more effectively with the children.

Staff members at an agency that provided services for the visually impaired indicated in structured interviews and surveys that they often felt quite frustrated with clients who did not respond to counseling. They also felt isolated from co-workers and thought that it was unprofessional to reveal their feelings and failures. After discussing the results of the survey and the idea of staff support groups, they decided to use team meetings to discuss their feelings, get feedback on their efforts, and openly discuss their work with individual clients. They also shared clients with complex problems and the frustration and learning they experienced in dealing with these clients.

These development teams required members to be persistent and skillful. They had to overcome inertia to meet and take the risks to ask for and give feedback. Many staff members were unaccustomed to sharing their feelings or having their behavior examined; as professionals they thought that they should already be highly competent. Groups that overcame initial barriers became cohesive, discussed clients, got feedback on their behavior, found help and support in their groups, and enjoyed their camaraderie.

Procedures for Reflection

Most organizations, even today, discourage discussions about how persons work together. Employees are expected to keep their feelings to themselves and not waste time arguing and discussing personal issues. Relationships should be businesslike—task-oriented, rational, impersonal, and devoid of discussions of interpersonal experiences and troubles. Thinking about relationships is considered time-wasting brooding; talking to others is gossiping and spreading rumors. These norms and attitudes, although they do not stop people from thinking about their work relationships, make open, constructive discussion difficult. How can reflecting on experiences be constructive?

Cooperative Goals

Employees recognize that the purpose of discussing how they work as a team is for all to learn and improve their work situations. They recognize that everyone is responsible for the present situation and that everyone must work to improve it. All employees benefit when their relationships are strengthened. Their goal is not to find who is at fault or to focus on individuals' weaknesses but to help each other become more confident. They guard against distractions and stick to the issues. Their common goal is to develop their skills and to improve how they work together.

Openness

All employees, regardless of their power and prestige in the company, have the opportunity to express their opinions and feelings and the information and reasoning that lie behind them. They do not just do their own thing or assert themselves but communicate their feelings so that others feel more informed and able to express their feelings.[16] They listen carefully and paraphrase each other's comments to make sure they understand.

Feedback Skills

Employees describe their perceptions and feelings about each other's behavior in specific terms. The emphasis is on sharing information and understanding rather than evaluating. They talk about their feelings and reactions to the team and its members and describe what led them to draw their conclusions. They minimize labeling and judging because such evaluation interferes with communication. People who feel that they are being evaluated often become defensive and closed-minded. Labels and abstract terms also do not clearly communicate people's observations and reactions to the team.

Problem Solving

Managers and employees work to understand the situation and problems rather than jump quickly to a solution. They want to investigate the past, not to find fault but to understand it and the reasons why problems arise. They develop a common understanding of their strengths and weaknesses. They use all available information and reasoning to dig into the issues, understand their relationships, and identify barriers and obstacles. They compare their present skills and work relationships with ideally effective ones.

They work to develop realistic solutions. They are not rigidly committed to their original position, but encourage opposing views and combine ideas to create a workable, effective solution. The best ideas, information, and reasoning are combined to formulate ways of improving work relationships. They focus on the issues and select a solution based on the facts of the situation that promotes everyone's interests. The responsibilities to implement the solution are shared so that all employees know concretely how they should act to improve how they work together.

A Developmental View

Skills and relationships need time to develop, and problems often are difficult to solve. The goal should be to make progress rather than to solve all issues quickly and become a completely successful team. Open reflection and discussion should be a regular, accepted part of working together. People should take the open, successful discussions as convincing evidence that they are making progress. They celebrate small as well as major gains in their ability and confidence to work as a team.

Concluding Comments

Teamwork is essential for a competent work force and a productive company. By working with others, tasks get accomplished and problems solved. Learning to work with others is much more than simply getting along; it is learning how to produce, solve problems, and manage. Learning cooperative ideas, procedures, and skills is not just something nice to know but the key to personal and organizational success.

Reading this book and learning from experience complement each other. Experience is necessary to apply and understand fully the ideas discussed here. But experience itself does not teach. Employees need to know their present ideas, understand new ones and their implications, experiment with applying ideas, and reflect on their ideas and strategies. In teams, employees help each other test their ideas and approaches, receive feedback and understand the impact of their style, and consider and adopt more effective ways to work. *Cooperation is a double-edged strategy: People work effectively and learn skills that will help them to work more effectively in the future.*

13
Creating a Productive Organization

When I started to sacrifice, I saw other people do whatever was necessary. And that's how Chrysler pulled through. . . . It was like a family getting together. . . . This was cooperation and democracy at their best. I'm not talking about a Bible lesson here. I'm talking about real life. We went through it. It works. It's like magic and it awes you.

—Lee Iacocca

In their search to improve productivity, deliver new products, make use of emerging technology, penetrate world markets, and build employee commitment, entrepreneurial managers are creating new ways to organize. They want innovative management that nurtures people, for people are the key to organizational excellence. People working together create the company's strategy, select its employees, invent and use its technology, and market its products. Managers must demand quality and performance but, simultaneously, respect and care for the people who make the organization work. How can organizations be both efficient and humane? How can managers be both tender and tough-minded?

This book provides a powerful *method for managers to be passionate about productivity and compassionate about people.* By helping employees work together, managers develop an organization that serves its employees and its community. Through effective teamwork, companies create valued products and services, exploit opportunities, and adapt to changes. Cooperative work binds employees together and to the company. People feel appreciated and cared for and are proud to be a part of a winning team.

Challenges for Managers

Managers have a special, challenging role: They are the architects of cooperation and relationships through which work gets done, problems are solved, and people feel enhanced. As this and other recent books suggest, managerial leaders facilitate, cheer, and encourage rather than do, order, and dominate. Contrary to the belief that this role takes away from managers and supervisors, behaving in this way enhances what they have to contribute.

Cooperative Goals and Skills

To develop teamwork, managers must work to have employees conclude that their goals are cooperatively linked: As one succeeds, others also succeed; as one fails, they all fail. It is not enough that managers believe that employees do or should see their goals as positively related; employees themselves must be committed to goals that they believe make them all better off. Managers must promote a shared vision and the values of teamwork and support. Tasks are assigned to groups and rewards given for successful collaborative work. Employees openly discuss their aspirations to understand that their goals are cooperative and commit themselves to assisting each other.

Managers also must see to it that employees develop the skills and procedures to work cooperatively. Employees must recognize and use each other's abilities and openly discuss their opposing views to solve problems and make decisions. They must be able to discuss interpersonal difficulties and conflicts productively so that they continue to work cooperatively. Some individuals exploit cooperation by shirking their responsibilities. Employees who try to take a free ride should be held accountable and confronted.

Nurturing Teamwork

Working together demands constant attention and care. Misunderstandings obscure cooperative goals. It seems easy for persons, especially groups, to compete unless they have strong evidence that cooperation is more advantageous. Although cooperation reinforces itself, some of its consequences can make future collaboration difficult.[1] Individuals and groups, as they specialize to complete common tasks, develop their own language and form cliques that may be more committed to their own interests than company goals. The openness to influence in cooperation can turn to strong pressures to conform and avoid conflicts that undermine the group.

Working together must be nurtured, strengthened, and managed. Managers must continually remind employees that their goals are cooperative and that they need to refine their skills and procedures to work cooperatively. Employees must periodically reflect on their work relationships, solve problems, and create more effective ways to work together. Cooperative skills must be sharpened; conflict with new people and issues can require additional skills. Teamwork is a double-edged productivity strategy: It not only gets the job done, but it also helps employees learn from their experiences, develop their competence, and be more productive in the future.

This book has summarized ideas and their research support, discussed implications, identified procedures and skills, and shown through examples how to apply ideas. But it has not devised a concrete plan that automatically results in productive teamwork. With your understanding of cooperative work, you must create your own plans that will be useful for your group, department, and company. You must adapt approaches and procedures to fit your style and circumstance. But you need not do this alone. A cooperative team can help managers identify problems and opportunities and develop approaches to inspire everyone to work together. The problem-solving group described in chapter 4 can be used as a guide.

Working with Customers, Suppliers, and Investors

Cooperation spreads out far beyond an organization's boundaries. Companies are becoming highly market-oriented. They are urged to move beyond reading surveys and projections to listening to the customer.[2] But more than listening is required. Employees must talk with customers, discuss new products, understand their perspective, know how they use and view the company's products, and solicit their suggestions to develop new ones. In addition, managers, technicians, sales representatives, and workers must discuss what they have learned from customers. At 3M, employee teams collaborate with customers and develop a relationship in which the customer works with them on the common goal of improved products and services.

Companies also must work with suppliers. Ford, GM, and Chrysler realized that they needed high-quality components to deliver high-quality cars that could compete with imports. They have adopted just-in-time delivery to reduce inventory and hold the line on costs.

Citicorp, under its new president, John Reed, is moving away from a style of unalloyed aggressiveness that alienated its regulators and created doubts in the investment community.[3] They have recognized the costs of this approach and have decided to work more cooperatively. In the words of Lawrence M. Small, the new head of commercial banking, "We have a clear tendency toward arrogance [and] occasionally demonstrate an almost uncontrollable urge for confrontation when regulators or other authority figures differ with us. . . . What we want is to [become a] . . . high-performance machine with great power and handling ability, but with a touch more grace, elegance, and dignity."

Cooperation within an organization reinforces working effectively with those outside it. Employees who cooperate with each other develop the skills and are emotionally prepared to work together with those outside the organization.

An international airlines is in danger of losing its reputation for friendly, helpful service. The stewards and attendants on my last flight were abrupt, preoccupied, and unhelpful. In an interview with company officials who manage the flight crews, the following picture emerged. The company had decided that it owed its success to service, therefore it must be very diligent about its flight crews. Unfortunately, the managers did not initiate programs to have flight crews work as a cooperative team in which they could support each other, help each other cope with the rigors of long flights, and learn to serve passengers. Instead, they put heavy pressure on each individual. Attendants knew that their steward had to rate them after each flight and that the company hired more evaluators to fly incognito.

Many attendants were reprimanded, several lost their jobs, and others quit. Under these conditions, few attendants could manage their stress so that they could work effectively, make passengers feel relaxed and welcome, and solve problems. The personnel department had to undertake a very expensive international recruiting program to maintain standards. But partly because of company efforts, one basis for the airline's success is threatened.

The ideas and skills explained in this book, though discussed in terms of developing teamwork between the individuals and groups that make up a company, are useful for working with persons outside its boundaries. Of course, companies must compete for markets, but they also must develop strong, cooperative links with customers, suppliers, investors, experts, and regulators.

Competitive and Independent Work

Proctor & Gamble, Johnson & Johnson, 3M, Campbell Soup, Mervyn's, and IBM all use internal competition.[4] Several teams work in parallel to develop new products. The company chooses the prototype that it believes has the most potential. Divisions compete in the same market. Groups and individuals have successfully competed to sign up the most new customers, reduce the most costs, and make the most sales.

Competition can be useful—if certain conditions are created. The individuals and groups should have sufficient knowledge, resources, and confidence that they can win and have no need to share each other's abilities. Although individuals and groups in serious competition cannot be expected to assist each other and work together, competition can at times be productive and fun.

Independent employees can accomplish many tasks efficiently. Not all tasks warrant the combined attention and talents of several persons; coordinating with others is a costly nuisance for many tasks. To work independently, employees should have all the abilities and information needed to do the job, feel challenged by the task, and be rewarded when they have completed it themselves.

Competition and independence have their place, but cooperation best accomplishes important, complex tasks. Cooperation should be the underlying dependence in the organization. Individuals who work alone then recognize that their typing a letter, making a sale, or operating a machine are all part of a larger, common enterprise. They realize that their performing well helps others and themselves; they know that others will help them when needed. Their task takes on more meaning, for it is related to important goals shared by the others in the company.

Useful competition also occurs within a larger cooperative context. Two teams want to win the competition for the new product, but they also recognize that they and the company are best served when the better product wins or when they are able to combine their ideas to develop the best product. Two supervisors compete for a job promotion but do not let that interfere with getting the job done. Competition and independent work are constructive when the underlying cooperative links are present and strong.

Doubts about Cooperation

Cooperation evokes some fears and disquieting questions. Doesn't cooperation suppress individuality, ignore individual interests, and deny individual rights? Won't cooperation produce a conformity and an oppressive equality where the group, not the individual, is served? Managers, economists, and philosophers have long argued whether cooperation stifles the human spirit and productivity. Competition is much lauded in traditional free-market and U.S. economic and social thought. A full examination of these issues would take books, but the following comments based on the research reviewed in this book shed some light.

Individuality

Cooperation fosters individuality. People contribute in different ways to the common project. If one member of the group completes the drawing, there is no need for others to do the same. As they specialize, persons develop their own expertise and point of view. Independent ideas and abilities are appreciated and valued in cooperation. People realize that the more capable and diligent others are, the more successful they all will be. They express their opposing views more freely because they feel confident that the controversy will be productive.

Through cooperation, persons get to know each other as individuals, take each other's perspective, and value each other as persons. Cooperative interaction repeatedly has been found to break down stereotypes and develop liking and appreciation for people with different ethnic, economic, and racial backgrounds.[5]

Cooperation serves the individual. It is a vehicle for individuals to reach their goals and promote their interests. Cooperation does not ask for self-denial and altruism but only that people see that by working together they can all attain their objectives.

Cooperation supports the well-being and psychological development of individuals. Through cooperative interaction, persons get feedback and support that helps them become more self-aware and more self-confident. They learn social competence, emotional maturity, problem solving, and technical skills through cooperation. Cooperators, compared to persons who prefer to compete or work independently, have high, unconditional self-regard, positive mental health, and an absence of psychological pathologies.[6]

But cooperation must be well structured and properly carried out to be so beneficial. Cooperation can result in oppressive conformity and, as some cults illustrate, can be used to manipulate and exploit. Individual abilities and power must be recognized, opposing views encouraged to solve problems, and norms established to discuss conflicts productively. Cooperative teamwork has great potential for individuals, but it is not magic and must be skillfully and humanely managed.

Equality

Does cooperation push for an unrealistic equality? Rewards in cooperation are distributed to the extent that the group, department, and organization as a whole has been successful. But that does not mean that everyone gets the same rewards. A venture group is cooperatively rewarded when everyone receives a bonus as their product increases sales, but not everyone need get the same bonus. The group leader or a person who has worked the longest and hardest may be rewarded more than others. The CEO draws a higher salary than the vice presidents, but they can still work cooperatively.

Cooperation does not imply that everyone has the same power and authority; managers need power and authority to do their job. Cooperative goals do encourage people to use their power for mutual advantage. Cooperative work does not require employee ownership, democratic management, or forming a cooperative. These alternatives to traditional capitalist organizations can be viable,[7] but type of ownership does not determine an organization's success. All organizations need to be skillfully managed so that people work together to get things done.

Cooperation, though, does appear to foster an equality in that it demands that unequal rewards be justified. Team members want to know why others receive more. If they are not convinced that there are good reasons for this, they are apt to concentrate on getting more for themselves rather than on contributing to the group as a whole. More generally, invidious comparisons break down cooperation.[8] Differences in preferences, needs, and abilities must be recognized, but highly evaluative comparisons between people heighten competition. The emphasis on cooperation is on community and valuing everyone, not determining who are winners and who are losers.

Fairness

Many people doubt that cooperation is fair and reasonable. They worry that people will be rewarded for what the group does rather than for what individuals do and that some will exploit the opportunity and slacken their personal effort. As was already discussed, cooperators can be rewarded differently, and persons who shirk their responsibilities must be confronted. Team rewards are fair for the many tasks that individuals cannot complete alone.

Establishing an effective, fair reward system is difficult and time-consuming, but group rewards actually are more practical than individual rewards. To reward effectively, meaningful rewards must be selected, standards accurately communicated, and performance validly measured. In addition, employees must accept the system.[9] Group rewards have the advantage because managers must do these tasks for each team rather than for each individual.

We typically think in terms of the individual versus the group. But this either-or thinking is misleading. The individual depends on others and thrives by working and living with others. Cooperative teamwork fosters individuality and group solidarity.

A New Organizational Chart

In addition to identifying procedures to make teams and organizations more productive, the ideas developed in this book outline a general perspective on how organizations can and should work. This perspective suggests a new kind of organizational chart.

Most companies use some form of a pyramid to indicate how they should operate. The board of directors and the CEO are at the top, followed by executives, middle managers, supervisors, and workers. Authority follows these levels. Persons on top exert control by making decisions, instructing those below, and using their power to reward compliance. But this view is increasingly obsolete.

The new chart must recognize that the group, not the individual, is the basic building block of the organization. Departments, project teams, task forces, and other cooperative teams complete the important assignments; employees working independently understand that their tasks contribute to the success of the group. The chart also recognizes that managers and other leaders work in the middle of their groups to encourage and assist; they do not lord over them from above.

Let's take an example. The $4 million Siegal Corporation makes Allen wrenches and balldrives for manufacturing companies. The company's fifty-five employees are in four major departments: production, marketing, human resources, and administration. Each department is critical to the company's success, and each uses teams for important tasks.

Because of its limited product line, need for economies of scale, and de-

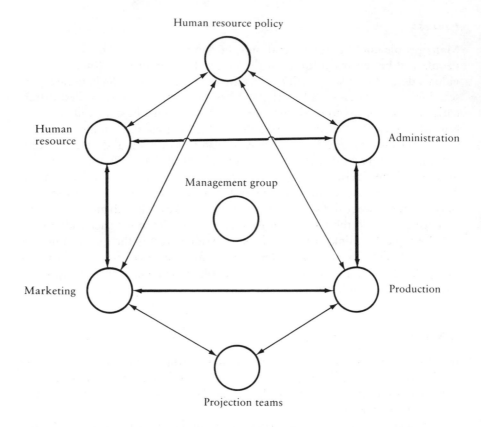

Figure 13–1. Siegal Corporation Organizational Chart

sire to learn, Siegal aggressively developed exports and was able to earn more than 50 percent of the Japanese market for balldrives. Every year, the marketing department prepares an elaborate fact sheet on the world economy, the gross national products of the countries in which Siegal does business, user-industry indicators, median incomes, and other conditions that affect sales. Then for each product line, marketing specialists join with production managers to develop the sales projections and production plans that will guide their work for the rest of the year.

Siegal needs high-quality products to maintain its exports. In production, groups of workers meet regularly to improve the quality of the tools and discuss work issues; supervisors use a consensus style of management to work more efficiently and improve quality.

The human-resource policy committee, chaired by the department's head, oversees Siegal's progressive employment practices. President James Siegal, the vice president of administration, and one salaried and one hourly representative from each department serve on the committee. This group determines vacation policy, benefit package, allowances for safety apparel, and company layoffs. The committee decided that if the company was unable to reach its profit goals, everyone would take a 20 percent cut in salary before any other retrenchment measures were taken.

Siegal's organizational chart (figure 13–1) shows the prominence of teams. Assignments to departments are permanent, whereas membership in the human-resource policy group and sales and production projection groups is temporary. The production department is itself broken down into groups. Siegal Corporation is participative, and employees feel cared for, respected, and powerful. But James Siegal and the department managers are still central to the company's success. They are more accurately portrayed, however, in the middle of the company and their groups, not on top of them.

Closing Remarks

The great experiment in organizing is on, and this is an exciting, challenging, and rewarding time to be a manager. Companies are testing new strategies and designs. Some companies will thrive by being low-cost producers, others by high value-added products; some will flourish through high tech and others through low tech. Companies are using project teams, matrix management, division decentralization, and other designs. But because the forms and procedures that work for one company do not necessarily work for others, managers are trying alternative ways of organizing to see what works best for them.

Regardless of the organization's strategy or design, the ideas, procedures, and skills outlined in this book are critical because combined performance is what counts. Within and across departments, people must work together; an organization is much more than a collection of individuals doing their own thing. Bright strategic, financial, and marketing specialists are very useful, but by themselves they do not make an organization productive. Strategy, finances, and salesmanship all are important, but specialists must work with each other as well as with executives, middle managers, supervisors, workers, and customers to create effective solutions and to put them in place. Managers have a vital mission, for they develop the collaboration essential for a successful organization.

Where will the experimenting in management lead us? What will future organizations look like? My guess is that we will be surprised by what we create. No matter what the organization's mission, design, or size, cooperative goals, positive power, constructive controversy, and productive conflict will be just as important in the future as they are today.

Notes

Introduction

1. P.F. Drucker, *Innovation and Entrepreneurship: Practices and Principles* (New York: Harper & Row, 1985).

2. W.G. Ouchi, *Theory Z: How American Business Can Meet the Japanese Challenge* (Reading, MA: Addison-Wesley, 1981); T.J. Peters & R.H. Waterman, *In Search of Excellence: Lessons from America's Best-Run Companies* (New York: Harper & Row, 1982).

Chapter 1. Working Together and Management

1. K. Weick, *The Social Psychology of Organizing* (Reading, MA: Addison-Wesley, 1979).

2. R. Levering, M. Moskowitz, & M. Katz, *The One Hundred Best Companies to Work For in America* (Reading, MA: Addison-Wesley, 1984). W.G. Ouchi, *Theory Z: How American Business Can Meet the Japanese Challenge* (Reading, MA: Addison-Wesley, 1981); T.J. Peters & R.H. Waterman, *In Search of Excellence: Lessons from America's Best-Run Companies* (New York: Harper & Row, 1982).

3. T.J. Peters & R.H. Waterman, *In Search of Excellence: Lessons from America's Best-Run Companies* (New York: Harper & Row, 1982).

4. M.M. Lombardo & M.W. McCall, Jr., *Coping with an Intolerable Boss* (Greensboro, NC: Center for Creative Leadership, 1984).

5. D.W. Johnson & R.T. Johnson, "The Socialization and Achievement Crisis: Are Cooperative Learning Experiences the Solution," in L. Bickman (ed.), *Applied Social Psychology Annual* 4 (Beverly Hills, CA: Sage Publications, 1983): 119–164. D. Tjosvold, "Cooperation Theory and Organizations," *Human Relations* 37 (1984): 743–767.

6. D. Tjosvold, I.R. Andrews, & H. Jones, "Cooperative and Competitive Relationships Between Leaders and Subordinates," *Human Relations* 36 (1983): 1111–1124. D. Robertson & D. Tjosvold, "Staff Relations, Job Commitment, and Acceptance of Elderly in Long Term Care Facilities," paper, Academy of Management Meetings, Chicago, 1986.

7. T. Peters & N. Austin, *A Passion for Excellence* (New York: Random House, 1985).

8. M.D. Cohen & J.G. March, *Leadership and Ambiguity* (New York: McGraw-Hill, 1974). R.H. Guest, "Of Time and the Foreman," *Personnel* 32 (1956): 478–486. C.M. Pavett & A.W. Lau, "Managerial Work: The Influence of Hierarchical Level and Functional Specialty," *Academy of Management Journal* 26 (1983): 170–177.

9. E. Brewer & J.W.C. Tomlinson, "The Manager's Working Day," *The Journal of Industrial Economics* 12 (1964): 191–197. T. Burns, "Management in Action," *Operational Research Quarterly* 8 (1957): 45–60. M.D. Cohen & J.G. March, *Leadership and Ambiguity* (New York: McGraw-Hill, 1974). J.H. Horne & T. Lupton, "The Work Activities of 'Middle' Managers: An Exploratory Study," *The Journal of Management Studies* 2 (1965): 14–33. H. Mintzberg, "Structured Observation as a Method to Study Managerial Work," *The Journal of Management Studies* 7 (1970): 87–104.

10. M.D. Cohen & J.G. March, *Leadership and Ambiguity* (New York: McGraw-Hill, 1974). R. Stewart, *Managers and Their Jobs: A Study of the Similarities and Differences in the Way Managers Spend Their Time* (London: MacMillan, 1967).

11. H. Mintzberg, "Structured Observation as a Method to Study Managerial Work," *The Journal of Management Studies* 7 (1970): 87–104.

12. T. Dahl & D.R. Lewis, "Random Sampling Device Used in Time Management Study," *Evaluation* 2 (1975): 20–22. H. Mintzberg, "Structured Observation as a Method to Study Managerial Work," *The Journal of Management Studies* 7 (1970): 87–104.

13. T. Dahl & D.R. Lewis, "Random Sampling Device Used in Time Management Study," *Evaluation* 2 (1975): 20–22. F. de P. Hanika, "How to Study Your Executive Day," in G. Copeman, H. Luijk, & F. de P. Hanika, *How the Executive Spends His Day* (London: Business Publications, 1963). J.R. Hinrichs, "Communications Activity of Industrial Research Personnel," *Personnel Psychology* 17 (1964): 193–204.

14. T. Janz & D. Tjosvold, "Costing Effective Versus Ineffective Work Relationships: A Method and A First Look," *Canadian Journal of Administrative Sciences* 2 (1985): 43–51.

15. E.E. Sampson, "Psychology and the American Ideal," *Journal of Personality and Social Psychology* 35 (1977): 767–782.

16. E. Mayo, *The Human Problems of an Industrial Civilization* (New York: Macmillan, 1933). J.A. Sonnenfield, "Shedding Light on the Hawthorne Studies," *Journal of Occupational Behaviour* 6 (1985): 110–130.

17. K. Lewin, R. Lippitt, & R.K. White, "Patterns of Aggressive Behavior in Experimentally Created Social Climates," *Journal of Social Psychology* 10 (1939): 271–299.

18. L. Coch & J.R.P. French, Jr., "Overcoming Resistance to Change," *Human Relations* 1 (1948): 512–532.

19. S. Strasser & T.S. Bateman, "What We Should Study, Problems We Should Solve: Perspectives of Two Constituencies," *Personnel Psychology* 37 (1984): 77–92.

20. C. Argyris, *Intervention Theory and Method: A Behavioral Science View* (Reading, MA: Addison-Wesley, 1970). C. Argyris & D. Schon, *Organizational*

Learning (Reading, MA: Addison-Wesley, 1978). R. Likert, *The Human Organization* (New York: McGraw-Hill, 1967). C.A. Schriesheim, & S. Kerr, "Theories and Measures of Leadership: A Critical Appraisal of Current and Future Directions," in J.G. Hunt & L.L. Larson (eds.), *Leadership: The Cutting Edge* (Carbondale, IL: Southern Illinois University Press, (1977): 9–45. R.M. Stogdill, *Handbook of Leadership* (New York: Free Press, 1974).

21. J. Pfeffer, *Power in Organizations* (Boston: Pittman, 1981).

22. H.P. Sims, Jr., & C.C. Manz, "Observing Leader Verbal Behavior: Toward Reciprocal Determinism in Leadership Theory," *Journal of Applied Psychology* 69 (1984): 222–232.

23. J.D. Thompson, *Organizations in Action* (New York: McGraw-Hill, 1967).

24. "Who's Excellent Now?" *Business Week,* 5 November 1984: 46–48. D.T. Carroll, "A Disappointing Search for Excellence," *Harvard Business Review,* November-December 1983: 78–88.

What Makes an Organization Productive?

1. D. Katz and R.L. Kahn, *The Social Psychology of Organizations* (New York: John Wiley & Sons, 1978). D. Tjosvold & D.W. Johnson, *Productive Conflict Management: Perspectives for Organizations* (New York: Irvington Publishers, 1983).

Chapter 2. Alternative Ways to Work with People

1. R. Likert, *The Human Organization* (New York: McGraw-Hill, 1967). H.C. Katz, T.A. Kochan, & M.R. Weber, "Assessing the Effects of Industrial Relations Systems and Efforts to Improve the Quality of Working Life on Organizational Effectiveness," *Academy of Management Journal* 28 (1985): 509–526.

2. T.E. Deal & A.A. Kennedy, *Corporate Culture: The Rites and Rituals of Corporate Life* (Reading, MA: Addison-Wesley, 1982). W.G. Ouchi & A.L. Wilkins, "Organizational Cultures," in R.H. Tuner & J.F. Short, Jr. (eds.), *Annual Review of Sociology* 11 (Palo Alto, CA: Annual Review, Inc., 1985): 457–483. A.L. Wilkins & W.G. Ouchi, "Efficient Cultures: Exploring the Relationships Between Culture and Organizational Performance," *Administrative Science Quarterly* 28 (1983): 468–481.

3. R.H.G. Field & M.A. Abelson, "Climate: A Reconceptualization and Proposed Model," *Human Relations* 35 (1982): 181–201. R.D. Pritchard & B.W. Karasick, "The Effects of Organizational Climate on Managerial Job Performance and Job Satisfaction," *Organizational Behavior and Human Performance* 9 (1973): 126–146.

4. J.D. Thompson, *Organizations in Action* (New York: McGraw-Hill, 1967).

5. P. Lawrence & J. Lorsch, *Organizations and Environment* (Boston: Division of Research, Harvard Business School, 1967). J. McCann & J.R. Galbraith, "Interdepartmental Relations," in P.C. Nystrom & W.H. Starbuck (eds.), *Handbook of Organizational Design* 1 (New York: Oxford University Press, 1981): 60–84. A.H. Van De Ven, A.H. Delbecq, & R. Koenig, Jr., "Determinants of Coordination Modes Within Organizations," *American Sociological Review* 41 (1976): 322–338.

6. J.L. Cheng, "Interdependence and Coordination in Organizations: A Role-System Analysis," *Academy of Management Review* 26 (1983): 156–162. L.L. Roos, Jr., & F.A. Starke, "Organizational Roles," in P.C. Nystrom & W.H. Starbuck (eds.), *Handbook of Organizational Design* 1 (New York: Oxford University Press, 1981): 290–308.

7. D.W. Johnson, R.T. Johnson, & G. Maruyama, "Interdependence and Interpersonal Attraction among Heterogeneous and Homogeneous Individuals: A Theoretical Formulation and a Meta-Analysis of the Research," *Review of Educational Research* 53 (1983): 5–54. D. Tjosvold, "Effects of Cooperative and Competitive Interdependence and Task Complexity on Subordinates' Productivity, Perception of Leader, and Group Development," *Canadian Journal of Behavioural Science* 14 (1982): 24–34.

8. M. Schuster, "The Scanlon Plan: A Longitudinal Analysis," *Journal of Applied Behavioral Science* 20 (1984): 23–38. J.K. White, "The Scanlon Plan: Causes and Correlates of Success," *Academy of Management Journal* 22 (1979): 292–312.

9. J.P. Campbell, & R.D. Pritchard, "Motivation Theory in Industrial and Organizational Psychology," in M. Dunnette (ed.), *Handbook of Industrial and Organizational Psychology* (Chicago: Rand McNally, 1976): 63–130. T.R. Mitchell, "Motivation: New Directions for Theory, Research, and Practice," *Academy of Management Review* 7 (1982): 80–88. B. Schneider, "Organizational Behavior," in M.R. Rosenzweig & L.W. Porter (eds.), *Annual Review of Psychology* 36 (Palo Alto, CA: Annual Reviews, Inc., 1985): 573–611.

10. M. Deutsch, *Distributive Justice: A Social-Psychological Perspective* (New Haven, CT: Yale University Press, 1985). M. Deutsch, "Fifty years of conflict," in L. Festinger (ed.), *Retrospections on Social Psychology* (New York: Oxford University Press, 1980): 46–77. M. Deutsch, *The Resolution of Conflict* (New Haven, CT: Yale University Press, 1973). M. Deutsch, "A Theory of Cooperation and Competition," *Human Relations* 2 (1949): 129–152. M. Deutsch, "Cooperation and Trust: Some Theoretical Notes" in M.R. Jones (ed.), *Nebraska Symposium on Motivation* 10 (Lincoln: University of Nebraska Press, 1962): 275–320.

11. D.W. Johnson, R.T. Johnson, & G. Maruyama, "Interdependence and Interpersonal Attraction Among Heterogeneous and Homogeneous Individuals: A Theoretical Formulation and a Meta-Analysis of the Research," *Review of Educational Research* 53 (1983): 5–54. D.W. Johnson et al., "Effects of Cooperative, Competitive, and Individualistic Goal Structures on Achievement: A Meta-Analysis," *Psychological Bulletin* 89 (1981): 47–62. D. Tjosvold, "Cooperation Theory and Organizations," *Human Relations* 37 (1984): 743–767.

12. M. Deutsch & R.M. Krauss, "Studies in Interpersonal Bargaining," *Journal of Conflict Resolution* 6 (1962): 52–76. R.M. Krauss, "Structural and Attitudinal Factors in Interpersonal Bargaining," *Journal of Experimental Social Psychology* 2 (1966): 42–55. D.G. Pruitt & H. Syna, "Successful Problem Solving," in D. Tjosvold & D.W. Johnson (eds.), *Productive Conflict Management: Perspectives for Organizations* (New York: Irvington, 1983): 62–81. J. Rubin & B.R. Brown, *The Social Psychology of Bargaining and Negotiations* (New York: Academic Press, 1975).

13. R.A. Baron, "Reducing Organizational Conflict: An Incompatible Response Approach," *Journal of Applied Psychology* 69 (1984): 272–279. D. Tjosvold, D.W. Johnson, & L. Fabrey, "The Effects of Affirmation and Acceptance on Incorporation

of an Opposing Opinion in Problem Solving," *Psychological Reports* 47 (1981): 1043–1053. D. Tjosvold, "Threat as a Low-Power Person's Strategy in Bargaining: Social Face and Tangible Outcomes," *International Journal of Group Tensions* 4 (1974): 494–510.

14. D. Tjosvold, "Testing Goal Linkage Theory in Organizations," *Journal of Occupational Behaviour* 7(1986): 77–88. D. Tjosvold, "Dynamics and Outcomes of Goal Interdependence in Organizations," *Journal of Psychology*, in press. D. Tjosvold, "Goal Interdependence Approach to Interdepartmental Relations," manuscript, Simon Fraser University, 1984. D. Tjosvold & L.C. Chia, "Dynamics and Outcomes of Goal Interdependence in Organizational Conflict," manuscript, Simon Fraser University, 1985.

The Reality of Mutual Dependence

1. J.W. Thibaut & H.H. Kelley, *The Social Psychology of Groups* (New York: John Wiley & Sons, 1959).

2. J. Pfeffer & G.R. Salancik, *The External Control of Organizations* (New York: Harper & Row, 1978).

Chapter 3. Motivation, Productivity, and Entrepreneurship

1. T.R. Mitchell, "Motivation: New Directions for Theory, Research, and Practice," *Academy of Management Review* 7 (1982): 80–88.

2. J.P. Campbell & R.D. Pritchard, "Motivation Theory in Industrial and Organizational Psychology," in M. Dunnette (ed.), *Handbook of Industrial and Organizational Psychology* (Chicago: Rand McNally, 1976): 63–130. K. Lewin, *A Theory of Personality* (New York: McGraw-Hill, 1935). T.R. Mitchell, "Motivation: New Directions for Theory, Research, and Practice," *Academy of Management Review* 7 (1982): 80–88.

3. H.J. Arnold, "A Test of the Validity of the Multiplicative Hypothesis of Expectancy-Valence Theories of Work Motivation," *Academy of Management Journal* 24 (1981): 128–141. J.P. Campbell & R.D. Pritchard, "Motivation Theory in Industrial and Organizational Psychology," in M. Dunnette (ed.), *Handbook of Industrial and Organizational Psychology* (Chicago: Rand McNally, 1976): 63–130. R.A. Reber & J.A. Qallin, "The Effects of Training, Goal Setting, and Knowledge of Results on Safe Behavior: A Component Analysis," *Academy of Management Journal* 27 (1984): 544–560.

4. R. Halverson & M. Pallak, "Commitment, Ego-Involvement, and Resistance to Attack," *Journal of Experimental Social Psychology* 14 (1978): 1–12. C. Kiesler, *The Psychology of Commitment: Experiments Linking Behavior to Belief* (New York: Academic Press, 1971). M. Pallak, D. Cook, & J. Sullivan, "Commitment and Energy Conservation," in L. Bickman (ed.), *Applied Social Psychology Annual* 1 (Beverly Hills, CA: Sage Publications, 1980). R. Wicklund & J. Brehm, *Perspectives on Cognitive Dissonance* (Hillsdale, NJ: Lawrence Erlbaum Associates, 1976).

5. J.M. Ivancevich & J.T. McMahon, "The Effects of Goal Setting, External Feedback, and Self-Generated Feedback on Outcome Variables: A Field Experiment," *Academy of Management Journal* 25 (1982): 359–372. K.D. McCaul & J.T. Kopp, "Effects of Goal Setting and Commitment on Increasing Metal Recycling," *Journal of Applied Psychology* 67 (1982): 377–379. E.A. Locke et al., "Goal Setting and Task Performance: 1969–1980," *Psychological Bulletin* 90 (1981): 125–152.

6. G.W. Hill, "Group Versus Individual Performance: Are N + 1 Heads Better than One?" *Psychological Bulletin* 91 (1982): 517–539. H.H. Kelley & J.W. Thibaut, "Group Problem Solving," in G. Lindzey & E. Aronson (eds.), *Handbook of Social Psychology* 3 (Reading, MA: Addison-Wesley, 1968): 1–105. P.R. Laughlin, "Ability and Group Problem Solving," *Journal of Research and Development in Education* 12 (1978): 114–120. A. Zander & D. Wolfe, "Administrative Rewards and Coordination Among Committee Members," *Administrative Science Quarterly* 9 (1964): 50–69.

7. J.W. Atkinson & J.O. Raynor, *Motivation and Achievement* (Washington, DC: R.H. Winston & Sons, 1974).

8. T. Janz, "Manipulating Subjective Expectancy Through Feedback: A Laboratory Study of the Expectancy-Performance Relationship," *Journal of Applied Psychology* 67 (1982): 480–485.

9. D.W. Johnson & S. Johnson, "The Effects of Attitude Similarity, Expectation of Goal Facilitation, and Actual Goal Facilitation on Interpersonal Attraction," *Journal of Experimental Social Psychology* 8 (1972): 197–206. D. Tjosvold, "Unequal Power Relationships Within a Cooperative or Competitive Context," *Journal of Applied Social Psychology* 11 (1981): 137–150.

10. D.W. Johnson & R.T. Johnson, "Motivational Processes in Cooperative, Competitive, and Individualistic Learning Situations," in C. Ames & R. Ames (eds.), *Research on Motivation in Education* 2 (New York: Academic Press, 1985): D.W. Johnson et al., "Effects of Cooperative, Competitive, and Individualistic Goal Structures on Achievement: A Meta-Analysis," *Psychological Bulletin* 89 (1981): 47–62.

11. G.W. Hill, "Group Versus Individual Performance: Are N + 1 Heads Better than One?" *Psychological Bulletin* 91 (1982): 517–539. L. Hayes, "The Use of Group Contingencies for Behavioral Control: A Review," *Psychological Bulletin* 83 (1976): 628–648. J. Michaels, "Classroom Reward Structures and Academic Performance," *Review of Educational Research* 47 (1977): 87–99. H.H. Kelley & J.W. Thibaut, "Group Problem Solving," in G. Lindzey & E. Aronson (eds.), *Handbook of Social Psychology* 3 (Reading, MA: Addison-Wesley, 1968): 1–105.

12. D.W. Johnson et al., "Effects of Cooperative, Competitive, and Individualistic Goal Structures on Achievement: A Meta-Analysis," *Psychological Bulletin* 89 (1981): 47–62.

13. D.W. Johnson & R.T. Johnson, "Motivational Processes in Cooperative, Competitive, and Individualistic Learning Situations," in C. Ames & R. Ames (eds.), *Research on Motivation in Education* 2 (New York: Academic Press, 1985):

14. B. Winer et al., *Perceiving the Causes of Success and Failure* (Morristown, NJ: General Learning Press, 1977).

15. C. Ames, "Competitive Versus Cooperative Reward Structures: The Influence of Individual and Group Performance Factors on Achievement Attributions and Affect," *American Educational Research Journal* 18 (1981): 273–287. C. Ames & R.

Ames, "Competitive Versus Individualistic Goal Structures: The Salience of Past Performance Information for Causal Attributions and Affect," *Journal of Educational Psychology* 73 (1981): 411–418.

16. D. Tjosvold, I.R. Andrews, & H. Jones, "Cooperative and Competitive Relationships Between Leaders and Subordinates," *Human Relations* 36 (1983): 1111–1124. R. Robertson & D. Tjosvold, "Staff Relations, Job Commitment, and Acceptance of Elderly in Long Term Care Facilities," paper, Academy of Management Meetings, Chicago, 1986.

17. T.J. Peters & R.H. Waterman, *In Search of Excellence: Lessons from America's Best-Run Companies* (New York: Harper & Row, 1982).

18. D.W. Johnson et al., "Effects of Cooperative, Competitive, and Individualistic Goal Structures on Achievement: A Meta-Analysis," *Psychological Bulletin* 89 (1981): 47–62.

Chapter 4. Groups and Teamwork: Putting Cooperation to Work

1. G. Gyllenhammar, "How Volvo Adapts Work to People," *Harvard Business Review,* July-August 1977: 102–113.

2. M. Schuster, "The Scanlon Plan: A Longitudinal Analysis," *The Journal of Applied Behavioral Science* 20 (1984): 23–38.

3. S.L. Gallucci, "Increasing Profits Through Teamwork," *Training and Development Journal,* March 1985: 56–57.

4. W.H. Davidson, "Small Group Activity at Musashi Semiconductor Works," *Sloan Management Review,* Spring 1982: 3–14.

5. W.W. George, "Task Teams for Rapid Growth," *Harvard Business Review,* March-April 1977: 71–80.

6. W. Pasmore & F. Friedlander, "An Action-Research Program for Increasing Employee Involvement in Problem-Solving," *Administrative Science Quarterly* 27 (1982): 343–362.

7. R. Albanese & D.D. Van Fleet, "Rational Behavior in Groups: The Free-Riding Tendency," *Academy of Management Review* 10 (1985): 244–255. S.G. Harkin & R.E. Petty, "The Effects of Task Difficulty and Task Uniqueness on Social Loafing," *Journal of Personality and Social Psychology* 43 (1982): 1214–1229. G.R. Jones, "Task Visibility, "Free Riding, and Shirking: Explaining the Effect of Structure and Technology on Employee Behavior," *Academy of Management Review* 9 (1984): 684–695. N. Kerr "The Dispensability of Member Effort and Group Motivation Losses: Free-Rider Effects," *Journal of Personality and Social Psychology* 44 (1983): 78–94. J.M. Jackson & K. D. Williams, "Social Loafing on Difficult Tasks: Working Collectively Can Improve Performance," *Journal of Personality and Social Psychology* 49 (1985): 937–942. K. Williams, S. Harkins, & B. Latane, "Identifiability as a Deterrent to Social Loafing: Two Cheering Experiments," *Journal of Personality and Social Psychology* 40 (1981): 303–311.

8. R.J. Boyle, "Wrestling with Jellyfish," *Harvard Business Review,* January-February 1984: 74–83.

9. S. Seashore, *Group Cohesiveness in the Industrial Work Group* (Ann Arbor: Institute for Social Research, 1954). J.A. Sonnenfield, "Shedding Light on the Hawthorne Studies," *Journal of Occupational Behaviour* 6 (1985): 110–130.

10. E. Mayo, *The Human Problems of an Industrial Civilization* (New York: Macmillan, 1933).

Chapter 5.   Becoming a Team: How to Develop Cooperative Goals

1. H.A. Hornstein, "Promotive Tension: The Basis of Prosocial Behavior from a Lewinian Perspective," *Journal of Social Issues* 28 (1972): 191–218. D.W. Johnson & S. Johnson, "The Effects of Attitude Similarity, Expectation of Goal Facilitation, and Actual Goal Facilitation on Interpersonal Attraction," *Journal of Experimental Social Psychology* 8 (1972): 197–206.

2. A.L. Wilkins, "The Creation of Company Cultures: The Role of Stories and Human Resource Symbols," *Human Resource Management* 23 (1984): 41–60.

3. D.W. Johnson, "Role Reversal: A Summary and Review of the Research," *International Journal of Group Tensions* 1 (1971): 318–334. D. Tjosvold, "Effects of Leader Warmth and Directiveness on Subordinate Performance on a Subsequent Task," *Journal of Applied Psychology* 69 (1984): 422–427. D. Tjosvold, "Social Face in Conflict: A Critique," *International Journal of Group Tensions* 13 (1983): 49–64.

4. T.E. Deal & A.A. Kennedy, *Corporate Culture: The Rites and Rituals of Corporate Life* (Reading, MA: Addison-Wesley, 1982). T.J. Peters & R.H. Waterman, *In Search of Excellence: Lessons from America's Best-Run Companies* (New York: Harper & Row, 1982). T. Peters & N. Austin, *A Passion for Excellence* (New York: Random House, 1985). A. L. Wilkins, "The Creation of Company Cultures: The Role of Stories and Human Resource Symbols," *Human Resource Management* 23 (1984): 41–60.

5. W.G. Ouchi, *Theory Z: How American Business Can Meet the Japanese Challenge* (Reading, MA: Addison-Wesley, 1981).

6. P. Lawrence, & J. Lorsch, *Organizations and Environment* (Boston: Division of Research, Harvard Business School, 1967). J. McCann & J.R. Galbraith, "Interdepartmental Relations," in P.C. Nystrom & W.H. Starbuck (eds.), *Handbook of Organizational Design* 1 (New York: Oxford University Press, 1981): 60–84.

7. J.D. Thompson, *Organizations in Action* (New York: McGraw-Hill, 1967). A.H. Van De Ven, A.H. Delbecq, & R. Koenig, Jr., "Determinants of Coordination Modes Within Organizations," *American Sociological Review* 41 (1976): 322–338.

8. M. Deutsch, *Distributive Justice: A Social-Psychological Perspective* (New Haven, CT: Yale University Press, 1985).

9. L. Mann & I.L. Janis, "A Follow-up Study on the Long-Term Effects of Emotional Role Playing," *Journal of Personality and Social Psychology* 18 (1968): 339–342. W.G. Ouchi, *Theory Z: How American Business Can Meet the Japanese Challenge* (Reading, MA: Addison-Wesley, 1981).

10. D.W. Johnson, "Role Reversal: A Summary and Review of the Research," *International Journal of Group Tensions* 1 (1971): 318–334. D. Tjosvold, "Effects of

Leader Warmth and Directiveness on Subordinate Performance on a Subsequent Task," *Journal of Applied Psychology* 69 (1984): 422–427. D. Tjosvold, "Social Face in Conflict: A Critique," *International Journal of Group Tensions* 13 (1983): 49–64.

Chapter 6. Forming One Company: How to Integrate Groups into an Organization

1. M.E. Porter, *Competitive Advantage* (New York: Free Press, 1985). M.E. Porter, *Competitive Strategy* (New York: Free Press, 1980).

2. "TRW Leads a Revolution in Managing Technology," *Business Week,* 15 November 1982: 259–266.

3. R.R. Blake & J.S. Mouton, "Lateral Conflict," in D. Tjosvold & D.W. Johnson (eds.), *Productive Conflict Management: Perspectives for Organizations* (New York: Irvington, 1983): 83–134. J. Gandz & V.V. Murray, "The Experience of Workplace Politics," *Academy of Management Journal* 23 (1980): 237–251.

4. J. Galbraith, *Designing Complex Organizations* (Reading, MA: Addison-Wesley, 1973). S. Gannes, "Marketing is the Message at McGraw-Hill," *Fortune,* 17 February 1986: 34–37. P. Lawrence & J. Lorsch, *Organizations and Environment* (Boston: Division of Research, Harvard Business School, 1967). J. McCann & J.R. Galbraith, "Interdepartmental Relations," in P.C. Nystrom & W.H. Starbuck (eds.), *Handbook of Organizational Design* 1 (New York: Oxford University Press, 1981): 60–84. H. Mintzberg, *Structuring Organizations* (Englewood Cliffs, NJ: Prentice-Hall, 1979).

5. J. Galbraith, *Designing Complex Organizations* (Reading, MA: Addison-Wesley, 1973).

6. R.R. Blake & J.S. Mouton, "Lateral Conflict," in D. Tjosvold & D.W. Johnson (eds.), *Productive Conflict Management: Perspectives for Organizations* (New York: Irvington, 1983): 83–134. R.R. Blake & J.S. Mouton, "Reactions to Intergroup Competition under Win-Lose Conditions," *Management Science* 7 (1961): 420–435. G.L. Clore et al., "Interracial Attitudes and Behavior at a Summer Camp," *Journal of Personality and Social Psychology* 36 (1978): 107–116. M. Deutsch, "Fifty Years of Conflict," in L. Festinger (ed.), *Retrospections on Social Psychology* (New York: Oxford University Press, 1980): 46–77. M. Deutsch, *The Resolution of Conflict* (New Haven, CT: Yale University Press, 1973). D.W. Johnson, R.T. Johnson, & G. Maruyama, "Interdependence and Interpersonal Attraction Among Heterogeneous and Homogeneous Individuals: A Theoretical Formulation and a Meta-Analysis of the Research," *Review of Educational Research* 53 (1983): 5–54. M. Sherif et al., *Intergroup Cooperation and Competition: The Robbers' Cave Experiment* (Norma, OK: University Book Exchange, 1961). H. Tajfel, "Social Psychology of Intergroup Relations," in M. Rosenzweig & L.M. Porter (eds.), *Annual Review of Psychology* (Palo Alto, CA: Annual Review, Inc. 1982): 1–39. D. Tjosvold, "Cooperation Theory and Organizations," *Human Relations* 37 (1984): 743–767. D. Tjosvold, "Effects of Departments' Interdependence on Organizational Decision Making," *Psychological Reports* 53 (1983): 851–857. D. Tjosvold, "Goal Interdependence Approach to Relations Between Departments," manuscript, Simon Fraser University, 1984. S. Wor-

schel, V.A. Anderoli, & R. Folger, "Intergroup Cooperation and Intergroup Attraction: The Effects of Previous Interaction and Outcome of Combined Effort," *Journal of Experimental Social Psychology* 13 (1977): 131–140.

7. D.W. Johnson, et al. "Effects of Cooperative, Competitive, and Individualistic Goal Structures on Achievement: A Meta-Analysis," *Psychological Bulletin* 89 (1981): 47–62.

8. D.W. Johnson, R.T. Johnson, & G. Maruyama, "Interdependence and Interpersonal Attraction Among Heterogeneous and Homogeneous Individuals: A Theoretical Formulation and a Meta-Analysis of the Research," *Review of Educational Research* 53 (1983): 5–54.

9. J.W. Jullian, D.W. Bishop, & F.E. Fielder, "Quasitherapeutic Effects of Intergroup Competition," *Journal of Personality and Social Psychology* 3 (1966): 321–327. T.J. Peters & R.H. Waterman, *In Search of Excellence: Lessons from America's Best-Run Companies* (New York: Harper & Row, 1982). J.M. Rabbie et al., "Differential Power and Effects of Expected Competitive and Cooperative Intergroup on Intragroup and Outgroup Attitudes," *Journal of Personality and Social Psychology* 39 (1974): 46–56.

10. M.G. Billig & H. Tajfel, "Social Categorization and the Similarity in Intergroup Behavior," *European Journal of Social Psychology* 3 (1973): 27–51. C.K. Ferguson & H.H. Kelley, "Significant Factors in Overevaluation of Own Group's Product," *Journal of Abnormal and Social Psychology* 69 (1963): 223–238.

11. W.G. Ouchi, *Theory Z: How American Business Can Meet the Japanese Challenge* (Reading, MA: Addison-Wesley, 1981). T. Peters & N. Austin, *A Passion for Excellence* (New York: Random House, 1985). T.J. Peters & R.H. Waterman, *In Search of Excellence: Lessons from America's Best-Run Companies* (New York: Harper & Row, 1982).

12. W. Keichel III, "Celebrating a Corporate Triumph," *Fortune,* 20 August 1984: 259–266.

13. "TRW Leads a Revolution in Managing Technology," *Business Week* 15 November 1982: 124–130.

14. R.R. Blake & J.S. Mouton, "Lateral Conflict," in D. Tjosvold & D.W. Johnson (eds.), *Productive Conflict Management: Perspectives for Organizations* (New York: Irvington, 1983): 83–134.

15. R.F. Vancil & C.H. Green, "How CEOs use top management committees," *Harvard Business Review,* January-February 1984: 65–73.

16. D.F. Ephlin, "The UAW-Ford Agreement—Joint Problem Solving," *Sloan Management Review* 24 (1983): 61–65.

17. R.F. Vancil & C.H. Green, "How CEOs use top management committees," *Harvard Business Review,* January-February 1984: 65–73.

Chapter 7. Power and Recognition

1. R.M. Kanter, "Power Failure in Management Circuits," *Harvard Business Review,* July-August 1979: 65–75. R.M. Kanter, *Men and Women of the Corporation* (New York: Basic Books, 1977).

2. D.C. McClelland, *Power: The Inner Experience* (New York: Irvington, 1975). D.C. McClelland, "The Two Faces of Power," *Journal of International Affairs* 24 (1970): 29–47. D.C. McClelland & R.E. Boyatzis, "Leadership Motive Pattern and Long-Term Success in Management," *Journal of Applied Psychology* 67 (1982): 737–743.

3. E.E. Jones, *Ingratiation* (New York: Appleton-Century-Crofts, 1964). D. Kipnis, *The Powerholders* (Chicago: University of Chicago Press, 1976), D. Kipnis, S.M. Schmidt, & I. Wilkinson, "Intraorganizational Influence Tactics: Explorations in Getting One's Way," *Journal of Applied Psychology* 65 (1980): 440–452. R. Walton, *Interpersonal Peacemaking* (Reading, MA: Addison-Wesley, 1969).

4. S.B. Bacharach & E.J. Lawler, *Bargaining: Power, Tactics, and Outcomes* (San Francisco: Jossey-Bass, 1981). R. Bierstedt, "An Analysis of Social Power," *American Sociological Review* 15 (1950): 730–738. R.P. Dahl, "The Concept of Power," *Behavioral Science* 2 (1957): 201–218. R.M. Emerson, "Power-Dependence Relations," *American Sociological Review* 27 (1962): 31–41. J. Pfeffer, *Power in Organizations* (Boston: Pitman, 1981). G.R. Salancik & J. Pfeffer, "Who Gets Power—And How They Hold on to It: A Strategic-Contingency Model of Power," *Organizational Dynamics* 5 (1977): 3–21. M. Weber, *The Theory of Social and Economic Organization* (New York: Oxford University Press, 1947).

5. J. Pfeffer, *Power in Organizations* (Boston: Pitman, 1981).

6. R.M. Emerson, "Power-Dependence Relations," *American Sociological Review* 27 (1962): 31–41. J.R.P. French, Jr., & B. Raven, "The Bases of Social Power," in D. Cartwright (ed.), *Studies in Social Power* (Ann Arbor: University of Michigan Press, 1959). J. Pfeffer, *Power in Organizations* (Boston: Pittman, 1981).

7. R.M. Emerson, "Power-Dependence Relations," *American Sociological Review* 27 (1962): 31–41. J.R.P. French, Jr., & B. Raven, "The Bases of Social Power," in D. Cartwright (ed.), *Studies in Social Power* (Ann Arbor: University of Michigan Press, 1959). J.W. Thibaut & H.H. Kelley, *The Social Psychology of Groups* (New York: John Wiley & Sons, 1959).

8. D. Tjosvold, "Power and Goal Interdependencies in Organizations," manuscript, Simon Fraser University, 1985. D. Tjosvold, I.R. Andrews, & J. Struthers, "Power and Social Context: Superior and Subordinate Views," manuscript, Simon Fraser University, 1985.

9. M. Deutsch, *The Resolution of Conflict* (New Haven, CT: Yale University Press, 1973). D. Tjosvold, "Power and Social Context in Superior-Subordinate Interaction," *Organizational Behavior and Human Decision Processes* 35 (1985): 281–293. D. Tjosvold, "Power and Goal Interdependencies in Organizations," manuscript, Simon Fraser University, 1985. D. Tjosvold, "Effects of the Approach to Controversy on Superiors' Incorporation of Subordinates' Information in Decision Making," *Journal of Applied Psychology* 67 (1982): 189–193. M. Van Berklom & D. Tjosvold, "Effects of Social Context on Engaging in Controversy," *Journal of Psychology* 107 (1981): 141–145.

10. D. Tjosvold, "Power and Social Context in Superior-Subordinate Interaction," *Organizational Behavior and Human Decision Processes* 35 (1985): 281–293. D. Tjosvold, "Unequal Power Relationships Within a Cooperative or Competitive Context," *Journal of Applied Social Psychology* 11 (1981): 137–150. D. Tjosvold, "Power and Goal Interdependencies in Organizations," manuscript, Simon Fraser

University, 1985. D. Tjosvold, D.W. Johnson, & R.T. Johnson, "Influence Strategy, Perspective-Taking, and Relationships Between High- and Low-Power Individuals in Cooperative and Competitive Contexts," *Journal of Psychology* 116 (1984): 187–202.

11. R.M. Kanter, "Power Failure in Management Circuits," *Harvard Business Review,* July-August 1979: 65–75. R.M. Kanter, *Men and Women of the Corporation* (New York: Basic Books, 1977).

12. D. Tjosvold, "Power and Social Context in Superior-Subordinate Interaction," *Organizational Behavior and Human Decision Processes* 35 (1985): 281–293.

13. D. Tjosvold, D.W. Johnson, & R.T. Johnson, "Influence Strategy, Perspective-Taking, and Relationships Between High and Low Power Individuals in Cooperative and Competitive Contexts," *Journal of Psychology* 116 (1984): 187–202.

14. D. Tjosvold, "The Effects of Attribution and Social Context on Superiors' Influence and Interaction with Low Performing Subordinates," *Personnel Psychology* 38 (1985): 361–376.

15. D. Tjosvold, I.R. Andrews, & H. Jones, "Cooperative and Competitive Relationships Between Leaders and Subordinates," *Human Relations* 36 (1983): 1111–1124. D. Tjosvold, "Power and Goal Interdependencies in Organizations," manuscript, Simon Fraser University, 1985.

16. H.H. Kelley, "Communication in Experimentally Created Hierarchies," *Human Relations* 4 (1951): 39–56. L. Solomon, "The Influence of Some Types of Power Relationships and Game Strategies Upon the Development of Interpersonal Trust," *Journal of Abnormal and Social Psychology* 61 (1960): 223–230. D. Tjosvold & L. Fabrey, "Effects of Interdependence and Dependence on Cognitive Perspective-Taking," *Psychological Reports* 46 (1980): 755–765. D. Tjosvold & M. Okun, "Effects of Unequal Power on Cooperation in Conflict," *Psychological Reports* 44 (1979): 239–242. D. Tjosvold & S. Sabato, "Effects of Relative Power on Cognitive Perspective-Taking," *Personality and Social Psychological Bulletin* 4 (1978): 256–259.

17. D.W. Johnson, "Role Reversal: A Summary and Review of the Research," *International Journal of Group Tensions* 1 (1971): 318–334.

18. M. Deutsch, *Distributive Justice: A Social-Psychological Perspective* (New Haven, CT: Yale University Press, 1985).

19. P.F. Levin & A.M. Isen, "Further Studies on the Effects of Feeling Good on Helping," *Sociometry* 38 (1975): 141–147.

Power and Recognition in a Growing Company

1. T. Melohn, "How to Build Employee Trust and Productivity," *Harvard Business Review,* January-February 1983: 56–61.

Chapter 8. Solving Problems and Making Decisions

1. R.M. Cyert & J.G. March, *A Behavioral Theory of the Firm* (Englewood Cliffs, NJ: Prentice-Hall, 1963). R.L. Keeney & H. Raiffa, *Decisions with Multiple*

Objectives: Preferences and Value Tradeoffs (New York: John Wiley & Sons, 1976). D.E. Lindbloom, "The Science of Muddling Through," *Public Administrative Review* 15 (1959): 79–88. H.A. Simon, *Administrative Behavior* (New York: The Free Press, 1976).

2. L. Fahey, "On Strategic Management Decision Processes," *Strategic Management Journal* 2 (1981): 43–60. H.P. Mintzberg, "Patterns in Strategy Formation," *Management Science* 24 (1976): 934–948.

3. H.H. Barnes, Jr., "Cognitive Biases and their Impact on Strategic Planning," *Strategic Management Journal* 4 (1984): 129–137. R.M. Hogarth & S. Makridakis, "Forecasting and Planning: An Evaluation," *Management Science* 27 (1981): 115–138. J.D. Steinbruner, *The Cybernetic Theory of Decision* (Princeton, NJ: Princeton University Press, 1974).

4. C.R. Schwenk, "Cognitive Simplification Processes in Strategic Decision-Making," *Strategic Management Journal* 5 (1984): 111–128.

5. A. Tversky & D. Kahneman, "Judgment Under Uncertainty: Heuristics and Biases," *Science* 185 (1974): 1124–1131.

6. P. Slovic, B. Fischhoff, & S. Lichtenstein, "Behavioral Decision Theory," *Annual Review of Psychology* 28 (1977): 1–39.

7. C.R. Schwenk, "Cognitive Simplification Processes in Strategic Decision-Making," *Strategic Management Journal* 5 (1984): 111–128.

8. A. Pettigrew, *The Politics of Organizational Decision Making* (London: Tavistock, 1973). J. Pfeffer & G.R. Salancik, *The External Control of Organizations* (New York: Harper & Row, 1978).

9. M.R. Callaway, R.G. Marriott, & J.K. Esser, "Effects of Dominance on Group Decision Making: Towards a Stress-Reduction Explanation of Groupthink," *Journal of Personality and Social Psychology* 49 (1985): 949–952. I.L. Janis, *Victims of Groupthink* (Boston: Houghton Mifflin, 1972). L. Mann & I.L. Janis, "Decisional Conflict in Organizations," in D. Tjosvold & D.W. Johnson (eds.), *Productive Conflict Management: Perspectives for Organizations* (New York: Irvington, 1983): 19–40. J.D. Stanley, "Dissent in Organizations," *The Academy of Management Review* 6 (1981): 13–19.

10. H.C. Foushee, "Dyads and Triads at 35,000 Feet: Factors Affecting Group Process and Aircrew Performance," *American Psychologist* 39 (1984): 885–893.

11. H.S. Geneen, "Why Directors Can't Protect the Shareholders," *Fortune* 17 September 1984: 28–32.

12. T. Janz & D. Tjosvold, "Costing Effective Versus Ineffective Work Relationships: A Method and A First Look," *Canadian Journal of Administrative Sciences* 2 (1985): 43–51.

13. J. Hall, "Decisions, Decisions, Decisions," *Psychology Today*, November 1971: 51–54, 86, 88. N.R.F. Maier, *Problem-Solving and Creativity in Individuals and Groups* (Belmont, CA: Brooks/Cole, 1970).

14. L.J. Bourgeois, III, "Strategic Goals, Perceived Uncertainty, and Economic Performance in Volatile Environments," *Academy of Management Journal* 28 (1985): 548–573. R.A. Cosier, "The Effects of Three Potential Aids for Making Strategic Decisions on Prediction Accuracy," *Organizational Behavior and Human Performance* 22 (1978): 295–306. R.A. Cosier & P.R. Rechner, "Inquiry Method Effects on Performance in a Simulated Business Environment," *Organizational Behavior and Hu-*

man Decision Processes, in press. R.O. Mason, & I. Mitroff, *Challenging Strategic Planning Assumptions* (New York: John Wiley & Sons, 1981).

15. D. Tjosvold, "Implications of Controversy Research for Management," *Journal of Management* 11 (1985): 19–35.

16. D. Tjosvold, "Dynamics within Participation: An Experimental Investigation," *Group and Organizational Studies* 10 (1985): 260–277. D. Tjosvold, "Effects of Departments' Interdependence on Organizational Decision Making," *Psychological Reports* 53 (1983): 851–857. D. Tjosvold, "Effects of the Approach to Controversy on Superiors' Incorporation of Subordinates' Information in Decision Making," *Journal of Applied Psychology* 67 (1982): 189–193. D. Tjosvold & D.K. Deemer, "Effects of Controversy Within a Cooperative or Competitive Context on Organizational Decision Making," *Journal of Applied Psychology* 65 (1980): 590–595. D. Tjosvold & R.H.G. Field, "Effects of Social Context on Consensus and Majority Vote Decision Making," *Academy of Management Journal* 26 (1983): 500–506. D. Tjosvold & R.H.G. Field, "Managers' Structuring Cooperative and Competitive Controversy in Group Decision Making," *International Journal of Management* 1 (1984): 26–32. D. Tjosvold & D.W. Johnson, "The Effects of Controversy on Cognitive Perspective Taking," *Journal of Educational Psychology* 69 (1977): 679–685. D. Tjosvold & D.W. Johnson, "Controversy Within a Cooperative or Competitive Context and Cognitive Perspective Taking," *Contemporary Educational Psychology* 3 (1978): 376–386.

17. D. Tjosvold, D.W. Johnson, & L. Fabrey, "Effects of Defensiveness on Cognitive Perspective-Taking, *Psychological Reports* 47 (1980): 1043–1053. D. Tjosvold, D.W. Johnson, & J. Lerner, "The Effects of Affirmation and Acceptance on Incorporation of an Opposing Opinion in Problem-Solving," *Journal of Social Psychology* 114 (1981): 103–110. D. Tjosvold, "Social Face in Conflict: A Critique," *International Journal of Group Tensions* 13 (1983): 49–64.

18. D. Tjosvold, "Effects of Crisis Orientation on Managers' Approach to Controversy in Decision Making," *Academy of Management Journal* 27 (1984): 130–138. D. Tjosvold, "Control strategies and own group evaluation in intergroup conflict," *Journal of Psychology* 100 (1979): 305–314. D. Tjosvold & D.K. Deemer, "Effects of a Control or Collaborative Orientation on Participation in Organizational Decision Making," *Canadian Journal of Behavioural Science* 13 (1981): 33–43.

19. D. Tjosvold, W. C. Wedley, & R.H.G. Field, "Constructive Controversy, the Vroom-Yetton Model, and Managerial Decision Making," *Journal of Occupational Behaviour* 7(1986): 125–138.

20. J. Barker, D. Tjosvold, & I.R. Andrews, "Project Manager's Approach to Conflict in a Matrix Organization," manuscript, Simon Fraser University, 1985. M. Van Berklom & D. Tjosvold, "Effects of Social Context on Engaging in Controversy," *Journal of Psychology* 107 (1981): 141–145.

21. C. Argyris, *Intervention Theory and Method: A Behavioral Science View* (Reading, MA: Addison-Wesley, 1970). C. Argyris & D.A. Schon, *Organizational Learning: A Theory of Action Perspective* (Reading, MA: Addison-Wesley, 1978).

22. M. Magnet, "How Top Managers Make a Company's Toughest Decision," *Fortune,* 18 March 1985: 52–57.

23. J. Hall, "Decisions, Decisions, Decisions," *Psychology Today,* November 1971: 51–54, 86, 88. D. Tjosvold & R.H.G. Field, "Effects of Social Context on Consensus and Majority Vote Decision Making," *Academy of Management Journal* 26 (1983): 500–506.

24. M. Shashkin, "Participative Management Is an Ethical Imperative," *Organizational Dynamics,* Spring 1984: 4–22.

25. E. Locke & D.M. Schweiger, "Participation in Decision-Making: One More Look," in B.M. Staw (ed.), *Research in Organizational Behavior* 1 (Greenwich, CT: JAI Press, 1979): 265–339. M. Shashkin, "Participative Management Is an Ethical Imperative," *Organizational Dynamics,* Spring 1984: 4–22. A. Lowin, "Participative Decision Making: A Model, Literature Critique, and Prescriptions for Research," *Organizational Behavior and Human Performance* 3 (1968): 68–106.

26. A. George, "Adaptation to Stress in Political Decision-Making: The Individual, Small Group, and Organizational Contexts," in G.V. Coelho, D.A. Hamburg, & J.E. Adams (eds.), *Coping and Adaptation* (New York: Basic Books, 1974). M. Mulder & H. Wilkie, "Participation and Power Equalization," *Organizational Behavior and Human Performance* 5 (1970): 430–448. D. Tjosvold, "Dynamics within Participation: An Experimental Investigation," *Group and Organizational Studies* 10 (1985): 260–277.

IBM and Controversy

1. R.F. Vancil & C.H. Green, "How CEOs Use Top Management Committees," *Harvard Business Review,* January-February 1984: 65–73.

Participation Research

1. E. Locke & D. M. Schweiger, "Participation in Decision-Making: One More Look," in B.M. Staw (ed.), *Research in Organizational Behavior* 1 (Greenwich, CT: JAI Press, 1979): 265–339. V.H. Vroom & P.W. Yetton, *Leadership and Decision-Making* (Pittsburgh: University of Pittsburgh Press, 1973).

2. L. Coch & J.R.P. French, Jr., "Overcoming Resistance to Change," *Human Relations* 1 (1948): 512–532. N.C. Morse & E. Reimer, "The Experimental Change of a Major Organizational Variable," *Journal of Abnormal and Social Psychology* 56 (1956): 120–129. F. Richter & D. Tjosvold, "Effects of Student Participation in Classroom Decision-Making on Attitudes, Peer Interaction, Motivation, and Learning," *Journal of Applied Psycholotgy* 65 (1980): 74–80.

3. I.D. Steiner, *Group Process and Productivity* (New York: Academic Press, 1972). I.L. Janis, *Victims of Groupthink* (Boston: Houghton Mifflin, 1972).

4. A. George, "Adaptation to Stress in Political Decision-Making: The Individual, Small Group, and Organizational Contexts," in G.V. Coelho, D.A. Hamburg, & J.E. Adams (eds.), *Coping and Adaptation* (New York: Basic Books, 1974). D. Tjosvold, "Dynamics within Participation: An Experimental Investigation," *Group and Organizational Studies* 10 (1985): 260–277.

Chapter 9.   Making Conflict Productive

1. J.R. Averill, *Anger and Aggression: An Essay on Emotion* (New York: Springer-Verlag, 1982).

2. K.W. Thomas & W.H. Schmidt, "A Survey of Managerial Interests with Respect to Conflict," *Academy of Management Journal* 19 (1976): 315–318.

3. S.P. Robins, *Managing Organizational Conflict* (Englewood Cliffs, NJ: Prentice-Hall, 1974).

4. M.H. Bazerman & R.J. Lewicki (eds.), *Negotiations in Organizations* (Beverly Hills, CA: Sage Publications, 1982). R.J. Lewicki, B.H. Sheppard, & M.H. Bazerman (eds.), *Research on Negotiations in Organizations* (Greenwich, CT: JAI Publishing, 1986). D. Tjosvold & D.W. Johnson (eds.), *Productive Conflict Management: Perspectives for Organizations* (New York: Irvington, 1983).

5. S.B. Bacharach & E.J. Lawler, *Bargaining: Power, Tactics, and Outcomes.* (San Francisco: Jossey-Bass, 1981). R.E. Walton & R.B. McKersie, *A Behavioral Theory of Labor Negotiations* (New York: McGraw-Hill, 1965).

6. M. Deutsch, "Fifty Years of Conflict," in L. Festinger (ed.), *Retrospections on Social Psychology* (New York: Oxford University Press, 1980): 46–77. M. Deutsch, *The Resolution of Conflict* (New Haven, CT: Yale University Press, 1973). M. Deutsch, "Conflicts: Productive and Destructive," *Journal of Social Issues* 15 (1969): 7–41.

7. J.R. Averill, *Anger and Aggression: An Essay on Emotion* (New York: Springer-Verlag, 1982).

8. M. Deutsch & R.M. Krauss, "Studies in Interpersonal Bargaining," *Journal of Conflict Resolution* 6 (1962): 52–76. H.H. Kelley, "Experimental Studies of Threats in Interpersonal Negotiations," *Journal of Conflict Resolution* 9 (1965): 80–102. D. Tjosvold, "Low-Power Person's Strategies in Bargaining: Negotiability of Demand, Maintaining Face, and Race," *International Journal of Group Tensions* 7 (1977): 29–42. D. Tjosvold, "Threat as a Low-Power Person's Strategy in Bargaining: Social Face and Tangible Outcomes," *International Journal of Group Tensions* 4 (1974): 494–510.

9. R. Axelrod, *The Induction of Cooperation* (New York: Basic Books, 1984). M. Deutsch, "Fifty Years of Conflict," in L. Festinger (ed.), *Retrospections on Social Psychology* (New York: Oxford University Press, 1980): 46–77. M. Deutsch, *The Resolution of Conflict* (New Haven, CT: Yale University Press, 1973). M. Deutsch, "Conflicts: Productive and Destructive," *Journal of Social Issues* 15, (1969): 7–41. D.G. Pruitt & H. Syna, "Successful Problem Solving," in D. Tjosvold & D.W. Johnson (eds.), *Productive Conflict Management: Perspectives for Organizations* (New York: Irvington, 1983): 62–81. J. Rubin & B. R. Brown, *The Social Psychology of Bargaining and Negotiations* (New York: Academic Press, 1975). D. Tjosvold & D.W. Johnson (eds.), *Productive Conflict Management: Perspectives for Organizations* (New York: Irvington, 1983).

10. M. Deutsch & R.M. Krauss, "Studies in Interpersonal Bargaining," *Journal of Conflict Resolution* 6 (1962): 52–76.

11. R. Fisher & W. Ury, *Getting to Yes* (Boston: Houghton Mifflin, 1981).

12. R.A. Baron, "Reducing Organizational Conflict: An Incompatible Response Approach," *Journal of Applied Psychology* 69 (1984): 272–279. D. Tjosvold, "Social Face in Conflict: A Critique," *International Journal of Group Tensions* 13 (1983): 49–64. D. Tjosvold & T. Huston, "Social Face and Resistance to Compromise in Bargaining," *Journal of Social Psychology* 104 (1978): 57–68.

13. D. Tjosvold, "Control Strategies and Own Group Evaluation in Intergroup Conflict," *Journal of Psychology* 100 (1979): 305–314.

14. R.J. Boyle, "Wrestling with Jellyfish," *Harvard Business Review,* January-February 1984: 74–83.

Coping with Labor-Management Conflict

1. R. Kuttner, "Sharing Power at Eastern Air Lines," *Harvard Business Review,* November-December 1985: 91–99.

Chapter 10. Stimulating and Managing Innovation

1. P.F. Drucker, *Innovation and Entrepreneurship: Practices and Principles* (New York: Harper & Row, 1985). M.E. Porter, *Competitive Advantage* (New York: Free Press, 1985). M.E. Porter, *Competitive Strategy* (New York: Free Press, 1980).

2. P.F. Drucker, *Innovation and Entrepreneurship: Practices and Principles* (New York: Harper & Row, 1985). R.M. Kanter, *The Change Masters* (New York: Simon Schuster, 1984). T. Peters & N. Austin, *A Passion for Excellence* (New York: Random House, 1985). T.J. Peters & R.H. Waterman, *In Search of Excellence: Lessons from America's Best-Run Companies* (New York: Harper & Row, 1982). S.P. Sherman, "Eight Big Masters of Innovation," *Fortune,* 15 October 1984: 66–84.

3. R.T. Keller & W.E. Hovland, "Communicators and innovators in research and development organizations," *Academy of Management Journal* 26 (1983): 742–749. S.P. Sherman, "Eight Big Masters of Innovation," *Fortune,* 15 October 1984: 66–84.

4. J.V. Baldrige & R.A. Burnham, "Organizational Innovation: Individual, Organizational, and Environmental Impacts," *Administrative Science Quarterly* 20 (1975): 165–176. T. Peters & N. Austin, *A Passion for Excellence* (New York: Random House, 1985).

5. T. Peters & N. Austin, *A Passion for Excellence* (New York: Random House, 1985). S.P. Sherman, "Eight Big Masters of Innovation," *Fortune,* 15 October 1984: 66–84.

6. R. Norman, "Organizational Innovativeness: Product Variation and Reorientation," *Administrative Science Quarterly* 16 (1971): 203–215. N. Lin & G. Zaltman, "Dimensions of Innovations," in G. Zaltman (ed.), *Processes and Phenomena of Social Change* (New York: John Wiley & Sons, 1973):

7. J.G. March & H.A. Simon, *Organizations* (New York: John Wiley & Sons, 1958).

8. P.F. Drucker, *Innovation and Entrepreneurship: Practices and Principles* (New York: Harper & Row, 1985).

9. C. Pine & S. Mundale, "Manuel Villafana: The Heart of the Matter," *Self-Made* (Minneapolis: Dorn Books, 1982): 161–172.

10. W. H. Davidson, "Small Group Activity at Musashi Semiconductor Works," *Sloan Management Review,* Spring 1982: 3–14.

11. R.G. Havelock, *Planning for Innovation* (Ann Arbor: University of Michigan, 1970). G.R. Zaltman, R. Duncan, & J. Holbek, *Innovations and Organizations* (New York: John Wiley & Sons, 1973). J.R. Kimberly, "Managerial Innovation," in P.C. Nystrom & W.H. Starbuck (eds.), *Handbook of Organizational Design* 1 (London: Oxford University Press, 1981): 84–104.

12. H. Sapolsky, "Organizational Structure and Innovation," *Journal of Business* 40 (1967): 497–510.

13. N.R.F. Maier, *Problem-Solving and Creativity in Individuals and Groups* (Belmont, CA: Brooks/Cole, 1970). G.R. Zaltman, R. Duncan, & J. Holbek, *Innovations and Organizations* (New York: John Wiley & Sons, 1973).

14. F. Friedlander & B. Schott, "The Use of Task Groups and Task Forces in Organizational Change," in R. Payne and G.L. Cooper (eds.), *Groups at Work* (New York: John Wiley & Sons, 1981): 191–217.

15. L. Coch & J.R.P. French, Jr., "Overcoming Resistance to Change," *Human Relations* 1 (1948): 512–532.

16. T.J. Peters & R.H. Waterman, *In Search of Excellence: Lessons from America's Best-Run Companies* (New York: Harper & Row, 1982).

17. L. Mann & I. Janis, "Decisional Conflict in Organizations," in D. Tjosvold & D.W. Johnson (eds.), *Productive Conflict Management: Perspectives for Organizations* (New York: Irvington, 1983): 14–40. D. Tjosvold, "Effects of Crisis Orientation on Managers' Approach to Controversy in Decision Making," *Academy of Management Journal* 27 (1984): 130–138.

18. P.F. Drucker, *Innovation and Entrepreneurship: Practices and Principles* (New York: Harper & Row, 1985).

19. F. Friedlander & B. Schott, "The Use of Task Groups and Task Forces in Organizational Change," in R. Payne and G.L. Cooper (eds.), *Groups at Work* (New York: John Wiley & Sons, 1981): 191–217.

Chapter 11.   Managerial Leadership

1. E. Brewer & J.W.C. Tomlinson, "The Manager's Working Day," *The Journal of Industrial Economics* 12 (1964): 191–197. J.H. Horne & T. Lupton, "The Work Activities of 'Middle' Managers: An Exploratory Study," *The Journal of Management Studies* 2 (1965): 14–33.

2. T.R. Davis & F. Luthans, "Defining and Researching Leadership as a Behavioral Construct: An Idiopathic Approach," *Journal of Applied Behavioral Science* 20 (1984): 237–252. H. Mintzberg, "If You Are Not Serving Bill and Barbara, Then You Are Not Serving Leadership," in J.G. Hunt, U. Sekaran, & C.A. Schriesheim (eds.), *Leadership: Beyond Establishment Views* (Carbondale, IL: Southern Illinois University Press, 1982): 239–259. C.A. Schriesheim & S. Kerr, "Theories and Measures of Leadership: A Critical Appraisal of Current and Future Directions," in J.G. Hunt & L.L. Larson (eds.), *Leadership: The Cutting Edge* (Carbondale, IL: Southern Illinois University Press, 1977): 9–45. G.A. Yukl & W.E. Nemeroff, "Identification and Measurement of Specific Categories of Leadership Behavior: A Progress Report," in J.G.

Hunt & L.L. Larson (eds.). *Cross-currents in Leadership* (Carbondale, IL: Southern Illinois University Press, 1979).

3. J.B. Miner, "The Uncertain Future of the Leadership Concept: An Overview," in J.G. Hunt & L.L. Larson (eds.), *Leadership Frontiers* (Kent, OH: Kent State University Press, 1975). J. Pfeffer, "The Ambiguity of Leadership," in M.W. McCall, Jr., & M.M. Lombardo (eds.), *Leadership: Where Else Can We Go?* (Durham, NC: Duke University Press, 1978): 13–34.

4. T. Peters & N. Austin, *A Passion for Excellence* (New York: Random House, 1985).

5. R. Dubin, "Metaphors of Leadership: An Overview," in J.G. Hunt & L.L. Larson (eds.), *Cross-currents in Leadership* (Carbondale, IL: Southern Illinois University Press, 1979).

6. J.E. Smith, K.P. Carson, & R.A. Alexander, "Leadership: It Can Make a Difference," *Academy of Management Journal* 27 (1984): 765–776.

7. D.L. Bradford & A.R. Cohen, *Managing for Excellence* (New York: John Wiley & Sons, 1984).

8. J. Campbell, "The Cutting Edge of Leadership: An Overview," in J.G. Hunt & L.L. Larson (eds.), *Leadership: The Cutting Edge* (Carbondale, IL: Southern Illinois University Press, 1977): 221–234. R. Dubin, "Metaphors of Leadership: An Overview," in J.G. Hunt & L.L. Larson (eds.), *Cross-currents in Leadership* (Carbondale, IL: Southern Illinois University Press, 1979). R.M. Stogdill, *Handbook of Leadership* (New York: Free Press, 1974).

9. D.A. Kenny & S.J. Zaccaro, "An Estimate of Variance Due to Traits in Leadership," *Journal of Applied Psychology* 68 (1983): 678–685.

10. M.M. Lombardo & M.W. McCall, Jr., *Coping with an Intolerable Boss,* (Greensboro, NC: Center for Creative Leadership, 1984).

11. D. Tjosvold & L. Fabrey, "Effects of Interdependence and Dependence on Cognitive Perspective-Taking," *Psychological Reports* 46 (1980): 755–765. D. Tjosvold & M. Okun, "Effects of Unequal Power on Cooperation in Conflict," *Psychological Reports* 44 (1979): 239–242. D. Tjosvold & S. Sabato, "Effects of Relative Power on Cognitive Perspective-Taking," *Personality and Social Psychological Bulletin* 4 (1978): 256–259.

12. E.E. Jones, *Ingratiation* (New York: Appleton-Century-Crofts, 1964).

13. H.H. Kelley, "Communication in Experimentally Created Hierarchies," *Human Relations* 4 (1951): 39–56. E.E. Jones, *Ingratiation* (New York: Appleton-Century-Crofts, 1964).

14. C. Argyris, *Intervention Theory and Method: A Behavioral Science View* (Reading, MA: Addison-Wesley, 1970). C. Argyris & D.A. Schon, *Organizational Learning: A Theory of Action Perspective* (Reading, MA: Addison-Wesley, 1978).

15. D. Kipnis, *The Powerholders* (Chicago: University of Chicago Press, 1976). D. Kipnis, S.M. Schmidt, & I. Wilkinson, "Intraorganizational Influence Tactics: Explorations in Getting One's Way," *Journal of Applied Psychology* 65 (1980): 440–452.

16. L. Solomon, "The Influence of Some Types of Power Relationships and Game Strategies Upon the Development of Interpersonal Trust," *Journal of Abnormal and Social Psychology* 61 (1960): 223–230.

17. D. Tjosvold, "Effects of Superiors' Influence Orientation on Their Decision

Making in Controversy," *Journal of Psychology* 113 (1983): 175–182. D. Tjosvold, "The Other's Controlling Strategies and Own Group's Evaluation in Intergroup Conflict," *Journal of Psychology* 100 (1978): 305–314. D. Tjosvold & D.W. Johnson, "Conflict and Authority Hierarchies," in D. Tjosvold & D.W. Johnson (eds.), *Productive Conflict Management: Perspectives for Organizations* (New York: Irvington, 1983): 135–156. D. Tjosvold & D.K. Deemer, "Effects of a Control or Collaborative Orientation on Participation in Organizational Decision Making," *Canadian Journal of Behavioural Science* 13 (1981): 33–43.

18. D. Tjosvold & D.W. Johnson, "Conflict and Authority Hierarchies," in D. Tjosvold & D.W. Johnson (eds.), *Productive Conflict Management: Perspectives for Organizations* (New York: Irvington, 1983): 135–156.

19. D. Tjosvold & D.W. Johnson, "Conflict and Authority Hierarchies," in D. Tjosvold & D.W. Johnson (eds.), *Productive Conflict Management: Perspectives for Organizations* (New York: Irvington, 1983): 135–156. D. Tjosvold, I.R. Andrews, & J. Struthers, "Power and Social Context: Superior and Subordinate Views," manuscript, Simon Fraser University, 1985. D. Tjosvold, I.R. Andrews, & H. Jones, "Alternative Uses of Authority," *Canadian Journal of Administrative Sciences* 2 (1985): 307–317.

20. T. Peters & N. Austin, *A Passion for Excellence* (New York: Random House, 1985). T.J. Peters & R.H. Waterman, *In Search of Excellence: Lessons from America's Best-Run Companies* (New York: Harper & Row, 1982).

21. J.J. Gabarro & J.P. Kotter, "Managing Your Boss," *Harvard Business Review,* January-February 1980: 92–100.

22. M.M. Lombardo & M.W. McCall, Jr., *Coping with an Intolerable Boss* (Greensboro, NC: Center for Creative Leadership, 1984).

Complaint-Handling Systems

1. M.P. Rowe & M. Baker, "Are You Hearing Enough Employee Concerns? *Harvard Business Review,* May-June 1984: 127–135.

Chapter 12. Learning Together

1. J. Main, "New Ways to Teach Workers What's New," *Fortune,* 1 October 1984: 85–94.

2. U. Bronfrenbrenner, "Who Cares for America's Children?" in V. Vaughan & T. Brazelton (eds.), *The Family—Can It Be Saved?* (New York: Year Book Medical Publishers, 1976). D.W. Johnson & R.T. Johnson, "The Socialization and Achievement Crisis: Are Cooperative Learning Experiences the Solution?" in L. Bickman (ed.), *Applied Social Psychology Annual* 4 (Beverly Hills, CA: Sage Publications, 1983): 119–164.

3. R. Bybee & E. Gee, *Violence, Values, and Justice in the Schools* (Boston: Allyn & Bacon, 1982).

4. S. Flax, "The Executive Addict," *Forbes,* 24 June 1985: 24–31.

5. D.L. Bradford & A.R. Cohen, *Managing for Excellence* (New York: John Wiley & Sons, 1983). T. Peters & N. Austin, *A Passion for Excellence* (New York: Random House, 1985).

6. M.M. Lombardo & M.W. McCall, Jr., *Coping with an Intolerable Boss,* (Greensboro, NC: Center for Creative Leadership, 1984).

7. D.W. Johnson & F.P. Johnson, *Joining Together: Group Theory and Group Skills* (Englewood Cliffs, NJ: Prentice-Hall, 1982).

8. C. Argyris, & D.A. Schon, *Organizational Learning: A Theory of Action Perspective* (Reading, MA: Addison-Wesley, 1978).

9. D. Tjosvold, "Social Face in Conflict: A Critique," *International Journal of Group Tensions* 13 (1983): 49–64.

10. C. Argyris & D.A. Schon, *Organizational Learning: A Theory of Action Perspective* (Reading, MA: Addison-Wesley, 1978).

11. K.E. Kram & L.A. Isabella, "Alternatives to Mentoring: The Role of Peer Relationships in Career Development," *Academy of Management Journal* 28 (1985): 110–132.

12. K.K. Kram, *Mentoring at Work* (Glenview, IL: Scott, Foresman, 1985).

13. "Everyone Who Makes it Has a Mentor," *Harvard Business Review,* July-August 1978: 89–101.

14. L. Phillips-Jones, "Establishing a Formalized Mentoring Program," *Training and Development Journal,* February 1983: 38–42.

15. P. Petre, "Games that Teach You to Manage," *Fortune,* 29 October 1984: 65–72.

16. C. Argyris, *Intervention Theory and Method: A Behavioral Science View* (Reading, MA: Addison Wesley, 1970).

Chapter 13. Creating a Productive Organization

1. M. Deutsch, *Distributive Justice: A Social-Psychological Perspective* (New Haven, CT: Yale University Press, 1985).

2. T. Peters & N. Austin, *A Passion for Excellence* (New York: Random House, 1985).

3. E. Boyer, "Citicorp: What the New Boss Is Up To," *Fortune,* 17 February 1986: 40–44.

4. T. Peters & N. Austin, *A Passion for Excellence* (New York: Random House, 1985).

5. D.W. Johnson, R.T. Johnson, & G. Maruyama, "Independence and Interpersonal Attraction Among Heterogeneous and Homogeneous Individuals: A Theoretical Formulation and a Meta-Analysis of the Research," *Review of Educational Research* 53 (1983): 5–54.

6. D.W. Johnson & A. Horem-Hebeisen, "Attitudes Toward Interdependence Among Persons and Psychological Health," *Psychological Reports* 40 (1977): 843–850.

7. F. Lindenfeld & J. Rothschild-Whitt, *Workplace Democracy and Social*

Change (Boston: Porter-Sargent, 1982). F.W. Whyte & J.R. Blasi, "Worker Ownership, Participation and Control: Toward a Theoretical Model," *Policy Sciences* 4 (1982): 137–163.

8. M. Deutsch, *Distributive Justice: A Social-Psychological Perspective* (New Haven, CT: Yale University Press, 1985).

9. E.E. Lawler, *Pay and Organizational Effectiveness: A Psychological View* (Reading, MA: Addison-Wesley, 1981).

Index

About the Author

After graduating from Princeton University, **Dean Tjosvold** earned his Ph.D. in the social psychology of organizations at the University of Minnesota in 1972, and is now professor of organizational behavior at Simon Fraser University. Before that he taught at Pennsylvania State University and was a visiting scholar at the National University of Singapore. He has published over 80 articles on managing conflict, cooperation and competition, decision making, power, and other management issues. With David W. Johnson, he edited *Productive Conflict Management* and with Mary Tjosvold wrote two books for health care professionals. He consults and conducts seminars on how people can work together to get things done, and he is a partner in several health care businesses in Minnesota.